CHARACTER IN CRISIS

Character in Crisis

A Fresh Approach to the
Wisdom Literature
of the Old Testament

WILLIAM P. BROWN

WILLIAM B. EERDMANS PUBLISHING COMPANY
GRAND RAPIDS, MICHIGAN / CAMBRIDGE, U.K.

© 1996 Wm. B. Eerdmans Publishing Co.
255 Jefferson Ave. S.E., Grand Rapids, Michigan 49503
P.O. Box 163, Cambridge CB3 9BA U.K.

Printed in the United States of America

01 00 99 98 97 96   7 6 5 4 3 2 1

Library of Congress Cataloging-in-Publication Data

Brown, William P., 1958-
    Character in crisis : a fresh approach to the Wisdom literature
    of the Old Testament / William P. Brown.
        p.   cm.
    Includes bibliographical references and index.
    ISBN 0-8028-4135-X (pbk.: alk. paper)
    1. Wisdom literature — Criticism, interpretation, etc.   I. Title.
    BS1455.B76   1996
    223'.06 dc20   95-50895
                                                         CIP

Scripture quotations are from the *New Revised Standard Version of the Bible*, © 1989 by
the Division of Christian Education, National Council of the Churches of Christ in the
United States of America, and used by permission.

Contents

Preface

In American society renewed interest in the value of character has recently galvanized public and political discussion.[1] Phrases such as "character education" and "politics of virtue" are quickly entering the household of vernacular discourse. Former drug czar and Secretary of Education William J. Bennett's best-seller *The Book of Virtues* has sold over a million copies, and plans are underway for a sequel as well as a myriad of textbooks. Politicians and social analysts who focus on ethical character and how the government can play an instrumental role are now called "virtuecrats."[2] However the issues of virtue and character become defined and caricatured in public discourse, they address growing fears about the general direction society seems to be taking: the predominance of self-interest in corporate and private spheres, the violent fragmentation of American society, and the destructive effects of institutions on the character of young people.[3]

To add to the list, many have noted the vast and fertile fields of multiculturalism, which have been a source of pride and enrichment in American society, fast becoming desolate wastelands due to the withering effects of "culture wars."[4] Public discourse, with its ideal of providing an arena of free exchange and learning, has become a veritable battlefield dominated by the rhetoric of divisiveness and victimization. Columnist Lance Morrow echoes many a social critic when he makes the following diagnosis:

1. See James Q. Wilson, *On Character; idem, The Moral Sense;* William J. Bennett, ed., *The Book of Virtues.*
2. See Howard Fineman, "The Virtuecrats."
3. William A. Galston, "Introduction: The Revival of the Virtues," 2.
4. See James D. Hunter, *Culture Wars; idem, Before the Shooting Begins.*

vii

A somewhat violent, highly mobile information-television society of short moral attention span, of merciless scrutiny of its role models and of crazed blasts of overstimulation tends to subside into a psychology of grievance and entitlement.[5]

In short, there is a growing realization that without certain common values and virtues firmly in place, any public policy or program is doomed to failure.

It is commonplace now to hear social critics decry the failure among certain communities and institutions to act as agents of moral and cultural development. The call is made to rethink the ways in which individuals currently conceive of their duties to themselves, their obligations to each other, and, for some, their responsibilities before God. Blame has been affixed particularly on the family and the church, institutions that have been considered indispensable in fostering ethical development and right character.

As an ordained minister in the Presbyterian Church and student of the Bible, I want to take an inside look at the challenge such observations present the church as it seeks to respond with integrity in dialogue with Scripture. During the last presidential debates (1992) — like most political debates — when words like "character," "integrity," and "family values" were batted about, I began to ask myself what I thought were simple questions: Where in Scripture is the issue of character most explicitly addressed and what does it say about it? Although the concern for ethical character runs throughout the Bible, I was surprised to discover that it finds its most immediate home within a frequently neglected part of the biblical canon, the wisdom literature of the (Protestant) Old Testament: the books of Proverbs, Job, and Ecclesiastes.

And so began a journey. Little did I know when I embarked of the remarkably diverse and provocative ways in which the wisdom corpus addressed the issues of character and ethical practice. Along the way I felt challenged and changed. Many "scholarly" presuppositions and personal biases were called into question. The rich and evocative language of these wisdom books became a source of wonder I never thought possible. Equally surprising to me in the course of human events was the explosive controversy that erupted among mainline denominations surrounding an ecumenical conference that boldly introduced wisdom

5. Lance Morrow, "The Search for Virtues."

("Sophia") into its liturgy and discussion.[6] Still in need of a proper introduction, the character of wisdom is receiving an inordinate amount of press these days, both positive and negative, distorted and informed. No longer just the object of erudite study, biblical wisdom has, like ethical character, entered into the household of the vernacular, and, like character, a pervasive uncertainty remains over her role. This study is one attempt to find her place in ethical discourse among Christians.

Many are to be thanked in the development of this study, including my friend M. Patrick Graham of Pitts Theological Library at Emory University, whose insights and collegial support introduced me to issues related to character and biblical interpretation. In addition, Carol Newsom and Bruce Birch, two gifted teachers with distinctly different approaches, have proved to me that the study of moral character in the Old Testament need not be colored with a particular ideological hue.

In the preparation of the manuscript, special thanks goes to Kathy Davis of Union Seminary for reviewing my early drafts and vigilantly reminding me of my intended audience. I must also thank Allen C. Myers, Senior Editor at Wm. B. Eerdmans Publishing Company, for his patience and support throughout the editorial process, which in itself was a journey in wisdom. Finally, thanks must go to the community of peers that has nurtured and guided me as a teacher and scholar, Union Theological Seminary in Virginia. To that family of sages I dedicate this work.

6. "Re-imagining . . . God, Community and the Church," held in November 1993 in Minneapolis.

Abbreviations

AB	Anchor Bible
ANET	James B. Pritchard, ed., *Ancient Near Eastern Texts*
ATD	Das Alte Testament Deutsch
BBB	Bonner biblische Beiträge
BDB	Francis Brown, S. R. Driver, and Charles A. Briggs, ed., *A Hebrew and English Lexicon of the Old Testament*
BHT	Beiträge zur historischen Theologie
BJS	Brown Judaic Studies
BLS	Bible and Literature Series
BibRev	*Bible Review*
BZAW	Beihefte zur *ZAW*
CBQ	*Catholic Biblical Quarterly*
Ebib	Etudes bibliques
FRLANT	Forschungen zur Religion und Literatur des Alten und Neuen Testaments
HAR	*Hebrew Annual Review*
HAT	Handbuch zum Alten Testament
HBT	*Horizons in Biblical Theology*
HSM	Harvard Semitic Monographs
HTR	*Harvard Theological Review*
IRT	Issues in Religion and Theology
JAAR	*Journal of the American Academy of Religion*
JBL	*Journal of Biblical Literature*
JBR	*Journal of Bible and Religion*
JP	*Journal of Philosophy*
JRE	*The Journal of Religious Ethics*
JSOT	*Journal for the Study of the Old Testament*

JSOTSup	Journal for the Study of the Old Testament Supplement Series
KAT	Kommentar zum Alten Testament
LD	Lectio divina
LLA	The Library of Liberal Arts
MBS	Message of Biblical Spirituality
NCBC	New Century Bible Commentary
OTL	Old Testament Library
PSB	*Princeton Seminary Bulletin*
SBL	Society of Biblical Literature
SBLDS	SBL Dissertation Series
SBT	Studies in Biblical Theology
SJT	*Scottish Journal of Theology*
ThViat	*Theologia Viatorum*
TUMSR	Trinity University Monograph Series
VT	*Vetus Testamentum*
VTS	Supplements to *Vetus Testamentum*
WBC	Word Biblical Commentary
WMANT	Wissenschaftliche Monographien zum Alten und Neuen Testament
ZAW	*Zeitschrift für die alttestamentliche Wissenschaft*
ZTK	*Zeitschrift für Theologie und Kirche*

1 Introduction: The Ethics and Ethos of Biblical Wisdom

At a time when the chasm between academic scholarship and theological reflection seems to be widening, both the academic guild and the church share in common an uncertainty over how to study and appropriate the wisdom literature of the Old Testament. On the one hand, mainline denominations have for the most part avoided the books of Proverbs, Job, and Ecclesiastes in their preaching and educational curriculum.[1] Biblical scholars, on the other hand, have labored hard to identify the theological significance and thematic center of the wisdom literature, but without much consensus.

The impasse stems from the fact that this body of literature holds a unique, if not troubling, position within the biblical canon. The wisdom corpus is unique in that its literary forms by and large do not belong to either narrative or law. In addition, the nature of its discourse is troubling to Jews, and more so to Christians, since the literature appears to lack a readily identifiable theological center. Consequently, biblical wisdom has been studied from a variety of approaches. In particular, many exegetes have regarded biblical wisdom as uniquely *anthropocentric* in character, that is, as reflective of the human, pragmatic quest to secure wholeness and prosperity.[2] Others, however, have noted that much of the wisdom

---

1. One need only note the dearth of scriptural references to wisdom books in the latest revision of the common lectionary for Sundays and major festivals. The three-year cycle contains only five passages from Proverbs, three from Job, and one from Ecclesiastes.

2. Although most approaches to the study of wisdom literature differ only in degree, it is helpful to identify those who stress the anthropological or experiential side

1

corpus focuses on *creation theology* and thus find wisdom's *theocentric* side to provide the best entry point into the ethos of biblical wisdom.[3] To be sure, both approaches highlight two essential sides of biblical wisdom. Yet the question still remains whether there is an organizing principle or center to biblical wisdom that can account for both these theocentric and anthropocentric poles. Leo G. Perdue has recently suggested a synthesis of these poles, a "dialectic of anthropology and cosmology." But such a framework is of limited use, since it merely defines the problem rather than offers a heuristically constructive solution.[4] Determining the precise

---

of wisdom in relation to those who highlight wisdom's cosmological or theological dimensions. To the former belong Gerhard von Rad's earlier work on wisdom in *Old Testament Theology*, 1:418-441 (note particularly his definition on 418); John F. Priest, "Where is Wisdom to be Placed?"; *idem*, "Humanism, Skepticism, and Pessimism in Israel"; Walter Brueggemann, *In Man We Trust*; W. Sibley Towner, "The Renewed Authority of Old Testament Wisdom for Contemporary Faith"; with appropriate acknowledgment of the prominent role of cosmology in wisdom, Walther Zimmerli, "Concerning the Structure of Old Testament Wisdom"; *idem*, "The Place and Limit of the Wisdom in the Framework of the Old Testament Theology." Although James L. Crenshaw finds multiple levels of definition for wisdom, it is noteworthy that he begins in his introduction with a discussion of "sapiential ethics" in Job 31, namely Job's defense of his moral integrity (*Old Testament Wisdom*, 14-19).

3. E.g., Hartmut Gese, *Lehre und Wirklichkeit in der alten Weisheit*; Hans-Jürgen Hermisson, "Observations on the Creation Theology in Wisdom"; Hans Heinrich Schmid, *Gerechtigkeit als Weltordnung*; *idem*, "Creation, Righteousness, and Salvation"; and Leo G. Perdue, "Cosmology and the Social Order in the Wisdom Tradition."

For more novel approaches, see Samuel Terrien, "The Play of Wisdom"; and Roland E. Murphy, "Wisdom and Creation." Both Terrien and Murphy focus on the transcendent, theocentric role of personified wisdom in Proverbs 1–9, and thus eschew creation language per se.

4. Leo G. Perdue, *Wisdom in Revolt*, 20; *idem*, *Wisdom and Creation*, 48. The dialectic that Perdue draws from von Rad's classic treatment on wisdom functioned quite differently for von Rad. Von Rad repeatedly stressed the practical or experiential side of wisdom without subsuming it under the overarching framework of creation theology the way Perdue has attempted to do (e.g., Gerhard von Rad, *Wisdom in Israel*, 3-5, 312-18; *Old Testament Theology*, 1:418-441). As Perdue contends, "In my estimation, [the dialectic of anthropology and cosmology] should be regarded as a true dialectic, and not as a development from one (anthropology) to another (cosmology) or from an emphasis on one to a greater stress on the other" (*Wisdom and Creation*, 48). The statement in and of itself is commendable; however, one wonders if Perdue's polar counterparts represent a "*true* dialectic" when he considers anthropology and cosmology as simply two sides of creation theology.

In his discussion on Job, Perdue reductively regards anthropology as another

relationship between these two sides of the same coin still bedevils any interpreter who wants to grasp the full range and depth of the sapiential traditions.

Perhaps one helpful point of departure is to consider the roles that the anthropocentric and theocentric dimensions assume in the wisdom corpus. From a discursive level, they denote complementary frames of reference, but it is the anthropocentric framework that is clearly primary. Wisdom begins and ends with the self, in recognition that knowledge of God cannot be divorced from human knowledge of the self. In the book of Proverbs, for example, knowledge of God and creation is framed in human discourse and observation: It opens with parental discourse on proper conduct and attitude (Prov. 1:8) and ends in homage to the "woman of excellence" (Prov. 31:10-31). In Ecclesiastes,

---

creation tradition to be set alongside cosmology (*Wisdom in Revolt*, 21-22). Consequently, his discussions are decidedly weighted toward creation and mythological texts (*Wisdom in Revolt*, 61-72), which is appropriate for a discussion of *creation* theology in Job but is of limited use for discerning the main point of the book, much less the center of the wisdom corpus as a whole. Elsewhere, Perdue claims a cosmological center in wisdom, as reflected in his definition of "the fear of God": "the conviction that the structures of life were created and sustained by the just and beneficent rule of God (Prov. 1:7, 14:27)" ("Cosmology and the Social Order," 460; cf. *Wisdom and Creation*, 79).

Stripped of all its methodological embellishments, Perdue's approach — "the metaphorical process" — appears in practice to favor the cosmological pole of the dialectic. Perdue hardly takes account of the anthropocentric frame of reference he outlines in the introduction to his study of Job or in his reflections on Proverbs (see *Wisdom and Creation*, 121-22). Rather, he slides from a balanced synthesis of contrasting frameworks to a one-sided approach that is almost entirely focused on the cosmological. How Perdue makes such a move stems from confusing anthropology as a methodological frame of reference — an anthropocentric framework — with ancient Near Eastern and biblical *creation* traditions concerning the genesis of humankind.

While acknowledging the pervasive role that creation has in biblical wisdom, Perdue in effect gives short shrift to the no less pervasive anthropocentric framework of sapiential discourse. One may legitimately question whether the traditions and perspectives of the wisdom corpus differ in principle from the creation traditions attested throughout the Old Testament outside of the wisdom corpus. Are the wisdom books of Proverbs, Job, and Ecclesiastes by and large treatises, mythological depictions, or poetic musings on the created order? Clearly more than simply variant creation perspectives comprise the ethos of biblical wisdom. With his appropriate emphasis upon human imagination and the metaphorical process in constructing worldviews peculiar to the sages, the synthesizing notion of character would have better served Perdue's attempt at identifying a comprehensive approach to the wisdom corpus.

the speaker Qoheleth recounts his personal experience in what is essentially a confession of failure. From Job's piercing cries of anguish to his final confession before God, wisdom cultivates the language of the self as a discerning moral agent in a world filled with choices, ambiguity, threat, and grace. Indeed, of all the books and genres of biblical literature, it is the wisdom corpus that most explicitly addresses the character and praxis of *both* the individual and the community.

It is within the anthropocentric framework of the self as moral agent that one can begin to talk about ancient Israelite wisdom in relation to the idea of character, a subject of much study among modern ethicists and literary critics. The appeal of suggesting character formation as the central framework and goal of biblical wisdom lies in the literature's focus on the developing self in relation to the perceived world, thus bridging the gulf between the anthropocentric and theocentric frames of reference that run throughout the wisdom corpus. Before exploring further the connection between character and biblical wisdom, it is necessary to assess what is meant by the notion of character in literary and moral discourse.

I. DESCRIPTIVE CHARACTER

In their revised study, Bruce Birch and Larry Rasmussen acknowledge two root meanings inherent in the notion of character, which for convenience can be labeled descriptive and prescriptive. From the Greek *charactēr*, originally meaning "engraving tool," the term has come to refer to certain qualities that distinguish one person from another.[5] At the most basic literary level, character refers to those figures (e.g., human beings, animals, communities, animate objects) that assume certain roles within a narrative and are designated by certain terms that denote characteristic traits.[6] The literary relationship between action and character in narrative is a matter of continued debate among literary critics. Aristotle, for example, argued that character is subordinate to action.[7] However, as the contemporary literary critic Shlomith Rimmon-Kennan

---

5. Bruce Birch and Larry Rasmussen, *Bible and Ethics in the Christian Life*, 75.
6. Shlomith Rimmon-Kennan, *Narrative Fiction*, 33.
7. See particularly chs. 2 and 6 in the *Poetics*. See discussion in Seymour B. Chatman, *Story and Discourse*, 109.

suggests, character and action must ultimately be construed as interdependent referents, in accordance with Henry James's famous dictum: "What is character but the determination of incident? What is incident but the illustration of character?"[8]

In literary discourse, character refers to a "paradigm" or distinctive cluster of personal traits, a trait being a "relatively stable or abiding personal quality."[9] More than "ephemeral psychological phenomena,"[10] character traits are attributes or predicates that exhibit a degree of consistency with respect to the subject. As formulated by E. M. Forster, characters in fiction can either be "flat" or "round."[11] Flat characters do not develop in the course of the plot and are restricted in qualities. Round characters, however, exhibit more than one quality or trait. Since Forster's pioneering distinction, literary critics have made further distinctions.

Biblical scholar Adele Berlin argues for no less than three categories of characters in narrative: the "full-fledged" or round character, the type or flat character, and the agent or functionary character.[12] Types are built around a single trait. To this category Berlin assigns the character of Abigail, "the perfect wife," and Nabal, the proverbial fool (1 Sam. 25).[13] An agent is a character that is merely functional and thus cannot be characterized.[14] The character of Abishag, the Shunamite who ministered to the ailing David and was the object of political intrigue, falls under this character type (1 Kgs. 1–2).[15] As for the full-fledged character, Berlin finds Michal and Bathsheba to be "realistically portrayed" and their emotions made explicit.[16]

The problem, however, with such cleanly packaged categories is the danger of forcing every literary character into one category, a move that invariably requires some reduction.[17] More helpful is Joseph Ewen's

---

8. Quoted from Rimmon-Kennan, 35. See also Frank Kermode's comments on the interrelationship between character and narration in *The Genesis of Secrecy*, 75-77.

9. Chatman, 126.

10. *Ibid.*, 126.

11. *Aspects of the Novel*, 75.

12. *Poetics and Interpretation of Biblical Narrative*, 23.

13. Berlin, 30-31.

14. This category is taken from M. H. Abrams, *A Glossary of Literary Terms*, 21.

15. Berlin, 30-32.

16. *Ibid.*, 31-32.

17. It is a problem that Berlin (32) also recognizes in stressing that character types differ only in degree.

classification of characters along three axes: complexity, development, and penetration into the "inner life."[18] At one end of the pole belong allegorical figures, caricatures, and types; that is, characters that exhibit a single or dominant trait. Such characters in narrative are essentially static and viewed from the outside. Fully developed characters, on the other hand, exhibit complexity, development, and reveal themselves from the inside out. In between the poles on each axis is an infinite degree of variation. As Berlin, Robert Alter, David Gunn, and others have fruitfully pointed out, biblical narrative is replete with characters that range from the infinitely complex to the uniformly simple.[19] What remains for further study are those biblical characters that do not have their primary home in narrative proper but nonetheless exhibit a wide range of complexity and variation, namely the characters profiled in the wisdom literature, the topic of this study.

In summary, literary character denotes both a body and a spectrum of distinctive traits that set one character apart from another. Identifying the traits and their range constitutes what is commonly called a character analysis, a thick description of a particular figure's personality, role, and function — in short, its defining characteristics. Students of literature have by and large limited their investigations of character within the narrative genres (e.g., novel, biography, fiction, history). However, insights gained from such studies have their value for other literary genres, as will be demonstrated.

II. PRESCRIPTIVE OR MORAL CHARACTER

Ethicists speak of character in a different, but not wholly unrelated sense. Both definitions of character — literary and moral — acknowledge that the morphologies of our lives express certain configurations of action, affect, and responsibility. Character is reflected in the tendency to act, feel, and think in certain definable ways. Generally speaking, ethical character refers to the sum and range of specifically *moral*

---

18. Rimmon-Kennan, 41-42.

19. Robert Alter, *The Art of Biblical Narrative;* David M. Gunn, *The Story of King David; idem, The Fate of King Saul;* Shim'on Bar-Efrat, *The Art of the Biblical Story,* 73-112; Meir Sternberg, *The Poetics of Biblical Narrative,* 321-364.

qualities or traits the individual or community possesses.[20] Thus the ethical domain of character consists of a particular class of distinctive traits embedded within the wider matrix of traits comprising an individual's full, descriptive character. One can speak of a person as having exemplary, credible, or unassailable character, or simply possessing character. Such language invests normative claim in certain qualities of a person's overall character, traits that are positively esteemed and therefore serve as a model for others. More specifically, someone who has character is one who is considered to possess sound judgment to know what is right and the courage to act on it.[21] When compared to the literary qualities of character that highlight a person's uniqueness, ethical character represents a *generalizing* aspect that sets in relief certain values and virtues that have a normative claim to be shared and embodied by others.

Ethicists identify several basic elements that comprise a person's moral life, irreducible social and psychological factors that render a full explanation of one's character. In addition to normative dispositions or *virtues*, Birch and Rasmussen posit *perception* and *intention* as basic structural elements that make up character.[22] It is important that some discussion be devoted to each of these three constituents of ethical character.

Perception

In the moral language of character, perception is more than simple observation; it involves the selective internalization and integration of events, thereby giving shape to the way people experience events and render them meaningful. Perception involves the way one selects, interprets, and evaluates events by means of certain fundamental symbols.[23] The role of perception in the definition of character cannot be overemphasized, for the subject matter of character is in essence the *self in*

20. See the common definition given in *The Oxford English Dictionary,* 2nd ed. (Oxford: Clarendon, 1989), 3.31.11, where the normative and descriptive dimensions of character are mentioned together.

21. Birch-Rasmussen, 75.

22. *Ibid.,* 74-81.

23. *Ibid.,* 77. See also Stanley Hauerwas, *Character and the Christian Life,* 203.

relation, in relation to the perceived world, including God, and to the history and pattern of one's choices.[24]

The particular orientation espoused by the ancient sages involved nothing less than perceiving the world from the perspective of all things subject to and ordered by God's will, be it discernible or inscrutable. Within the context of perception as it relates to character, creation or cosmology — broadly speaking, how one views the world — plays a vitally important role for the wise.[25] But it is within the purposeful context of living, in appropriating and embodying truth rather than simply apprehending it, that creation functioned for the ancient sages. Specific creation texts of wisdom literature (e.g., Prov. 8:22-31; Eccl. 1:2-11; Job 38–41) are contextualized in such a way so as to (re)construct the reader's perception of the world and God in accord with certain values, perspectives, and principles, the stuff of ethical character. Simply put, to alter one's perception of God and the world is to shape and reshape character, the goal of sapiential rhetoric.

Intention

The second element of moral character, intention, need only be briefly mentioned. Intentions consist of "expressions of character which show aim, direction, purpose; they express the volitional side of character."[26] Presupposing a degree of self-determination, intention expresses purpose and gives direction to choice.[27] Intention builds upon free choice and thus provides a basis for ethical accountability. More than discrete acts of the will, intentions provide coherence to the decisions and actions of an individual or community. They are by nature "goal-oriented determinations."[28] In short, through intention, the language of character casts the self as having duration and growth, the self in formation.[29]

---

24. Richard Bondi, "The Elements of Character," 204; *idem,* "Character," 83.
25. See above.
26. Birch-Rasmussen, 79.
27. *Ibid.,* 80.
28. *Ibid.,* 80.
29. Hauerwas, *Character and the Christian Life,* 3-4.

Virtue or Disposition

The character element that has received the most amount of attention in classical and contemporary discussions is virtue. The cultivation of virtue has traditionally been the aim of character formation. Virtue is a disposition, which denotes the pattern of choices an individual makes. Dispositions comprise persistent attitudes or "habits"[30] of the heart and mind that dispose one to a consistency of certain action and expression.[31] Bound up with perception, dispositions constitute the traits of character that are demonstrated in customary patterns of ethical behavior. Classically, such dispositions have been referred to as "virtues," a term that is finding renewed currency in moral discourse.

Aristotle defined virtue[32] as "a deliberated and permanent disposition, based on a standard applied to ourselves and defined by the reason displayed by the man of good sense."[33] Similarly, St. Thomas Aquinas described virtue as "that which makes good he who has it and renders good his work."[34] Together, these two definitions highlight several elements: Virtue is both a disposition and a standard; it is based on reason and the source of good conduct.[35] As dispositions that involve a tendency to do certain sorts of action in particular situations, virtues are by no means static qualities. They are dynamic and, hence, "determinable" as opposed to determinate.[36] Not wholly inborn, virtues are

30. Properly speaking, *habitus* in Latin or *hexis* in Greek.

31. Birch-Rasmussen, 79-80.

32. The Greek term *aretē* comprises a tremendous range of meaning. For Homer, *aretē* was synonymous with courage. Later the term came to signify "civic virtue" and moral qualities other than courage (see Martin Ostwald's discussion of the definition in *Nicomachean Ethics*, 303). The basic root meaning of the term was power or ability to do something; hence, it could denote whatever caused someone to perform a function well in relation to particular tasks. For the most thorough and comprehensive history of the term in Greek literature, see Werner W. Jaeger, *Paideia*, I.

33. *Nicomachean Ethics* 2.6.15 (quoted from Jean Baechler, "Virtue," 27). Aristotle's theory of the median between the extremes of excess and deficiency as it relates to defining the virtues (*Nicomachean Ethics* 2.6) is beyond the scope of this study. Suffice it to say that Aristotle makes the claim that the median is always "relative to us" (2.6.7), and hence is a matter of perception (see Hauerwas, *Character and the Christian Life*, 72).

34. Baechler, 27.

35. *Ibid.*, 27.

36. Edmund L. Pincoffs, *Quandaries and Virtues*, 77.

acquired through education and practice.[37] Once a particular virtue is developed, it is ever present, at least in potential form.

As determinable dispositions, virtues imply self-conscious, willful behavior and thus provide the material for assessing a person's character.[38] Unlike the modern sense of "habit," which denotes a psychologically automatic response, virtue is a "quality which permits the reason and will . . . to achieve their maximum capacity on the moral plane."[39] Moral virtues are virtues of character (Greek *ēthos*) and must be distinguished from abilities. One can possess the ability to think intelligently without having the disposition to use it.[40] Dispositions imply a lasting "readiness for action" formed through the agent's activity.[41] Furthermore, moral virtues must be distinguished from "skills for success" — sometimes called "instrumental virtues."[42] But the appeal of recent popular literature is in large measure due to a blurring of the boundaries between moral virtues and skills for success.[43] According to the classical ethicists, however, moral virtue is no guarantee of success, and success is not necessarily a sign of moral integrity. The appeal of the virtuous life is intrinsic. Distinct from professional skills, moral virtue is characteristic of a "unitary life."[44] In other words, moral virtues tend to cut

---

37. See Alasdair MacIntyre's definition of virtue in *After Virtue*, 178:

> A virtue is an acquired human quality the possession and exercise of which tends to enable us to achieve those goods which are internal to practices and the lack of which effectively prevents us from achieving any such goods.

38. So Pincoffs (77). Pincoffs goes on to define virtues and vices in purely functional terms as "dispositional properties that provide grounds for preference or avoidance of persons" (82). Although Pincoff's concern to find a nonreductive basis for virtue is commendable, establishing it in terms of rationales given for the preference of individuals is much too broad. Certain reasons given for preferring, as opposed to avoiding, someone do not necessarily imply that such a person possesses particularly normative qualities. Consistent with his approach, however, Pincoffs's chart of virtues makes moral virtues merely one category among other kinds of virtue (85).

39. Servais Pinckaers, "Virtue is Not a Habit," 71.

40. William K. Frankena, *Ethics*, 68.

41. Hauerwas, *Character and the Christian Life*, 71. Hauerwas, however, does suggest that it is an ability; but see *Nicomachean Ethics* 2.5.7-12.

42. Pincoffs, 84-86.

43. E.g., Stephen R. Covey, *The Seven Habits of Highly Effective People*; Kenneth H. Blanchard and Norman Vincent Peale, *The Power of Ethical Management*; Thomas J. Peters and Robert H. Waterman, Jr., *In Search of Excellence*.

44. MacIntyre, 191.

across all situations of conduct, from professional to personal. To compartmentalize the virtue of honesty by relegating it to, for example, one's personal life but excluding it from one's professional conduct, is no virtue. Virtues are by nature all encompassing.

The history of ethical discourse has attempted in various ways to prioritize or reduce the "swarm of virtues," to borrow a phrase from Plato's *Meno*. The most basic and highly esteemed virtues have traditionally been designated "cardinal" virtues. Plato and Aristotle identify four such virtues: prudence, justice, fortitude, and temperance. For Aristotle, prudence or practical wisdom[45] is primary, since it is both a moral virtue and one of the five intellectual virtues (the others are understanding, science, wisdom, and art).[46] As practical wisdom, prudence embodies wisdom in practice and in judging right action in particular situations. As a moral virtue, Aristotle defines prudence as "a reasoned and true state of capacity to act with regard to human goods."[47] By bringing the mind and heart, reason and inclination together, prudence enables the person to determine what is and how to do the right thing in every situation.[48]

For Aristotle, the four cardinal virtues exist not in isolation from each other but work in consort in the act of choice, particularly in the choice of an informed mean.[49] Hence, prudence, the primary virtue, is operative at all levels of virtuous conduct. Aristotle distinguishes the four moral virtues from the intellectual virtues in the way they are appropriated: Intellectual virtues are acquired through pedagogical instruction; virtues of character are gained primarily from habitual exercise.[50] Neither class of virtue is, according to Aristotle, implanted by nature.[51] "We become just by the practice of just actions, self-controlled by exercising self-control, and courageous by performing acts of courage."[52] The classroom for the instruction of virtue is life itself.

---

45. See Ostwald's discussion of the definition in *Nicomachean Ethics,* 312.

46. *Nicomachean Ethics* 6.3-7.

47. *Nicomachean Ethics* 6.5.20 (as quoted from Ross's translation with slight alteration [i.e., the translation for *hexis*] in Yves R. Simon, *The Definition of Moral Virtue,* 96).

48. See Simon's discussion (96).

49. *Nicomachean Ethics* 2.6.

50. *Ibid.,* 2.1; see MacIntyre, 144-45.

51. *Nicomachean Ethics* 2.1.

52. *Ibid.,* 2.1 (Ostwald translation, 34).

As is well known, St. Thomas Aquinas's contribution to the discussion is his addition of three theological virtues to the cardinal list: faith, hope, and charity (or love). A quick glance at his configuration of ethical character is important for the study of character in biblical wisdom literature, since Thomas was able to establish a distinctly *theological* context for *habitus* or virtue.[53] Like Aristotle, Thomas highlighted prudence for its unitive function of integrating practical reason and desires toward making moral judgments.[54] As the bridge between moral knowledge and virtuous action, prudence precedes choice and coordinates the activity of the other virtues.[55] For Thomas, however, a virtue other than prudence was to assume the head position, namely the theological virtue charity. Charity, along with faith and hope, was infused in human beings in order to direct them to God.[56] The primacy of charity is clear in the famous statement of Thomas: "Charity is the mother and the root of all the virtues, inasmuch as it is the form of them all."[57] In modern parlance, charity is the default drive in the exercise of any virtue.

Much more recently, ethicists such as Arthur Schopenhauer and William K. Frankena have either reduced the cardinal virtues to two (benevolence and justice)[58] or, like Edmund L. Pincoffs, have refused to limit the "swarm" altogether.[59] Common to most attempts at delineating and specifying the collage of virtues is the recognition that character is more than the sum of its constituent moral parts. The shape of character entails an organized, harmonious unity by which "the total determination of the self . . . is present through each particular virtue and habit."[60] From Aristotle's perspective, the exercise of the virtues requires a unity of the soul in its three elements — perception, intelligence, and desire.[61] Cast another way, there is an *integrity* to the person of character, a wholeness or completeness regarding the exercise of virtue. Such a holistic notion of integrity is crucial to biblical wisdom, particularly in the character of Job.[62]

---

53. See Romanus Cessario, *The Moral Virtues and Theological Ethics*, 7.
54. *Ibid.*, 82-95.
55. Daniel M. Nelson, *The Priority of Prudence*, 52.
56. Thomas Aquinas, *Summa Theologiae*, I-II, q. 62, a.1.
57. *Ibid.*, I-II, q. 62, a. 4.
58. Frankena, 64-65.
59. Pincoffs lists a total of sixty-seven virtues (85).
60. Hauerwas, *Character and the Christian Life*, 78.
61. *Nicomachean Ethics*, 6.1-2.
62. See Chapters 3 and 4.

The Ethic of Being and Ethic of Duty

Like character, the element of virtue cannot be identified with any moral principle. In contrast to the ethics of duty, virtue essentially points to an ethic of being or character. The relationship between duty and virtue is one that is no doubt complex, but however construed, it is clearly one of mutual interdependence. A system of morality that focuses exclusively on rules and principles can account for motivations and intentions to act on them only on an *ad hoc* basis.[63] Conversely, one cannot conceive of character traits except as including dispositions to act in certain ways according to moral principles. As Frankena puts it in his parody of Immanuel Kant, "principles without traits are impotent and traits without principles are blind."[64] Yet the cultivation of virtue is of *primary* necessity when it comes to situations that demand choosing between conflicting principles of duty or revising working rules of right and wrong.[65] It is precisely this necessity that suggests the primacy of "virtue ethics" in moral discourse: Rules can never be exhaustively specified so as to preclude the need for judgment that extends beyond the rules themselves.[66] Even when moral rules are adequate guides to conduct, they merely constitute the *form* of morality, not its *point*.[67]

An illustrative example of the limitations of moral rules comes from two conflicting maxims found side by side, no less, in the book of Proverbs. In Prov. 26:4 is the injunction: "Do not answer fools according to their folly, or you will be a fool yourself." In the very next verse is found its opposite: "Answer fools according to their folly, or they will be wise in their own eyes" (26:5). With such direct juxtapositioning, biblical wisdom fully acknowledges the limits of moral principles and rules. Since each maxim is followed immediately by a reason, the very structure of these proverbs accords a degree of freedom that invites personal judgment and engagement on the part of the intending moral subject with his or her environment, a freedom to decide which line of action is the most appropriate, given the situation. Proverbs are, prop-

---

63. Frankena, 65.
64. *Ibid.*, 53.
65. *Ibid.*, 66.
66. J. Budziszewski, "Religion and Civic Virtue," 57.
67. *Ibid.*, 57. For a radical statement of the primacy of moral virtue over value, see Pincoffs's criticism of MacIntyre's definition of virtue (Pincoffs, 97).

erly speaking, not universal rules; rather, they are situationally oriented, open-ended sayings, designed to exercise one's mental and moral faculties and thereby enable the moral agent to size up ethically demanding situations and to act appropriately. In short, a crucial aim of the proverb is to help develop practical wisdom, to cultivate what Aristotle would identify as the chief virtue, prudence.

In summary, the notion of character with the elements of perception, intention, and virtue provides a model of coherence to the moral life of the individual and community. As noted above, the relationship between moral principle and virtue is an interdependent one, yet virtue finds its primacy in situations of conflicting rules and in the community's need to revise them. Indeed, it has been claimed that character provides a comprehensive perspective on the shape of ethics itself.[68] Stephen E. Fowl and L. Gregory Jones observe that character is formed in and through "socially-embodied traditions,"[69] that is, through traditions carried and passed on by the community from one generation to the next. As Birch and Rasmussen put it, albeit simplistically, while character is the "chief architect of our decisions and actions," the community is the "chief architect of character."[70]

Moral rules, consequently, cannot operate independently of the formation of character in traditions transmitted and shaped by the community. Rather, principles and rules are part and parcel of the dynamics of character formation in that they contribute to the community's task of providing particular conceptions of the good through which character is formed.[71] Constantly subject to and in need of revision, ethical rules and principles constitute the achievement of the community as it both seeks to appropriate the wisdom of the past for every new social context and refine or reshape, if need be, the contours of normative character.[72]

Within the ethos of biblical wisdom, the reformulations of moral rules and principles by the community is particularly evident. Wisdom fully acknowledges its debt to antiquity as it seeks to appropriate and disseminate the values of the past for the present generation.[73] The

68. Stephen E. Fowl and L. Gregory Jones, *Reading in Communion*, 10.

69. *Ibid.,* 10.

70. Birch-Rasmussen, 81.

71. Fowl-Jones, 10.

72. *Ibid.,* 10.

73. For a discussion of the ethos of wisdom literature, see James L. Crenshaw, "Wisdom and Authority."

father figure in Prov. 4, for example, appeals to his own father as he instructs his son on the ways of wisdom. Eliphaz chides Job for deviating from conventional wisdom: "The gray-haired and the aged are on our side, those older than your father" (Job 15:10). "What the sages have told and their ancestors have not hidden" constitutes the conservative cultural basis upon which wisdom is frequently grounded.[74] The dynamic of recontextualization is particularly evident in the fact that the literary forms of wisdom distinguish themselves from the legal traditions of the Hebrew Bible in part by their exhortative tenor.[75] Although the imperative is an important component to the basic form of proverbial wisdom, wisdom places the language of command within the larger framework of moral experience.[76] As illustrated by the two contradictory injunctions, the very nature of the individual proverb requires an openness for reapplication and revision in light of the plethora of social phenomena life presents to the moral subject. And yet such "contradictions" do not undermine the direction and shape of the moral life. The final shape of Proverbs, with its various collections, renders in the end a comprehensive and consistent profile of normative character.[77]

In short, ethical character as an ethic of being places a much needed emphasis upon the human subject, for which abstracted rules and duties have difficulty accounting. The issues of identity and conduct, character and action are necessarily bound up together in the formation and maintenance of any viable community. In particular, the language of normative character necessarily focuses on two fundamental questions for members of Christian communities: who are we? and whose are we? The answers inseparably wed identity and conduct, embracing the dialectic of election

74. As will be demonstrated in Chapters 4 and 5, the book of Job radically questions and recontextualizes this traditional basis of wisdom.

75. The claim is not made that legal traditions are somehow immune to reconstrual in the face of new social contexts. One need only look at the variety of legal corpora in the Old Testament, including the two versions of the Decalogue in Exod. 20 and Deut. 5. Furthermore, the rhetorical value of motive clauses within the legal traditions, increasingly recognized in recent scholarship, reflects the dynamic nature of law in the development of communal chracter. See Waldemar Janzen, *Old Testament Ethics,* 60-61, 81n.12; Bruce Birch, *Let Justice Roll Down,* 160-62, 190nn.50, 51.

76. Zimmerli, "Concerning the Structure of Old Testament Wisdom," 183.

77. See Chapter 2. The often-asked question of whether a "proverb in a collection is dead" must be answered negatively (cf. Carole R. Fontaine, *Traditional Sayings in the Old Testament,* 54).

and sanctification, of God's sovereign initiative and the moral responsibilities of God's people. With its consistent focus upon human identity and agency, the wisdom corpus repeatedly returns to these two inseparably related issues of character by rendering powerfully compelling profiles of human and divine characters.

III. LITERARY AND MORAL CHARACTER

The relationship between descriptive and prescriptive character is of critical importance in the wisdom literature. It is no accident that much of the wisdom literature fashions and conveys the contours of normative character by certain definable literary characters. The book of Proverbs, for instance, introduces the reader to a veritable cavalcade of competing characters in lively, urgent discourse: the parental figures, rebellious adolescents, woman wisdom, the strange woman, the fool, and the sage, to name only a few. The book of Job profiles Job, his friends, and Yahweh, all in passionate interchange. Ecclesiastes portrays only Qoheleth, in a painfully poignant monologue. All are linked together primarily by their discourse and secondarily by their actions. Some bare their souls, while others are relatively flat and dispassionate. Nevertheless, all are *talking* characters who know who they are and what they are to do, whether enlightened or misguided. Through their discourse each character imparts certain values and perspectives that make for a vision of normative character.

In biblical wisdom, *literary* character and *moral* character are tightly interwoven. For example, a flat character by definition can assume *either* good or bad virtues, but hardly both. Appealing to well-established ethical norms and expectations, such a literary figure can be an ideal model of, or foil for, normative character. Flat characterizations such as the parental figures in Proverbs recall traditional values in an atmosphere of ambient challenge and conflict. Such is the case today with William J. Bennett's popular best-seller,[78] which profiles the contours of traditional virtues amid a perceived dissolute age. His work recalls a past of easily definable heroes and scoundrels, of virtues and vices. However, such appeals to the traditional contours of character run the danger of becoming lifeless typecasts that preclude the free

78. *The Book of Virtues.*

exercise of intention or judgment for new situations and generations, of unwittingly espousing a moral fascism "that feels like a breath of fresh air as it approaches, and like an apocalypse in its aftermath."[79]

More complex or "round" literary characters, on the other hand, exhibit a mixture of estimable and not-so-estimable qualities, a delicate balance of conservative and unorthodox traits. In addition, full-fledged characters demonstrate by personal example a candid *development* of character, displaying their turgid "inner life," because their integrity has become an open question. They are enfleshed with ambiguity and conflict, life and blood. Round characters connote a sense of personal realism with their own appeal and aim in the rhetoric of wisdom. Their task is in part to deconstruct, reform, or reconstruct of traditional contours of ethical character. In short, the way in which the *literary* character is portrayed bears direct relevance to the way in which *normative* character is profiled.

IV. NARRATIVE AND CHARACTER

Before exploring literary and normative character in the wisdom corpus, one item remains to be addressed. Most current work on character formation has focused on the role of narrative. Stanley Hauerwas is well known in Christian circles for exploring the interface between narrative and character formation: "The growth of character . . . is a correlative of our being initiated into a determinative story."[80] The development of an individual's character within the community is the result of a gradual conformity between a story and one's character. The precise relation between narrative and character as self is still a matter of debate, but the connection has been increasingly stressed by Hauerwas and others.[81]

For Hauerwas, the very formation of character involves the self's integration into a particular narrative. We are formed by stories and metaphors, not rules.[82] A narrative is what equips us with the requisite

79. Lance Morrow, "The Search for Virtues," 78.

80. Stanley Hauerwas, *A Community of Character,* 151.

81. See also Stanley Hauerwas, "The Self as Story," 68-89; *idem, The Peaceable Kingdom,* 17-34. See also Bondi, "The Elements of Character," 201-18; *idem,* "Character," 82-83.

82. Hauerwas, "The Self as Story," 71.

skills to "fit what we do and do not do into a coherent account sufficient to claim our life as our own."[83] How that is done, Hauerwas does not specify except to claim that "growing into" a narrative involves constantly challenging one's past achievements.[84] Similarly, Richard Bondi describes the power of narrative in shaping character:

> The power of stories lies not only in their subtle conveyance of truth, but in their ability to touch our hearts, to provide us with reasons of the heart, *acquaint us with lives of virtue,* offer a focus for the affections and a sense of order and discipline for the passions, and give us the vision necessary to reinterpret our subjection to the accidents of history. Character and story come necessarily together, then, exactly in their use as a practical language of the well-lived life, as we try to take part in the shaping of our character so as to better embody the truth of a story of the good life.[85]

While not denying the power of narrative in shaping character, I am inclined to think that the issue of what forms character is more complex and far-reaching than admitted by Hauerwas. It is a reductive mistake to identify that which shapes character as a specific genre, let alone the *only* genre. Hauerwas, in particular, plays fast and loose with the concept of story and its role in shaping character. On the one hand, story denotes the perceptions, beliefs, and social practices of the self in some historical sequence. On the other, it points to the story of the Christian faith, which is instrumental in forming Christian character.[86]

As suggested above, moral principles, rules, and expressed values can also play a significant role in the development of perception, disposition, and intention, the constitutive elements of character. Moral laws and principles and the reasons behind them can inform, even help select, those traits of character that require cultivation in communal life. Indeed, there are countless factors and diverse "genres" that can make moral conduct intelligible and shape the capacity for intentional action: legal codes, sermons, moral principles, liturgical traditions,

---

83. Hauerwas, *A Community of Character,* 151.
84. *Ibid.,* 144.
85. Bondi, "The Elements of Character," 205 (italics added).
86. Hauerwas, "The Self as Story," 87-88.

words of insight, and predictions of social consequences. As Hauerwas himself admits:

> Though moral principles are not sufficient in themselves for our moral existence, *neither are stories sufficient* if they do not generate principles that are morally significant. Principles without stories are subject to perverse interpretation . . . but stories without principles will have no way of concretely specifying the actions and practices consistent with the general orientation expressed by the story.[87]

More than simply "shorthand reminders" or summaries of stories, moral principles, rules, maxims, proverbs, and propositional insights can function decisively in the formation of character, indeed, in the formation of moral narratives.[88]

The factors that bear influence upon the formation of character are undoubtedly endless, though some have tried to reduce the swarm of factors to moral principles, on the one hand, or narrative, on the other. What the wisdom literature uniquely contributes to the contemporary discussion is neither hard-and-fast principles nor gripping narratives. This often neglected corpus essentially provides characterizations of character, that is to say, profiles of character embodied in certain "lives of virtue."[89] The wisdom corpus of the Old Testament, as well as much ancient Near Eastern wisdom literature, freely and readily embraces both narrative and nonnarrative forms of literary discourse to shape the contours of virtuous character.

V. CHARACTER AND WISDOM LITERATURE

Biblical wisdom's approach to character has its roots in certain ancient Near Eastern forms, particularly Egyptian. In the Egyptian "Instruction of Ptahhotep," for example, a certain figure is profiled that lends coher-

---

87. *Ibid.,* 89 (italics added).

88. To attempt to discern whether narrative or moral principle is primary is essentially a *chicken-or-egg* question that is of little relevance for constructive ethical discourse.

89. Bondi, "The Elements of Character," 205.

90. See Miriam Lichtheim's translation in *Ancient Egyptian Literature,* 1:62-80.

ence to the variety of proverbial and instructional sayings, namely the so-called *silent one*.[90] Together, these diverse sayings profile a figure that embodies prudent behavior and wise attitudes, one who is experienced and is successful with the intricacies of the moral life. The silent person avoids speaking rashly, diffuses conflict, is a peacemaker, and is sexually chaste, among other things. Far from comprising a narrative, these Egyptian instructions highlight the role of emulation as the central feature of the intended relationship between the reader, who is to appropriate the wise teachings, and the character profiled in the literature.[91] The "silent one" is presented as a role model, a character that bears striking similarity with several of the profiled characters in the book of Proverbs. In Proverbs certain characters embody such virtues as self-control, judiciousness in speech, and fidelity, to name only a few. Through complex networks of rhetorical images and strategies, all framed within a social hierarchy that correlates age with authority, the book of Proverbs presents a powerfully compelling profile of normative character.[92]

Although biblical wisdom is not narrative by nature, it must be acknowledged that the corpus is not without its narratival dimensions. As will be shown, the book of Proverbs is eminently more than a collection of terse proverbs and instructions; it bears the structure of a "meta-narrative" that exhibits an overall development that finds resolution only in the book's final chapter. For all of its heavy and turgid discourse, the final shape of the book of Job is fundamentally the story of one person's vindication and transformation of character. As for Ecclesiastes, the confessional tone that runs throughout the book presents an account of Qoheleth's achievements and reflections at the pinnacle of his status as a royal sage. With the exception of Job, the wisdom corpus does not exhibit the standard features that are constitutive of the *genre* of narrative.[93] Yet their narratival dimensions cohere with the language of the developing self and the formation of character.

These preliminary probes into the nature of character in ethical and literary discourse are meant to establish a heuristic framework from which a fresh approach to the wisdom traditions in the Hebrew Scrip-

91. See Hauerwas, *A Community of Character*, 131.
92. See Chapter 2.
93. One can also add to the wisdom corpus the extracanonical works of Ecclesiasticus and the Wisdom of Solomon, neither of which is narrative.

tures can be explored. The aim of this study is to demonstrate that the idea of character constitutes the unifying theme or center of the wisdom literature, whose *raison d'être* is to profile ethical character. In so doing, I hope to identify the contours of normative character that typify each of the wisdom books. In line with the elements of character and the factors that determine character discussed above, the following chapters will address three general issues for each biblical book:[94]

1. the way in which the diverse literary characters (e.g., the parent figures in Proverbs, the figure of wisdom, Elihu, Job, Yahweh) are profiled in the literature, including the particular values and virtues they embody;
2. the community's role in the formation of character and the individual's prescribed place within the community; and
3. the worldview, particularly the prescribed relationship of the self to the perceived world and to God.

This study is itself a journey through the changing ethos of biblical wisdom, as the contours of ethical character are shaped and reshaped for new generations. As will soon become clear, the three wisdom books by no means present a homogeneous view of normative character. Yet the fact that there is shared terminology and focus on character suggests certain lines of intertextual dependence among these works. Taken together, these works exhibit nothing less than an intellectual and cultural movement that begins with a particular mold and profile of character and continues with progressive recastings of that mold without altogether shattering the original. Together, the wisdom books of the Old Testament bear witness to the dangers of moral fascism, on the one hand, and moral confusion and anarchy, on the other. It is a biblical corpus whose time for renewed theological reflection has come.

---

94. I willl not focus upon the extracanonical works of Ecclesiasticus and the Wisdom of Solomon only because they deserve separate studies in themselves.

2 The Formation of Character in Proverbs; or, Virtue and the Art of Community Maintenance

In his best-seller, *The Book of Virtues,* William J. Bennett writes, "We must not permit our disputes over thorny political questions to obscure the obligation we have to offer instruction to all our young people in the area in which we have, as a society, reached a consensus: namely, on the importance of good character."[1] In an age of multiculturalism turned "culture wars," Bennett's words are underlined with a sense of urgency. They are meant to impart virtues for a dissolute age.

The book of Proverbs is also a book of virtues, written primarily for young people.[2] At least that is quite clear in the initial nine chapters, which comprise the first major unit of this rather complex book.[3] Whereas the bulk of Proverbs consists of thick jungles of terse, self-contained proverbs, somewhat haphazardly arranged (chs. 10–29),[4] these first nine chapters contain relatively lengthy, organized sections of sustained thought or "instructions" imparted from a parent to a youth.

---

1. Bennett, *The Book of Virtues,* 13.

2. See R. N. Whybray, *The Composition of the Book of Proverbs,* 11-12.

3. See William McKane, *Proverbs,* 262; see Claudia V. Camp's discussion on the thematic relations between Prov. 1–9 and the remainder of the book in *Wisdom and the Feminine in the Book of Proverbs,* 183-208. Camp has emended her dating of the first nine chapters (late sixth or early fifth century; pp. 233-38) for a later, Hellenistic one ("What's So Strange About the Strange Woman?" 23).

4. The section "The Words of the Wise" (Prov. 22:17–24:22) is a possible exception, but even so, this section consists essentially of some brief and not-so-brief commands. See R. N. Whybray, *Wisdom in Proverbs,* 31. For a discussion of the open genre of the proverb, see James L. Crenshaw, *Old Testament Wisdom,* 66-67.

In their final form, Prov. 1–9, along with ch. 31, provide a unifying focus for the book as a whole, a focus established by the voices of various characters and the values they impart. Much recent attention has been devoted to examining the literary profiles of these characters: the two parental figures, wisdom, and the alien or other woman.[5] Little has been done, however, in discerning the various ways these characters employ and nuance ethical language. This is surprising, since the seven verses that open the book of Proverbs present an unusually dense collage of ethical terms or, more accurately, virtues. Clearly, the specific nomenclature of wisdom discourse is equally worthy a topic of literary craft and development. How these technical terms of wisdom are developed with respect to the various voices featured in the first nine chapters will be the subject of this chapter.

I. PROVERBS 1:1-7

The first seven verses of the book of Proverbs introduce the purpose of the book as a whole. Though not in the lectionary, this passage is frequently used as a sermon text to mark the beginning of the Christian school year in the fall. In order to discern the nature and function of this introduction with some precision, a translation of the Hebrew text of Prov. 1:1-7 is offered.

1:1 The Proverbs of Solomon, Son of David, King of Israel
1:2 To appropriate wisdom and instruction;
    to understand insightful sayings;
1:3 To acquire effective instruction,
    righteousness, justice, and equity.
1:4 To teach the immature prudence,
    and the young knowledge in discretion.
1:5 Let the wise (also) attend and gain erudition,
    and the discerning acquire skill (in counseling).
1:6 To understand a proverb, a figure,
    words of the wise, and their enigmas.

5. E.g., Carol A. Newsom, "Woman and the Discourse of Patriarchal Wisdom," 142-160; Athalya Brenner, "Proverbs 1–9: An F Voice?" 113-130.

1:7 The fear of Yahweh is the beginning of knowledge;
fools despise wisdom and instruction.[6]

Following the superscription, these verses present an all-embracing purpose statement[7] of the Solomonic proverbs.[8] This ancient "course objective," as it were, is thick with sapiential terms, whose density is matched only by its comprehensive scope. Such a richness of wisdom terminology has an undeniably cumulative effect upon the reader. As Gerhard von Rad noted, "By the cumulation of many terms the text seems to aim at something larger, something more comprehensive which could not be expressed satisfactorily by means of any one of the terms used."[9]

Although von Rad may be correct in noting that the plethora of terms cannot be precisely delineated, there is undeniably a range of values conveyed in the introduction, extending from concrete skill or resourcefulness to more abstract qualities such as righteousness and justice. Moreover, a hodgepodge of ethical terms this list is not. Rather, a systematic arrangement is clearly in evidence. This litany of values and virtues opens and concludes with reference to the intellectual values of wisdom and instruction (vv. 2 and 7) as well as to their literary conventions: "words of insight" (v. 2) and their forms (v. 6). Sandwiched in between this literary envelope are particular distinctions in virtue. Effective instruction, skill, prudence, and discretion (vv. 3a and 5b) constitute eminently practical or instrumental virtues that enable the person to pursue successfully certain goals or objectives.[10] By definition, instrumental virtues are pragmatic and have the potential to be

6. Many scholars have argued that Prov. 1:7 is a later Yahwistic addition to these introductory verses, yet such judgment in the end is subjective and involves a complex model of development in which overtly religious themes are introduced into the corpus only at its latest stage. For our purposes, the arguments for or against such a diachronic literary development are not crucial.

7. This is particularly clear in the Hebrew, given the fact that each of the five bicola in vv. 2-6 is introduced with the preposition l^e adjoined to the infinitive construct.

8. On the significance of attributing the book of Proverbs to the royal figure of Solomon, see Walter A. Brueggemann, "The Social Significance of Solomon as a Patron of Wisdom," 117-132.

9. *Wisdom in Israel*, 13.

10. This method of classification is based on Edmund L. Pincoffs, *Quandaries and Virtues*, 84.

vices, depending upon the goal involved. At the center of this constellation of virtues are found the comprehensive moral traits of "righteousness, justice, and equity," which constitute normative communal relations and conduct (v. 3b).[11] All in all, the particular arrangement of ethical terms embedded in these introductory six verses exhibits a tightly wrought concentric structure.

> A   Comprehensive, intellectual values: 2a
> > B   Literary expression of wisdom: 2b
> > > C   Instrumental virtue: 3a
> > > _____
> > > **D   Moral, communal virtues: 3b**
> > > _____
> > > C′   Instrumental virtues: 4-5
> > B′   Literary expressions of wisdom: 6
> A′   Comprehensive, intellectual virtues: 7

With this programmatic arrangement proposed, it is necessary to examine briefly some of the individual terms.

1. Effective instruction *(mûsar haśkēl)*[12]

The virtue *haśkēl,* usually translated "wise dealing" in 1:3a, demonstrates a wide range of meaning. It can connote prosperity (Prov. 17:8; 1 Sam. 18:15; Jer. 10:21; 20:11) as well as that which brings about prosperity, such as reputation and good sense (Prov. 3:4; 12:8; 13:15). The term is action and outcome centered.[13] In its widest sense, *haśkēl* denotes action that ensures the successful pursuit of desired objectives and results.[14] Its wide range of meaning suggests more a *category* or *type* of virtue than a particular virtue per se.[15] Thus it is perhaps best to regard the

---

11. See below.

12. NRSV translates this phrase as "instruction in wise dealing."

13. For example, the one who is restrained in speech and has the foresight to gather in the summer is a *maśkîl* (Prov. 10:5, 19; 16:23).

14. Helmer Ringgren, *Sprüche/Prediger,* 13; McKane, 265.

15. Note, e.g., the diversity of translations for the term and its cognates in the variety of contexts in Proverbs in the NRSV: "good sense" (13:15), "repute" (3:4), "judicious" (16:23), "wisdom" (16:22; 23:9), "prudence" (10:5, 19), and "deals wisely" (14:35; 17:2).

term in this context as denoting the *class* of instrumental virtues. Within this broad class a variety of virtues may be included: prudence, resourcefulness, cool-headedness, caution, courage, good sense, and persistence, to name only a few.[16] The virtue of *haśkēl* is essentially pragmatic, fashioned and refined from well-tested experience and conduct.

2. Righteousness *(ṣedeq)*, Justice *(mišpāt)*, and Equity *(mêšārîm)*

Righteousness and justice are frequently paired in prophetic and psalmic literature. They carry a distinctly moral as well as communal connotation, particularly in the context of governance. The Hebrew term for "justice" can refer to any aspect of justice, from the process of litigation (Isa. 3:14) to the actual sentence of judgment (1 Kgs. 20:40). Righteousness similarly involves ethical relations between individuals and communities (e.g., Isa. 1:21). The righteous person is one who demonstrates *Gemeinschaftstreue* or "community loyalty."[17] "Equity," whose basic meaning is "straight" or "even," is also closely bound up with justice and judicious speech. In the Psalter, equity is used exclusively as a qualification of the way in which God judges the people Israel.[18] God is praised for rendering justice equitably and fairly. In short, all three virtues deal explicitly with the way social relations are to be structured and justice is to be executed.

3. Prudence *('ormâ)* and Discretion *(mᵉzimmâ)*

Prudence finds its opposite in those vices that are embodied by the "simple" *(petî;* Prov. 1:4; 19:25; 27:12). The prudent person heeds admonition (15:5), is cautious, and does not believe everything like the simple do (14:15). The prudent individual ignores insults rather than becomes inflamed with anger (12:16), understands and avoids danger (22:3; 27:12), and is endowed with knowledge but does not flaunt it (14:18; 12:23). The opposite of naïveté, prudence is founded upon caution and discretion (1:4b). Prudence is precisely what youth lack;

16. This is to be distinguished from exclusively task-oriented virtues (see the discussion of instrumental vs. task virtues in Pincoffs, 84).

17. Hans Heinrich Schmid, *Gerechtigkeit als Weltordnung*, 185-86.

18. Ps. 9:9(Eng. v. 8); 58:2(1); 75:3(2); 96:10; 98:9; 99:4.

thus, it is founded upon well-tested experience and developed in practice. Prudence is the paramount example of instrumental virtue.
Moreover, the fact that the term can also be used pejoratively to denote
craftiness (Job 5:12; 15:5; Gen. 3:1; Ps. 83:4[Eng. v. 3]) highlights the
instrumental force of this potential virtue-turned-vice.

Paired with prudence, "discretion" *(mᵉzimmâ)* is essentially synonymous to prudence (see also Prov. 8:12).[19] It is paired elsewhere with
"good sense" or resourcefulness *(tušiyyâ;* 3:21) and knowledge (5:2).
Like prudence, discretion can also turn sour in certain contexts by
connoting excessive scheming (12:2; 14:17; 24:8). Hence, the term is by
nature instrumental: this virtue gains its moral force in conjunction
with moral objectives.

4. Skill *(taḥbulôt)*

Etymologically this term conveys the concrete image of rope pulling for
the purpose of steering a ship.[20] Hence, the term perhaps means something akin to "the art of steering," as suggested by Walther Zimmerli, or
what could be colloquially translated "learning the ropes."[21] Elsewhere
in Proverbs the term refers concretely to the good advice given by royal
counselors in the context of the nation's livelihood (11:14; 20:18; 24:6).
The original sense of nautical expertise is transposed to the political
domain. In the context of sagacious discourse, the term denotes the art
of solving problems and meeting the challenges that face the body
politic, requiring an extensive amount of experience and intuition in
matters such as battle strategy, diplomacy, and negotiation. Such counsel, coming from the wicked, can be treacherous (12:5), however, and
thereby bring about disaster and ruin. In light of the fact that this term
applies to the wise, as opposed to the simple, the term denotes a high
degree of sophistication involving skill and insight in finding solutions
and rendering advice in leadership capacities.

19. Indeed, the NRSV renders the term "prudence" in 3:21 and 5:2.

20. Note the cognates: *ḥebel,* which means cord or rope; *ḥōbēl,* which denotes
sailor; and *ḥibbel,* which refers to the mast of a ship. See BDB, 287.

21. See Walther Zimmerli, "The Place and Limit of the Wisdom in the Framework
of the Old Testament Theology," 149 (repr. in *Studies in Ancient Israelite Wisdom,* ed.
James L. Crenshaw, 316); McKane, 265-66.

To sum up, the list in 1:2-7 is structured deliberately to cover a wide variety of virtue types, from cognitive[22] to instrumental to inherently moral dispositions, a veritable repertoire of virtues. Within this constellation, however, is another movement that underlies the concentric structure. The language becomes more specific. The "insightful words" briefly mentioned in v. 2b are thoroughly specified in v. 6. Effective instruction in v. 3 is exemplified in vv. 4 and 5. More striking is the fact that beginning in v. 4, certain characters are introduced: youths (v. 4), who in their immaturity stand in critical need of guidance; sages (v. 5), who cannot escape the need for further instruction; and fools (v. 7b), who delude themselves by thinking they have escaped. The constellation of values introduced in the first two verses are given personal rootage in the last four. The reader is introduced to the kinds of individuals who are to appropriate or reject such values. In short, the language moves from value to virtue: Youths become prudent and discreet; the wise become more resourceful; and the foolish remain intractably set in their ways. In the language of proverbial ethics, the movement toward specificity leads toward "virtue-osity," that is, the language of appropriation.

The culmination of this movement toward specificity and virtue is found in the phrase "the fear of the Lord is the beginning of knowledge" in v. 7. This *leitmotif* of proverbial wisdom is presented as a comprehensive *intellectual* virtue.[23] It marks the starting point as well as the end point of the journey of wisdom (2:3-5). Far from implying terror, holy reverence provides nothing less than a methodological base for the appropriation of wisdom. Instrumentally, it indicates the requisite posture one must assume in order to exercise and broaden one's repertoire of virtues. Yet more basic, "the fear of the Lord" introduces a relational dimension to the list of virtues that grounds this catalogue squarely within the parameters of normative character. Whereas the list of virtues delineates the external contours of ethical character, the "fear" of God deals fundamentally with the heart and center of character, namely the position of the person *in relation* to God.[24] A position of

---

22. The cognitive or intellectual values of wisdom, instruction, understanding, and insight presuppose a host of intellectual virtues such as attention, focus, imagination, discernment, and judgment.

23. See also Joachim Becker, *Gottesfurcht im Alten Testament*, 217-18; Michael Fox, "The Pedagogy of Proverbs 2," 238.

24. See Chapter 1 and Richard Bondi's definition of character as "the self *in*

humble, receptive reverence, an acknowledgment that all wisdom is divinely generated, this is not the kind of fear that walks on eggshells.[25]

In the center of this concentric structure (i.e., 1:3b) is located the series of moral virtues that are indispensable for the maintenance and governance of the community. Taken together, the plethora of terms appear to be weighted toward the intellectual and instrumental categories. It is such an observation that prompts one modern sage, William McKane, to claim that "the educational process [outlined in Prov. 1:1-6] was more occupied with developing mature intellectual attitudes than with morality."[26] To be sure, by sheer numbers alone, it would appear that the distinctly moral or communal virtues are in the minority. Yet these particular moral virtues comprise nothing less than the centerpiece of this prolegomena, enwrapped by a collage of instrumental values and framed with intellectual referents.

To address McKane's thesis more completely, it is necessary to determine how this constellation of virtues and values featured in the introduction are highlighted and arranged throughout the next nine chapters. In the subsequent material these virtues take on new depth, almost a life of their own. Rather than abstract categories systematically arranged, as in the prolegomena (1:1-7), such virtues take on new metaphorical dimensions: They become guardians, adornments, paths, street preachers, conversationalists, and intimate friends, all woven together into a rich rhetorical tapestry. No longer laid out black and white on a flat canvas, these categories of virtue are set in dramatic three-dimensional relief that heightens their rhetorical hold upon the reader, the student of wisdom. The added depth and color with which these virtues are imbued reflect a social situation of urgency, even crisis among our ancient sages, who perceived that the stakes could not be higher for their community as

---

relation" (italics added), "The Elements of Character," 204. "Fear of God" receives much attention in Deuteronomy as a posture of humble obedience the begins with the heart, the seat of understanding and will (e.g., Deut. 10:12).

25. It is such a perspective that prompts Jesus ben Sira, a Hellenistic Jewish sage and author of Ecclesiasticus, to proclaim, "the fear of the Lord delights the heart, and gives gladness and joy" (Sir. 1:12).

26. McKane, *Proverbs*, 265. McKane scarcely accounts for the presence of the moral virtues of justice, righteousness, and equity in v. 3. Such a bias is also reflected in Bruce Birch's discussion of the ethics of wisdom literature when he observes: "Thus, there is no concept of social responsibility which transcends the pursuit of personal righteousness" (*Let Justice Roll Down*, 334). See below.

they perceived it. For the final editors of Proverbs, it simply did not suffice to list series after series of terse proverbial sayings and instructions, as one finds in chs. 10 and following. Rather, new life was breathed into these values in order to profile them for a dissolute age.

II. THE ETHOS OF INSTRUCTION

Before analyzing the various ways this constellation of virtues is profiled in the subsequent chapters, a few observations need to be made concerning the formal literary setting in which these virtues are embedded. Following the introduction, a parental figure begins to speak in a series of instructions to a silent son in 1:8. "Hear, my son, your father's instruction" opens the discourse. Frequently, this form of "instruction" *(mûsār)* exhibits a disciplinary nuance in Proverbs, as in 6:23, which refers to "the reproofs of instruction."[27] This is confirmed extensively in the proverbial collections that follow ch. 9, in which "instruction" is frequently paired with reproof or rebuke.[28] Furthermore, in a significant number of cases the term "instruction" is used in the context of child rearing.[29]

It is no surprise, then, that such "instruction" is prominently highlighted in the parental speeches of chs. 1–9. Such instructions are filled with admonitions, commands, warnings, and reproofs. The first parental discourse is no exception (1:8-19). The father's instruction highlights the hierarchical relationship between him and his son, in stark contrast to the "sinners," who depict themselves as peers equal in relation to the son (1:10-19).[30] With the frequent use of cohorta-

---

27. *tôkᵉhôt mûsār.*
28. *tôkahat* and *gᵉʿârâ;* e.g., 13:1; 15:10; 10:17; 12:1; 13:18.
29. E.g., 13:1, 24; 22:15; 19:27; 4:1. Two lamentable examples stand out:

Do not withhold discipline *(mûsār)* from your children;
if you beat them with a rod, they will not die (23:13).

Folly is bound up in the heart of a boy,
but the rod of discipline *(mûsār)* drives it far away (22:15).

It is evident, however, that the term for discipline or instruction is not used in a physically abusive way in Prov. 1–9. See Fox, "The Pedagogy of Proverbs 2," 233, 241-43.
30. Newsom, "Woman and the Discourse of Patriarchal Wisdom," 144-45.

tives in place of commands, the sinners' speech embodies an enticing egalitarian ethos that in the end is thoroughly dismantled by the father's discourse. The father's rhetorical strategy is quite effective: He compels the son to take a step back from his peers' enticing invitation, enabling him to witness the consequences of their actions. Their rallying cry of "all for one and one for all" (see 1:14) is unveiled by the father as nothing more than greedy scheming for profits (1:19) that in the end will result in self-destruction. The father exposes their entrepreneurial spirit for what it is, violence against both the community (1:12) and themselves:

> For in vain is the net baited while the bird is looking on; yet they lie in wait — to kill [only] themselves! and set an ambush — for their own lives! (1:17-18)

The scenario depicted in these verses — the lure of quick profits through violence, the appeal of gangs, the conflict between youth and parents — is certainly not a distinctly contemporary, urban manifestation. Far from being a lecture on the intellectual virtues of prudence, the father's speech is passionately concerned about the preservation of his son's life and, thus, the preservation of the community.

In short, disciplinary instruction is what characterizes the parental language that runs throughout much of Prov. 1–9. Such parental discourse is even ascribed to Yahweh: "My son, do not despise YHWH's instruction or be weary of his reproof, for YHWH reproves the one he loves, as a father [reproves] the son in whom he delights" (3:11-12). In sum, instruction, as a form of sagacious discourse, has its primary home in parental discourse, particularly in connection with the pedagogy of reproof.

Tenor of reproof continues into wisdom's initial discourse (1:20-33). Indeed, the sternest rebuke in chs. 1–9 comes not from the parent but from wisdom herself. The term "reproof" is attested no less than three times in 1:22-33, the highest frequency of occurrence for this term within any literary unit in the Hebrew Bible.

> How long, O simple ones, will you love being simple?
> How long will scoffers delight in their scoffing
>   and fools hate knowledge?
> Give heed to my reproof;
> I will pour out my thoughts to you;

> I will make my words known to you.
> Because I have called and you refused,
>   have stretched out my hand and no one heeded,
> and because you have ignored all my counsel
>   and would have none of my reproof,
> I also will laugh at your calamity;
>   I will mock when panic strikes you. (1:22-26)

And it does not end there. It is clear up to this point that wisdom's rhetorical arsenal consists of nothing short of an *indictment* against her audience. While the father warns his son, wisdom indicts those who have rejected her counsel (1:25). At their own risk, simple ones and scoffers have refused to heed her summons. Wisdom's approach is clearly strategic: The force of her rhetoric lies in her ability to ascribe a guilty conscience to her listeners, thereby provoking a crisis of decision. This is clearly the rhetoric of rebuke at its sharpest!

The position of wisdom's rebuke immediately following the father's warning has the effect of extending the parental discourse into the realm of the community. Rather than mitigating the father's authoritative stance, wisdom heightens the hierarchical relationship between teacher and student. Indeed, whereas the father addresses exclusively the son, wisdom's audience is cast in the *plural*. The targets of wisdom's rebuke, the "simple ones" and "scoffers" of 1:22, stand in rhetorical continuity with the son's wayward peers, against whom the father warned his son. Not confined within the cloistered walls of hearth and home, wisdom's rhetoric wafts through the streets and central locales of public intercourse (1:20-21). She, unlike the father, is in a position to rebuke directly the scoffers who provoke only violence for quick gain. Such harsh discourse echoes Amos's injunction against those who promulgate injustice against the poor:

> They hate the one who *reproves* in the gate,
>   and they abhor the one who speaks the *truth*. (Amos 5:10)

It is at the city gate that wisdom reproves her detractors, speaking the plain truth of justice, righteousness, and equity. Her converts are few.

In short, by assuming a more critical stance, wisdom's discourse serves to sharpen, even heighten the hierarchical relationship between the wise and the immature. The son overhears, as it were, wisdom's indictment against those whose conduct is shared by his peers. What is cast as an indictment against them serves as a rebuke against the son.[31] Now the stage is set for the profiles of virtue that follow.

III. THE PROFILE OF VIRTUE IN PARENTAL DISCOURSE

The first dense cluster of virtues is found in the father's instruction in Prov. 2.[32] Here, the virtue of wisdom assumes the first position amid a cluster of intellectual virtues that also includes knowledge, insight, and understanding (2:2-6). Yet like our introduction in 1:1-7, the list does not remain on the level of intellectual generality. Similar to the movement in the introduction, there is a progression from intellectual virtues to instrumental to the distinctly moral, but they are all now embedded in an evocative metaphorical matrix. The instrumental virtue of good sense or resourcefulness that ensures success *(tušiyyâ)* acts as an effective shield for those who walk with integrity as well as guards the paths of justice.[33] Similarly, prudence and understanding play the roles of protective guardian on behalf of those who walk on "every good path," preventing the sojourner from veering off into the crooked "ways of darkness" (2:13, 15). At the center of this collage are the communal values of "righteousness, justice, and equity":

31. The way in which wisdom addresses a double audience that includes both the son and the fools confirms her as a consummate rhetorician. She appears to summon her audience for reproof (1:23) and yet at the same time indicts them for having rejected her reproof (vv. 25, 30). Note also the slide from second person address (1:22-27) into third person description (vv. 28-32). Such features enjoin a change of heart on the part of the son while decisively condemning the recalcitrant who are doomed for disaster.

32. For an analysis of the syntactical structure of Prov. 2, see Fox, "The Pedagogy of Proverbs 2," 235-36; Dennis Pardee, *Ugaritic and Hebrew Poetic Parallelism.*

33. NRSV, as with most translations, mistakenly identifies the shield with YHWH ("He is a shield . . ."). However, the semantic similarity with vv. 11-12 suggests otherwise: The virtues of discretion and understanding also assume the role of protectors. Vv. 7-8 read literally:

> [YHWH] stores up good sense for the upright,
> > a shield to those who walk with integrity,
> for guarding the paths of justice
> > and preserving the way of his faithful.

The "shield" in 7b refers to "good sense."

> Then you will understand righteousness, justice,
>   and equity, every good path. (2:9)

Appropriating the virtues of right communal relations is the natural result of receiving wisdom. That these three virtues are community oriented is confirmed by the way they are profiled in ch. 2. They comprise "every good path" (2:9), in direct contrast to evil ones, "whose paths are crooked" and lead to death (2:15, 18). An inherently communal metaphor, the path is a dominant motif in proverbial discourse. A path can only be formed by the passage of many feet; no lone individual can form a path.[34] As such, justice, righteousness, and equity constitute the guideposts of the community on the move.

The metaphor of the path or way serves to set in topographic relief the relationship between many of the virtues first delineated in 1:1-7. Communal values constitute the path along which the community must follow; certain instrumental virtues serve as protective guardians along the way, preserving the community from veering off into crooked ways and self-destruction. To welcome wisdom necessarily involves becoming a responsible and productive citizen of a community whose character is formed by justice and equity by those who have gone before, laying a foundation for those to come. Appropriating wisdom is realized by those who participate in molding the corporate identity of the community and directing its praxis. In stark contrast, the way of the wicked is essentially one that threatens to collapse the established structures of the community, undermining its ethical foundations. This anti-community ethos is most graphically represented by the personified form of the "strange" or "alien" woman, to whom the reader is first introduced in 2:16-19. From the very outset, this outsider is described as one who has severed and overturned the most basic of communal ties, the marriage covenant (2:17), an act considered no less destructive to the community than the sinners' schemes to ambush the innocent in ch. 1. In either case, at stake is the very survival of the covenant community, on behalf of which wisdom and her arsenal of virtues wage their defense.

Elsewhere, the constellation of virtues by and large echoes the profiles set forth in ch. 2. For example, the son is exhorted to "guard good sense (tušiyyâ) and discretion (mᵉzimmâ), for they will be life for

---

34. See Newsom, "Woman and the Discourse of Patriarchal Wisdom," 147.

your soul and adornment for your neck" (3:21). Such virtues ensure safe passage along the way (3:23). Like the prescribed phylacteries of Jewish tradition (cf. Deut. 6:6-9; 11:18-21), discretion and good sense are profiled as material objects to be worn by the wayfarer. The son is enjoined to grasp and wear them; they in turn serve to protect him on his way. The instrumental virtues of discretion and good sense establish the individual's point of departure into the realm of communal responsibility. Discretion serves to safeguard the individual from undermining communal structures and relationships based on equity and fairness.

The communal orientation of such instrumental virtues is no better specified than in the list of five negative commands in Prov. 3:27-31, which are designed to illustrate the contours of the sensibly prudent lifestyle. How they hang together is readily clear. All deal with the maintenance of harmonious relationships within the community. The importance of this list cannot be underestimated, since it clearly indicates that the instrumental virtues of discretion and good sense (3:21) are intimately bound up with the welfare of the community. The prudent lifestyle is profiled *relationally,* beyond the perspective of the efficient and successful attainment of individual goals.[35] The betterment of the individual per se is not the issue. Rather, instrumental virtues are nuanced in such a way as to highlight their beneficial impact upon the community. It is in service to the community that these virtues find their essential legitimacy.[36]

Other admonitions given by the father confirm such a profile. Marital faithfulness (5:15-20) is of utmost importance, since fidelity preserves family structures and prevents an unleash of violence caused by jealousy (6:24-35). Credit surety and money-lending are discouraged, since such arrangements upset the equilibrium of economic power between individuals (6:1-3). Even the most individualized and practical virtues are given a communal twist. Diligent labor, for example, as illustrated by the example of the ant, is profiled as the means to prevent the rapacious onslaught of poverty (6:6-11). It is not simply in passing that mention is made of the ant being part of a community that maintains itself

---

35. In contrast, e.g., to the way the instrumental virtue *tušiyyâ* is used in Job 5:12; 6:13.

36. Cf. the list of seven vices in 6:17-19, which culminates with the matter of causing strife within the family.

without chief, officer, or ruler (6:7). The community endures simply by each ant gathering for itself (a sort of precursor to Adam Smith's "invisible hand"?). Laziness, however, invites poverty, which is likened to a military attack (6:11) and, therefore, poses a liability to the community. Even the graphic description of the scoundrel's speech and body language (e.g., crooked discourse, winking, shuffling, pointing) is rooted in the proclivity to evoke destructive social tension, perhaps in its most damaging form through unnecessary and false litigation (6:12-14). In short, instrumental or practical values are profiled in the father's discourse specifically within the context of the community and its well-being.

IV. WISDOM'S DISCOURSE: FROM CHARACTER TO CREATION

It is no surprise that the densest cluster of virtues to be found in Prov. 1–9, with the exception of the introduction, is in wisdom's own discourse in ch. 8. As wisdom takes her usual position at the crossroads of public discourse, the virtues come fast and furious beginning with v. 5. Similar to her opening address in 1:4, wisdom targets the unintelligent. But unlike her first address, what follows is not so much a stern rebuke as a character sketch of wisdom herself. Wisdom opens with an analysis of the nature of her discourse (8:6-9). Listed first are her words concerning matters of leadership[37] and equity in 8:6, values constitutive of a just order. The values of truth and righteousness then follow (8:7-8). Such values, wisdom affirms, are part and parcel of "straight talk," the form of sagacious discourse. Straight talk is regarded as formative in upholding and maintaining the just community, for once speech loses its integrity, so also do the corporate relationships that sustain the community. Sagacious speech is the antonym of "doublespeak," to borrow from George Orwell. In short, the values imparted in wisdom's speech are finely interwoven in a way that tightly knits both the form and content of sagacious discourse: Plain truth is correlated with equity; righteousness and straight talk are inextricably bound up together.

The catalogue of virtues continues as wisdom's discourse turns from the topic of speech to character in 8:12-21: Wisdom lives with

---

37. *nᵉgîḏim*, lit., "princely matters"; cf. 8:15-16.

prudence,[38] discovers knowledge (v. 12), and walks along the paths of righteousness (v. 20). Such statements sound strange as a *self-description* of wisdom. Far from being statements concerning some metaphysical reality, the language seems more appropriate to the *recipient* of wisdom rather than to wisdom herself. But then that is the point. Wisdom presents a character résumé that is meant to bridge the inquirer and wisdom. Cast in the language of embodiment, the traits of wisdom are designed for appropriation. When wisdom claims she possesses "wise counsel and good sense," she casts herself in the role of the ideal character of her inquirer. By describing her own character in such a way, wisdom is able to forge an indelible link with the character of her disciple. Wisdom walks the paths of righteousness and justice, and so must also the community (8:20). This last statement concludes wisdom's confession of virtues before she launches into her cosmic role (8:22-31). Once again, the communal virtues stand at the apex of wisdom's discourse and character.

Wisdom's very concrete self-description, however, does not end with the profiling of normative character. Departing from the level of human character, wisdom rises to the cosmic realm after v. 21. Wisdom places herself at the very beginning of God's creative acts (vv. 22-23). She is created *(qnh)* by Yahweh, brought forth from birth *(ḥwl)* before the rest of earthly creation (vv. 24, 25).[39] The creative acts in vv. 24-29 all point to wisdom's primordial, albeit non-preexistent, nature. Yet the point of such cosmogonic language is to focus not so much on the process of creation as on wisdom's position *in relation* to creation and God. Wisdom's focus on her relationship to God and creation marks the culmination of her character description. While the created order was established, wisdom was beside God "like a little child" (8:30[40]), full

38. Scholars have deemed this a difficult verse, given the verb *škn,* "to abide," which seems inappropriate semantically and lacks a prepositional object. Elsewhere the term denotes an enduring, unassailable relationship, such as with the land (2:21, also without a preposition!). The wayward woman, on the other hand, does not abide at home (7:11). Such language vividly expresses the close correspondence between wisdom and prudence, a relationship in which wisdom's disciple must also share.

39. The base meaning of the Hebrew verb *ḥwl* refers to twisting or writhing, whether in dance or in pain, the latter frequently designating labor and birth.

40. See textual note in NRSV. The meaning behind the enigmatic term *'mn,* commonly translated as "master worker" (NRSV), takes on the nuance of buoyant youthfulness, given the immediate context both with what follows (v. 30b) and with the

of delight and joy. Wisdom revels in the created order, brimming with joy over the work of Yahweh's hands, particularly in the creation of humans (v. 31).[41]

Though wisdom's joy is primordial, humans can partake of it, for wisdom concludes her address in beatitudinal form: "Happy are those who keep my ways. . . . Happy is the one who listens to me" (8:32b, 34a; cf. 3:12-13). As the sabbath rest marks the culmination of creation in Gen. 1:1–2:3, the litany of creation of Prov. 8 finds its own climax in the phenomenon of joy. Wisdom's exuberant childlike delight in the inhabited world gushes over into the happiness she desires her children to experience. It is a joy that comes from having witnessed creation unfold in all of its grandeur much like an infant who begins to discover a world of bright colors and intriguing shapes. Wisdom's discourse concludes with an invitation to her children to share in the ebullient joy she herself experiences as a child. The language of admonition and instruction (1:20-33) slides into the language of beatitude. No imperatives or admonitions are needed here! Behind the stern cadences of wisdom's initial rebuke are the cosmic reverberations of her mirth.

For our ancient sages, the nature of wisdom's discourse was much more important than her metaphysical dimensions. Wisdom's discourse begins with a harsh rebuke (1:20-33) but ends in joyous acceptance. Wisdom does not come from within; our sages make that quite clear. Nor is she identified with God, the sole object of praise and petition. She is rather created, fashioned, and uttered by God. "The LORD gives wisdom; / from his mouth come knowledge and understanding" (2:6). At base, wisdom is profiled as the voice of God, the language of the Creator that is embodied and disseminated by the community. Wisdom

---

preceding references to wisdom's birth before creation (vv. 24-25). (So Christa Kayatz, *Studien zu Proverbien 1–9*, 93-94; Bernhard Lang, *Wisdom and the Book of Proverbs*, 65-66; Samuel Terrien, "The Play of Wisdom," 133-37. For an overview of all the issues, see R. B. Y. Scott, "Wisdom in Creation," 213-223.) Furthermore, there is no indication in this litany of creation that wisdom is assisting Yahweh in the process of creation. Rather, wisdom embodies the irrepressible joy of witnessing creation unfold and receiving God's "affections" (vv. 30b-31).

41. Wisdom is not the voice of creation; indeed, she precedes creation (contra von Rad, *Wisdom in Israel*, 144-165).

42. It is perhaps no coincidence that in Luke's narrative of the "Road to Emmaus" incident, Jesus' discourse to the two disciples moves through the same pedagogical stages as wisdom does in Prov. 1–9: rebuke (Luke 24:25), instruction (v. 27), and host (v. 30).

embodies that kind of discourse which is meant to mold and shape the community in its practice, moving strategically from rebuke, in response to the community's failure, to joy, in the community's success in embodying justice. When righteousness reigns, the community rejoices, to adapt a line from Prov. 11:10, and so also does wisdom. Wisdom's discursive journey begins in judgment and ends in grace. She is embodied when the community's discourse genuinely reflects divine discourse. With wisdom's creation, God establishes a community of discourse. When wisdom proclaims, "I was beside God like a little child," the community, like wisdom, becomes initiated into the grand and joyous ways of God that began in creation. Wisdom, like the community, experiences the ways of God as a journey of unbridled joy and awe, as well as discipline. Indeed, wisdom *is* the community, created to behold and follow the ways of God.

Wisdom's invitation to joy continues in her final discourse of ch. 9 in the form of open hospitality. Her banquet abounds with food and wine, and the only qualification for admittance is the commitment to "lay aside immaturity *(peṯāʾyîm)*, live and walk in the way of insight" (9:6). Wisdom's generosity is nothing short of gratuitous: "Come, eat of my bread / and drink of the wine I have mixed" (v. 5). But her invitation is only one of many that vie for the son's allegiance: "Come, let us lie in wait for blood," proclaim his peers (1:11); "come, let us take our fill of love" (7:18), says the strange woman (cf. 9:16). Again, wisdom's invitation to joy and her gracious hospitality complete her profile that began with the sternest of rebukes in ch. 1 but ends with a very different profile: wisdom receiving her disciple as an honored guest and friend, an approach that the father figure is unable to take.[43] The father in Proverbs can only exhort his son to love, embrace, and prize wisdom, actions that suggest a relationship between partners in marriage. The parental discourse of admonition is now replaced by the discourse of collegiality, of words among companions. In stark contrast to the protocol between father and son, the son is urged to address wisdom as "my sister" *(ʾaḥōṯî)* and "intimate friend" *(mōḏāʿ; 7:4)*, terms of endearment.

Wisdom's role in the pedagogical discourse of Prov. 1–9 is many faceted. Unlike the parent, she does not embody the age that separates the

---

43. At least such a role for the father is unprecedented until the Parable of the Prodigal Son, wherein the father surprisingly welcomes his lost son as a guest of highest honor, much to the dismay of the elder brother (Luke 15:11-32).

generations. Wisdom, rather, serves as the vital link that bridges the generational chasm between parent and child, as well as the social domains of family and community. Wisdom is ageless and thus absolutely youthful to the son (7:4). In this way, the values and virtues of the father are extended into the community as the son is beckoned to make the transition from family to society in a responsible manner. Wisdom extends in part the voice of the parent outside of the cloistered walls of hearth and home and becomes the voice of the larger community that legitimates all those who exercise authority, be they king or parent.[44] The family, to be sure, provides the foundation and training ground for responsible communal life. Family life, as framed in Prov. 1–9, offers a microcosm of the community as much as the temple presents a microcosm of creation in ancient Israelite religion.[45] Like the father, wisdom presupposes the virtues of self-restraint and fidelity, particularly in matters sexual. Prudence, straightforwardness, humility, discretion, hatred of evil, and fear of Yahweh are all featured in wisdom's discourse in ch. 8. But at the apex of the moral scale are the communal values of righteousness, justice, and equity. What the father can only claim secondhand, wisdom can attest directly in revelatory fashion, since she serves as the pedagogical link between God and humans. To embody true character is to put one in touch with creator, creation, *and* community.

The order of creation, as it is featured in 8:22-31, plays a defining role in the development of ethical character.[46] In Proverbs, the language of creation functions to establish wisdom's unequaled position within the conflictual context of the "strange woman." The similarities between these two female characters are striking: Both share the same social domains of street and square (7:12); they even share a common core of language. But the strange woman's speech is revealed by wisdom for what it is, crooked and devious. Her house is a facade of Sheol, whereas wisdom's seven-pillar abode is the fountain of life, perhaps suggesting the temple (cf. Ps. 36:7-9) or its literary replacement.[47] The source of life whose knowledge embraces the cosmos, wisdom alone is worthy of

---

44. Newsom, "Woman and the Discourse of Patriarchal Wisdom," 156.

45. See Jon D. Levenson's discussion of the temple in *Creation and the Persistence of Evil*, 90-99.

46. So also the litany of creation in the book of Job (chs. 38–41; see Chapter 4).

47. See discussion by McKane, 362-65; Harold C. Washington, *Wealth and Poverty in the Instruction of Amenemope and the Hebrew Proverbs*, 124-25.

appropriation. Whereas the strange woman comes on as predatory, lying in wait like the son's peers, not unlike the "doorstep" demon Cain is warned of (Gen. 4:7), wisdom's approach is direct and hospitable. For the one who attends to wisdom, all knowledge is freely shared. Nothing is held in secret. By wisdom Yahweh founded the earth (Prov. 3:19); by wisdom the contours of normative character are decisively shaped.

V. VIRTUES FOR THE WISE: PROVERBS 9:7-12

Last but not least is the constellation of virtues found in 9:7-12. Framed by the respective dinner invitations of woman wisdom and woman folly, this final matrix consists of several maxims from wisdom (see v. 11) that address the *advanced* student of wisdom (cf. 1:4-5). Sharing terminology with the last section of our introduction (1:5-7), the precepts that follow wisdom's profile as host repeat the sage's need for further instruction.

> Give instruction to the wise and they will become wiser still;[48]
> teach the righteous and they will gain in learning. (9:9)

In addition, the following verses make mention of the fear of God again as the methodological starting point of wisdom. The themes of instructing the wise and divine reverence round out the first nine chapters in the same way they concluded the introduction in the first seven verses in ch. 1. But what is striking in these final words of wisdom is that even the wise can warrant rebuke:

> A scoffer who is rebuked will only hate you;
> the wise, when rebuked, will love you. (9:8)

Rebuke also applies to the wise, but in a different way from the kind of rebuke that *indicts* one's peers as simpletons and scoffers, as in wisdom's initial speech in ch. 1. The sharp, heteronomous edge of rebuke is dulled a bit, or at the very least is recognized as a two-edged sword, for rebuking

---

48. Lit., "give to the wise." The verbal object is absent in the Hebrew (cf. 1:4). However, given the alliterative repetition of *ḥkm* in the first colon and the fact that it is wisdom herself who is speaking, *ḥokmâ* is the understood object.

the wise is an equal opportunity right. To count oneself among the wise is to be able to give as well as receive rebukes in love. Here the defining character trait of the wise is the capacity to receive correction with a sense of appreciative collegiality. In fact, it is this spirit of appreciation and love that distinguishes those who are wise from those who are not. Only the wise know most clearly that wisdom is their gain, even at the cost of self-certainty and pride. Although it is precisely this kind of pedagogy that is parodied in the book of Job, this ethos of collegiality among the sages mirrors the relationship between wisdom herself and her disciples.

> I love those who love me,
> > and those who seek me diligently find me. (8:17)

Such love is descriptive as well as prescriptive of the community of the wise. Transformed in the process, the pedagogy of rebuke now finds its home in the mutual edification of peers.

VI. CONCLUSION: PROLEGOMENA REVISITED

In conclusion, Prov. 1–9 is replete with sapiential virtues that are profiled in various ways that explicate the catalogue of values and virtues in Prov. 1:2-7. The material subsequent to this introduction seems to confirm the central place the moral/communal values of righteousness, justice, and equity assume within the whole spectrum of virtues. Though tersely delineated in the introduction, this triad of moral values constitutes nothing less than the pinnacle of moral and social development, the goal of proverbial *paideia*. Its inherently communal provenance readily corresponds to wisdom's own arena of activity at the centers of public discourse and practice. Indeed, her presence at the city gates (1:21; 8:3) implies involvement in the administration of justice.[49] The pairing of instruction and wisdom in 1:2 is more than simply the haphazard conjunction of two synonyms. Instruction and wisdom delineate two interrelated domains or

---

49. See, e.g., Deut. 21:19; 25:7; 2 Sam. 15:1-6; Amos 5:10; Ruth 4:1, 11. For a discussion on the place of law at the city gate, see Hans-Jochen Boecker, *Law and the Administration of Justice*, 31-33.

perhaps even stages of moral development, namely the home and the larger community, respectively. Disciplinary instruction is what characterizes parental discourse; the discourse of wisdom moves beyond rebuke to revelation and invitation (chs. 8 and 9).

To sum up, McKane's assessment that "the educational process was more occupied with developing mature *intellectual* attitudes than with *morality*"[50] misses the mark entirely. To dichotomize intellectual and moral values or, for that matter, instrumental and moral values is farthest from the mind of the ancient sage. That the terse list of moral virtues listed in 1:3b is wrapped with a host of instrumental and intellectual virtues is in no way meant to divert attention away from those virtues that most explicitly address the life of the community.[51] Rather, like spokes joined in the center, the surrounding virtues support the central concern of community maintenance. Cognitive and instrumental virtues are enlisted to enable the moral agent to size up ethically demanding situations accurately and to act appropriately within the community. In short, this comprehensive collage of virtues in 1:2-7 extends an invitation that is both broad enough to compel the reader to partake of the complex and compelling world of wisdom and yet focused enough to present in a new way the hard lessons of threat and tragedy experienced by the community.

VII. BEYOND PROVERBS 1–9: VIRTUES FOR A DISSOLUTE AGE

The central virtues of justice, righteousness, and equity remain, however, on the level of generality in the first nine chapters of Proverbs. They are simply profiled as representing the center and pinnacle of sapiential discourse, but without specific delineation. One could argue, then, that the virtues are simply vague, idealized abstractions that have lost their original force, as some have suggested. Are they simply code words meant to maintain the interests of the status quo?[52] What is clear

---

50. McKane, 265 (italics added); see above. McKane scarcely accounts for the presence of the moral virtues of justice, righteousness, and uprightness in v. 3.

51. Cf. Richard Clifford's one-sided assessment that the "moral route" of Prov. 1–9 is distinctively "individual, intellectual, [and] empirical" (*The Book of Proverbs*, 9).

52. So John David Pleins, "Poverty in the Social World of the Wise"; Birch, *Let*

in these introductory chapters is that the sages are witnesses to a community that they perceive to be on the verge of collapse. The father warns his son against greedy exploitation for the sake of profits in ch. 1. Exploitation and violence run rampant in a community struggling to restore itself during the postexilic period.

Some of the prophetic and historical works of the postexilic period attest to crushing poverty and assimilation in the struggling community. Zechariah tells of fear and rampant unemployment: "For before those days there were no wages for people or for animals, nor was there any safety from the foe for those who went out or came in, and I set them all against one another" (Zech. 8:10). The prophet Haggai likens poverty to earning low wages and placing them in a bag full of holes (Hag. 1:6). Nehemiah cites a severe drought that has led the community to pledge their property and sell their own children into slavery to their own leaders (Neh. 5:1-5).

As for the problem of foreign assimilation, one recalls the prophet Ezra denouncing mixed marriages to the point of espousing a policy of ethnic cleansing through divorce. "Separate yourselves from the peoples of the land and from the foreign wives," he commands (Ezra 10:11). Nehemiah cites severe opposition from the Horonites, Ammonites, Moabites, and Arabs, as the Jewish community begins the painful process of restoration. The problem of Jewish men marrying foreign women so vexed Nehemiah that he reports at one point: "I contended with them and cursed them and beat some of them and pulled out their hair; and I made them take an oath" not to give their children in marriage to foreigners (Neh. 13:25). No nondirective counseling here!

Justice Roll Down, 336-37. The inherent problem with both analyses stems from the much too generalized claim that the wisdom writers were simply purveyors of an urban elite or professional ethic that was by and large oblivious to the rights of the poor (so also Brian Kovacs, "Is There a Class-Ethic in Proverbs?"). Though the tradents of Proverbs by and large did not espouse an ethic of societal transformation *to the extent* promulgated by the prophets (e.g., Isa. 14:30; 26:6; 29:19; 32:7; Zeph. 3:12), the proverbial wisdom's diverse perspectives on the poor, nonetheless, exhibit strong points of correlation with the prophetic critique of urban society. By definition, social critiques presuppose some kind of vision of new order. The claim that "for the wise, poverty is a reality to be avoided, but *not protested against*" (Pleins, 67 [italics added]) fails to capture the nuance and depth of the sapiential critique of the community's responsibility to uphold justice and equity, particularly for the disenfranchised. See Washington's more balanced treatment of poverty in Proverbs (*Wealth and Poverty,* 2-4, 179-85, 205-6).

The first nine chapters of Proverbs also address a situation of social distress, a dissolute age in the eyes of some. To be sure, much of the attention is focused upon the family with the silent son listening at the feet of his parents. Why the family? Because it is seen as the invincible bastion of ideological innocence by virtue of the fact that everyone has or has had a family, a fact that is often exploited in public discourse today. Hence, of all social domains, the family provides the strongest appeal and basis for shaping and reorienting the praxis of the community. As noted above, such focus on the family in Proverbs does not end with this smallest and most basic of social structures.

As for these abstract categories of justice, righteousness, and equity, the hallmarks of wisdom's discourse, it is important to note that Prov. 1–9 was intended to provide a unifying focus to the book as a whole, serving as its introduction. The first nine chapters orient the ancient as well as modern reader to pick up amid the plethora of maxims and proverbs particular themes that delineate the chief virtues presented by the characters of parent and wisdom. In other words, these initial instructions and profiles provide an organizing paradigm designed to guide the reader in the act of reading, listening, and appropriating the myriad of proverbial sayings that begin in ch. 10. If the reader maintains the subject position of the silent adolescent beyond ch. 9, he or she will discover a host of various characters, a virtual cavalcade of heroes and scoundrels in the quest for wisdom, that expand this adolescent's social horizon from what was profiled initially by the parent. Kings and queens, wives and royal counselors, the righteous and the foolish, the poor and the rich, God and dogs all contribute to the youth's moral education and development. The life of the community, in all of its ambiguity and conflict, in its successes and failure, is unfolded in its variegated immensity.

Armed with the need to fill in and delineate the categories of communal virtues as profiled in the first nine chapters, the reader begins to make way through the jungle of competing voices and examples, through the enigmas and terse proverbs of the community's various traditions. Dispersed throughout the bulk of the book are specific sayings that give concrete shape and form to this triad of communal virtues. The reader finds, for example, that:

Righteousness exalts a nation. (14:34)

The throne is established by righteousness. (16:12; 20:28; 25:5)

The righteous know the rights of the poor;
    the wicked have no such understanding. (29:7)

The righteous give and do not hold back. (21:26)

The field of the poor may yield much food,
    but it is swept away through injustice. (13:23)[53]

There are those whose teeth are swords,
    whose teeth are knives,
to devour the poor from off the earth,
    the needy from among mortals. (30:14)

Indeed, there are innumerable sayings that delineate the rights of the vulnerable:

Those who oppress the poor insult their Maker. (14:31; 17:5)

The Lord . . . maintains the widow's boundaries. (15:25)

Whoever is kind to the poor lends to the Lord,
    and will be repaid in full. (19:17)

The rich and the poor have this in common:
    the Lord is the maker of them all. (22:2; cf. 29:13)[54]

Of particular note is the injunction in 22:22-23, wherein the theme of the gate corresponds precisely to wisdom's position at the city gate (1:21; 8:3), the center the administrative justice:[55]

Do not rob the poor because they are poor,
    or crush the afflicted at the gate;

---

53. This verse and 30:14 run contrary to Pleins's contention that "the wisdom writer draws no connection between the poverty of the poor and the wealth of the rich." Pleins cites 28:15 as "the sole exception" to his admitted generalized claim (67).

54. This verse, along with 29:13, does not imply so much that wealth and poverty are directly attributable to God's inscrutable providence as that there is a common bond of created humanity between the rich and the poor that requires equitable treatment of the poor (*contra* Pleins, 69).

55. See above. Overlooking the positioning of wisdom at the center of administrative justice, Pleins falsely claims that Prov. 22:22 is "the only instance in Proverbs of a concern for justice at the gate" (69).

> for the LORD pleads their cause
> and despoils of life those who despoil them. (cf. Amos 5:10-12)

The success of a ruler is measured by the way in which the poor are treated:

> A ruler who oppresses the poor
> is a beating rain that leaves no food. (Prov. 28:3)

> If a king judges the poor with equity,
> his throne will be established forever. (29:14)

In addition, ethical conduct in business was paramount for the sages:

> Honest balances and scales are the LORD's. (16:11)

> Diverse weights and diverse measures
> are both alike an abomination to the LORD.
> (20:10; cf. 11:1; 20:23; Amos 8:5-6; Mic. 6:10-11)

Are righteousness, justice, and equity, then, empty, inconsequential categories? Not in the least. They are rooted in specific action, on the levels of both communal structure and individual conduct. Such language is not unlike that of the classical prophets in many instances. The widow, the needy, and the poor assume significant positions in sapiential instruction as they do in prophetic discourse. As in the prophets, the way in which the poor are treated provides nothing short of a litmus test for determining the community's character, as it is defined by the moral triad of justice, righteousness, and equity.

To summarize, productive and responsible citizenship within the life of the community is of central concern to the editors who produced the book of Proverbs. An arm-chair document full of philosophical musings on wisdom this book is not. The maintenance of the community is given categorical preeminence in the first nine chapters, and then given particular expression in the following chapters to the end of the book. Where does that then leave the implied reader represented by the silent son? Beginning with the instruction of his parents and then wisdom's discourse, the youth moves out from the cloistered walls of hearth and home to the grand central stations of urban life. This silent figure is on the brink of adulthood and ready to strike out on his own into the larger social arena to carve out his own existence. In this state of betwixt and between, the son must adjudicate the competing voices that vie for his allegiance. Underlying these various profiles lies a tension that is not only left unresolved, but heightened by the fact that the last six verses of Prov. 9 profile the foolish woman and her alluring invitation. Will the son successfully appropriate the teachings of his parents and heed wisdom's words or like his contemporaries meet his doom through violence or sexual promiscuity? The text does not say. The book of Proverbs is not, properly speaking, a narrative.

And yet there is a resolution of sorts that is provided by the last chapter of the book. In the final chapter, the profile of the "woman of excellence" (NRSV "capable wife") features a matriarch who industriously provides for her household (31:10-31). In the background there stands — or more accurately sits — a patriarch who has taken his place at the city gate, the place where wisdom exercises her rhetorical skill (v. 31). The patriarch basks in the respect of his peers and with an economy of words praises his marriage partner (v. 28). The book of Proverbs began with a silent son, instructed in the responsibilities of communal life and family fidelity, and ends with an adult male who has successfully fulfilled them. Nothing could make a parent more proud.

Yet in the foreground of the beginning and ending of the book of Proverbs stand two other characters who are also linked by their common gender: wisdom, who dominates the discourse of the first nine chapters, and the silent matriarch in the final chapter, whose actions speak louder than any words of praise given by her mate. Like the son and the patriarch, wisdom and the matriarch switch social domains. Whereas wisdom takes her stand in the centers of public discourse, the matriarch has her home by the hearth. Yet the home serves as merely her base of operations for her activity in the community. Not only providing for her household, this woman conducts real estate and commercial ventures, even in remote lands (31:14). Indeed, language about her is adopted from traditionally masculine imagery: "She girds herself with strength, and makes her arms strong" (v. 17).[56] How is the triad of communal virtues embodied by this supermatriarch? They are fulfilled in v. 20: "She opens her hand to the poor, and reaches out her hands to the needy." It is in this very concrete act that righteousness, justice, and equity find their convergence; it is by this matriarch's act of

---

56. The language is reminiscent of military rhetoric (e.g., Nah. 2:2; Amos 2:14; Prov. 24:5).

hospitality that the covenantal community is sustained. For this she is praised as one who "fears Yahweh" (v. 30; cf. 1:7).

The book of Proverbs is eminently more than a catalogue of virtues. It is essentially about the journey from home to community and back again, a *rite de passage* that requires letting go of the parental ties of security to seek one's own security and identity through service to the community. One's destination on this path of wisdom is, to be sure, back home, but never to the original domicile. All the practical and intellectual virtues with which one was raised, from discipline to piety, from diligent labor to an openness for learning, find their ultimate significance within the larger network of the community and the values that sustain it. The balanced and comprehensive repertoire of virtues serves to open up new vistas of maturity that, in turn, provide new levels of engagement within the community, including the opportunity for authentic intimacy. As the home-bound parent urges the maturing son to discover true intimacy with his future spouse (5:15-20), so wisdom takes her student by the hand, finding clear avenues through the winding streets of public life, beckoning to be called "intimate friend."

3 The Deformation of Character: Job 1–31

The book of Job is one of those rare literary works that is both radical and profound. The work is radical in that it sharply breaks away from conventional norms and notions of ethical character, the moral coherence of the created order, and the nature of God. Indeed, it has been suggested that Job is the only book of the Bible that is *against* the Bible.[1] To be sure, there is a measure of iconoclastic zeal with which the Joban poet reshapes the contours of ethical character. Nevertheless, the book of Job is also profound in that it is not satisfied with simply dismantling conventional models of wisdom and morality. Job offers nothing less than a new framework for moral discourse, one that begins with posing unspeakable questions and ends with a new worldview that revises as well as broadens the horizons of the traditional model of character. To borrow from the language of science and intellectual history, the book of Job marks a "paradigm shift" in the formation of character.[2]

Attesting its profound character, the book of Job has, more than any other book of Scripture, generated a host of interpretive treatments, from the Testament of Job, a work of Hellenistic Judaism produced

1. Oral communication with Matitiahu Tsevat at the 1991 SBL meeting, Kansas City.

2. See Thomas S. Kuhn's seminal work *The Structure of Scientific Revolution*. Kuhn defines the term "paradigm" as "the entire constellation of beliefs, values, techniques, and so on shared by the members of a given community" (175). A paradigm is more than a conceptual system; it is a fundamental pattern of perception, explanation, and practice. And so it is only appropriate to talk about the reformation of character in the book of Job as a revolutionary paradigm shift.

between the first century B.C.E. and the first century C.E.,[3] to William Safire's *The First Dissident.*[4] From science fiction writers and columnists to politicians and playwrights, people have had a lot to say about Job. Perhaps it is because the book is profound both in what it says and in what it avoids saying. Both ancient and modern readers have noted the ability with which the Joban poet deftly dances around the issues of theodicy and individual suffering without providing clear solutions, leaving the reader to fill in the gaps.

In order to render a faithful interpretation of the book of Job, it is important to keep in mind that Job is *primarily* about Job and not someone else, even God, or something else, including theodicy. Job does not attempt to provide a solution to the universal problem of suffering. Rather, the book charts the journey of one person's character in response to an instance of seemingly inexplicable suffering, and in so doing, provides a new frame of reference and model of normative character that invites consideration for post-Joban generations.

I. THE PROLOGUE: THE PROFILE OF INTEGRITY (1:1–2:13)

The story of Job's journey begins, in effect, where the book of Proverbs ends. The silent son of Proverbs has successfully secured his life within the community as head of a successful and secure household (Prov. 31:10-31). Job's story begins with a character profile of such a successful patriarch. At the outset four key traits are identified: Job is "blameless," "upright," and one who "fears God" and "avoids evil" (Job 1:1). Each trait is integrally related to the other, together forming a comprehensive description of Job's character. Yet it is the first term, "blameless" (Heb. *tām*), that comes to the fore in the narrative, and thus may be considered the cardinal or overarching virtue, denoting ethical completeness or integrity.[5]

---

3. See Russell P. Spittler's introduction and translation of the Testament of Job in *The Old Testament Pseudepigrapha*, vol. 1, ed. James H. Charlesworth.

4. As the title suggests, Safire treats Job as a practical guide for effective dissent from prevailing political views.

5. The adjective's abstract cognate, *tummâ* ("integrity"), is attested in 2:3, 9. See below.

Taken together, these virtues profile Job's character as unassailable; they provide a thesis about Job, for which everything else provides ostensible confirmation. Job's vast wealth and status as the "greatest of all the people of the east" (1:3) gives material demonstration of his character. Job is first and foremost a "family man," whose honor as head of the household must be preserved and whose sacrificial actions on behalf of his children are motivated by fearful concern for his children's well-being and conduct (1:5). Job is the ever-concerned, preeminent patriarch.[6] Though never described as a professional sage, Job is a success story in the business of wisdom. Like the figure of the silent son turned patriarch in Proverbs, Job has successfully appropriated the wisdom of his elders. He has embodied the character of the listening heart, and it has literally paid off for him.

Yahweh assesses Job in the same way as our narrator (1:8). Job is singled out for his incomparable status among humans: "There is no one like him on the earth, a blameless and upright man who fears God and turns away from evil." In response, the satan[7] introduces a litmus test by which to evaluate Job's alleged integrity: "Does Job fear God for nothing?" By raising the issue of disinterested piety,[8] the satan cuts to the very heart of normative character, and in so doing, accuses Yahweh of having made it worth Job's while to behave in an ethically credible manner. If the satan is right, then Job's character is nothing more than a sham. Does Job perhaps have an ulterior motive behind his seemingly upright behavior? Perhaps his riches were gained by extortion. Perhaps Job's sacrifices for his children were selfishly conducted to protect his honor as head of the household. Though the satan's first question in 1:9 could lead one to reread Job's behavior in such ways, Job's accuser does not press such matters. Instead, the satan has brought God into the picture by recognizing correctly that Job's character is necessarily intertwined with Yahweh's character.

6. See Carol A. Newsom, "Job," 133-34.

7. The common translation "Satan" is avoided here, since the Hebrew term (haśśāṭān) is nothing more than a functionary title and, hence, not to be identified with the archenemy of God, as found in apocalyptic and New Testament literature. In the prologue, this character functions as a roving, semi-independent prosecutor within the heavenly council under Yahweh's charge. For a full discussion of the satan's place in Hebrew Scripture, see Peggy L. Day, *An Adversary in Heaven.*

8. For a full discussion of the issue of "disinterested piety" in the book of Job, see Matitiahu Tsevat's seminal essay, "The Meaning of the Book of Job."

The satan's accusation operates on two levels. On the one hand, if Job fears God *for something,* then his integrity is simply a facade. The question turns on whether Job's reverence for God has a telic twist to it, a hint of self-interest, and if so, then the curse will surely displace the deferential praise that has so far characterized Job's discourse, so the satan reasons. On the other hand, the satan's questioning of Job's integrity serves to point an accusing finger toward Yahweh. Ironically, the satan accuses Yahweh of acting in a way that echoes Job's own behavior toward his children: an overprotectiveness that shields their true character and preempts any degree of personal accountability. Yahweh stands accused of two related "crimes," according to this independent prosecutor: affording Job and his family special protection and effecting their prosperity. Yahweh does not refute these charges. Rather, Yahweh consents to the satan's challenge and the wheels of the plot are set in motion.

By enduring a progressively worsening series of disasters perpetrated by the satan with Yahweh's permission, Job succeeds in "holding fast to his integrity."[9] As he is known in the New Testament and in pseudepigraphical literature,[10] Job proves himself patient amid horrific circumstances by not uttering one word against God. He proves himself to be a man of few words, embodying a traditional ideal among the sages.[11] His character is one of patient endurance, accepting his misfortunes without a word, except in deference to God. Again, the key word that most sharply describes Job's character is *tām,* usually translated "blameless," along with the cognate term *tummâ,* "integrity." Integrity "denotes a person whose conduct is in complete accord with moral and religious norms and whose character is one of utter honesty."[12] One who is *tām* is one whose life is coherent and consistent in the ways he or she makes ethical choices within the life of the community.[13] Consequently, *tummâ* denotes a certain *wholeness* or coherence of character. While Proverbs focuses almost exclusively on the specific virtues, the book of Job begins with the issue of their internal coherence, specifically of their coherence in light of Job's world turned topsy-turvy.

9. In light of the Hebrew *(maḥᵃzîq bᵉtummātô),* the RSV translation is preferable to the NRSV in 2:3, 9.

10. See Jas. 5:11 and the Testament of Job.

11. See Chapter 2.

12. Newsom, "Job," 131.

13. See Ellen F. Davis, "Job and Jacob," 205.

In the prologue, Job keeps his integrity and therefore refuses to step out of character when he responds with uncompromising acceptance of his fate (1:21). Such acceptance also characterizes Job's response to his wife: One cannot receive the good without the bad and remain ethically complete (2:10). The voice of the narrator that intrudes makes quite explicit the connection between Job's integrity and God:

> In all this Job did not sin or charge God with wrong-doing. (1:22)

> In all this Job did not sin with his lips. (2:10)

Thus, the outcome of the test will be determined by what Job has to say about God.

As in proverbial wisdom, speech provides a window into one's integrity (or lack thereof); it is by nature revelatory of one's character. In Job's case, accusing God would irrevocably compromise Job's integrity. It is precisely this issue that dramatically contrasts the characters of the satan and Job. Job, the blameless one, would forsake his integrity if he were to assume the role of the satan by charging God with wrongdoing. Perhaps that is the sole prerogative of this heavenly prosecutor, or perhaps the satan has overstepped his boundaries. The text remains tantalizingly unclear. However, it is obvious that the satan is a foil for Job: Job adamantly refuses to do what the satan has done, namely accuse Yahweh of moral indiscretion. Moreover, the respective perspectives of Job and his accuser are entirely at odds. On the one hand, the satan accuses God of affording Job *special privileges,* making it worth Job's while to act piously. On the other hand, if Job were to accuse God of anything, it would be for having singled him out for *special oppression,* as he does in the poetic discharge that follows. But Job does no such thing in the opening chapters. Rather, his grip on integrity, as profiled in the prologue, remains firm.

The Character of God in the Prologue

One disconcerting element that has provoked concern among readers and commentators alike is the way in which God is depicted in the prologue. How could God allow such a thing to happen to Job? In response, Norman C. Habel describes the God featured in the prologue as a "jealous king, who is apparently willing to violate human life to gratify personal ends."[14] However, the prologue's characterization of God is much more nuanced. Yahweh is introduced at the very outset as the head of the divine council in typical ancient Near Eastern style. The image of the council connotes a distribution of power by Yahweh to the heavenly subordinates, including the satan. In both conversations with Job's accuser, Yahweh hands over Job and all that he has into the satan's power with certain inviolable provisos. To be sure, the royal image Habel invokes to describe God is appropriate, but the charge of petty jealousy is not.

Yahweh initiates the conversation with the satan by boasting of his servant Job. Like a proud patriarch boasting about his children, Yahweh clearly takes pride in Job. By repeating the narrator's description in 1:1, Yahweh is appropriately effusive. The sharp response of the satan, however, places such praise into question, casting doubt on Job's credibility. When Yahweh accepts the satan's challenge, which is cast in the form of an oath or self-curse,[15] it is neither out of jealousy nor doubt, but out of a confident trust that Job is worthy of divine praise. It is out of such confidence that Yahweh consents to a test of Job's integrity.

The description of God as tester is common throughout Hebrew Scripture. Indeed, it is a typical role that God assumes in relation to human beings. God, for example, tests Abraham's obedience in the *Akedah* story in Gen. 22.[16] Particularly relevant in the case of Job is Ps. 26, a lament, in which the psalmist petitions God to test his "heart and

---

14. "In Defense of God the Sage," 26.

15. The use of the oath formula *'im-lō'* in 1:11b, as well as in 2:5b, indicates that the satan has put his reputation on the line in the form of a self-imprecation. Perhaps the best translation of the satan's statement is the one offered by David J. A. Clines: "I'll be damned if he doesn't curse you to your face" (*Job 1–20*, 26). The fact that the satan appears nowhere in the epilogue suggests that the consequences of the self-curse have been implemented. See Edwin M. Good, "Job and the Literary Task," 475; and Day's discussion in *An Adversary in Heaven*, 81, n. 30.

16. In addition, God tests Israel's proclivity to obey in Exod. 15:25b-26; 16:4. In Exod. 20:20, Moses assures the people that the fearsome theophany at Mt. Sinai serves only to test rather than destroy. Deuteronomy locates the time of testing in the wilderness period: God tests in order to discern the heart and whether the commandments will be followed, in short, to determine whether Israel truly loves Yahweh (Deut. 8:2; 13:4[Eng. v. 3]). Similarly, Hezekiah is tested in order that God can determine "all that was in his heart" (2 Chr. 32:31).

mind" (26:2) in order to vindicate him. The psalmist testifies to his integrity at the outset as well as at the conclusion of the psalm (26:11):

> Vindicate me, Yahweh,
>   for I have walked in my integrity. (26:1)

For the psalmist, integrity involves unwavering trust (26:1b), truth (v. 3b), disassociation from the wicked (vv. 4, 5), innocence (v. 6), and praise (vv. 7, 8, 12), all behaviors and traits that comprise normative character. Relying upon God's justice and mercy (*hesed*, v. 3), the psalmist is confident that God will respond to his cries and vindicate him. In the case of Job, however, the test does not come out of any personal need of Job for vindication. The "need" comes rather from Yahweh. According to our narrator, Job's life is itself a sufficient testament to his integrity, and the test becomes necessary only when such integrity is challenged, both Job's and Yahweh's.

In the second conversation, Yahweh expresses confidence in Job, now vindicated, as well as regret for having allowed the satan to destroy (lit., "swallow") Job (2:3). The language is sarcastically hyperbolic, for Yahweh turns the satan's words against him: "You have incited me against him, to destroy him *for nothing*" (cf. 1:9). Yahweh boasts that the test has proved Job, thereby vindicating both him and Yahweh, and at the same time laments that it has done irreparable damage to Job's life. Yahweh's passionate protest gives voice to the theological dilemma of divine testing. The rationale of the test is pushed to an absurd extreme in the acknowledgment that in Job's case the means of testing outweighs the end. This act of vindication has backfired, devastating the defendant in the process.

Far from being a flat, one-dimensional, jealous God, Yahweh exhibits inner turmoil no less poignant than the regret described in Yahweh's decision to flood the earth (Gen. 6:6):

> Yahweh was sorry that he had made humankind on the earth,
> and it grieved him to his heart.

These two regrets are mirror images in a way. Owing to the irrevocable pervasiveness of wickedness among human beings, Yahweh regrets having created life and painfully arrives at the decision to destroy it. The God of the Joban prologue, on the other hand, regrets the destruction wrought upon his servant Job, owing to his unassailable righteousness. Both accounts depict a remorseful God. Unfortunately for Job, however, the story does not end there. That paragon of cynicism, the satan, is not satisfied and thus raises the demands of the test. The desire for vindication once again silences the voice of compassion, for Yahweh's very ability to judge character is at stake.

The downward turn in negotiations between Yahweh and the satan that results in further suffering for Job is precisely what generates the remainder of the plot, beginning with the wife's leading question and the consolation of the friends (see below). Had the narrator of the prologue intended to portray the deity as one who acted callously in testing Job's mettle, there would have been no need to bring in this second conversation between Yahweh and the satan. Rather, permission would simply have been granted to the satan to tighten the circle of disaster up to Job's very life without narrative interruption. Consequently, it is this *second* conversation that is the most revealing of Yahweh's character in the prologue, namely of a God who struggles with the whole business of testing, who senses the tug between compassion and vindication of right character regardless of the personal expense. In accordance with the dynamics of the plot, it is the boast and the protest in Job 2:3 that most vividly betrays a glimpse of the divine character, the struggling Tester. But it is only a glimpse, for the movement of the plot inexorably returns to Job, who remains center stage in the unfolding drama of his character.

How could God have sanctioned such suffering for Job? Similarly, how could God ever have commanded Abraham to sacrifice his only son?[17] Both questions are concerned with the moral legitimacy of divine testing. Behind such questions lies the more existential concern of whether God will ever again require someone to face what Job and Abraham had to undergo. In both cases, the biblical story suggests no. Both Job and Abraham have proved themselves faithful. As a result, their characters become efficacious for the subsequent community of faith. Both Abraham as the father of Israel and Job as the patriarch of integrity

---

17. Later Jewish revisionists understandably saw much in common between Gen. 22 and the book of Job. The pseudepigraphical work Jubilees, written in the mid-second century B.C.E., introduces the Abrahamic story by attributing the rationale of the test to a "Prince Mastema" or Satan, who suggests that God command Abraham to offer up Isaac (Jub. 17:16). Indeed, one of the marks of Abraham's character is that "his soul was not impatient" (17:18). See Orval S. Wintermute's translation and introduction in *The Old Testament Pseudepigrapha*, vol. 2, ed. James H. Charlesworth.

pass their tests that end such tests for future generations. The divine resolve never again to require the murder of children as a test of faith is rooted in the promise of grace given in response to Abraham's meritorious actions.[18] The divine resolve never again to subject a human being with suffering as the result of a wager to prove one's integrity is similarly rooted in the compassionate God who feels remorse.[19] The story of Job's life not only presents a model of character in the face of horrific tribulation but also suggests, in the end, a divine resolve to obviate the need to test the righteous with such severity. The prologue, thus, provides a candid view of God's pathos, but a glimpse is all it is. As for Job's character, much remains to be said.

Job's Character Revisited

The question and charge that Job's wife utters identifies the central concern of the prologue, namely Job's integrity. In the history of tradition, Job's wife is unfortunately given short shrift.[20] Nevertheless, what she has to say to the biblical Job strikes at the very heart of the matter, framing the focus of the entire book. In 1:21 Job has anticipated death and blessed Yahweh's name. Job's wife now advises Job to curse ("bless" used euphemistically in the Hebrew) God and die (2:9). Both blessing and cursing find common ground in the prospect of death. The blessing in 1:21 indicates Job's full acceptance of what he expects to be imminent death; the curse, on the other hand, is meant to quicken and ensure death's actualization. The way in which Job's wife casts the issue is significant. The central issue is whether she exhorts Job to step out of character: Does she exhort Job to let go of his integrity by cursing God *or* does she plead for Job to curse God *consonant* with his integrity? Her observation[21] that Job is still holding fast to his integrity is taken ver-

---

18. Jewish tradition predating the emergence of Christianity developed the notion of meritorial sacrifice in the *Akedah* story (see Shalom Spiegel, *The Last Trial*, esp. 77-120).

19. Moreover, the complete absence of the satan in the epilogue (42:7-17) suggests the absence of the need to test.

20. See, e.g., the Testament of Job and Susan R. Garrett, "The 'Weaker Sex' in the *Testament of Job*."

21. It is not clear whether she is asking a question or stating a simple fact, since the interrogative particle is absent in the Hebrew.

batim from the divine proclamation in 2:3b. The question is whether her observation is meant to be a form of approval or an indictment. If the latter, then Job's wife is clearly admonishing Job to compromise his integrity and curse God in order to insure a quick death. If the former, then Job's wife has introduced a new nuance to integrity that can provide the rationale for Job to curse God, the element of uncompromising honesty.[22]

In isolation, the wife's exhortation stands ambiguously open ended. Job's harsh reply, however, indicates that he regards his wife's exhortation as an admonishment to compromise his integrity, which he unequivocally rejects. Job again intones that unconditional acceptance of his fate, be it death or suffering subsistence, must be the crowning mark of his integrity. Overcome by grief, Job stands ready to accept his death, even welcome it, but not at the expense of his integrity. Death must come while his integrity is still intact. Yet the narrator has made it all too clear that such a scenario is impossible. On the heavenly plane, the divine stipulation limiting the satan's commission is a restraining order against outright murder. On the earthly plane, Job's reliance on his integrity also precludes death, but from the perspective of Job's wife, survival is more bane than blessing. Broached by Job's wife, the relationship between integrity, curse, and death remains an open issue, around which the whole book of Job revolves.

So Job lingers on. Either by sanction from above or by integrity from below, death does not come to release Job from his misery. What does come, however, are three friends, whose mission is to "console and comfort" him. Beginning with silence, this trio sets the stage for the rest of the discourse that follows. Their very presence raises an interesting question: If Job is indeed so accepting of his fate, regardless of the outcome, and remains willing to bless Yahweh, does he after all need consolation? Job has just rebuked his wife, and in so doing, rejected death as the final solution. His integrity excludes death, but it cannot

---

22. See Rick D. Moore's discussion of Job's integrity in the poetry ("The Integrity of Job"). Newsom has sharpened the issue by locating the ambiguity squarely in the wife's question ("Job," 132). My reading suggests that the prologue makes clear that the wife's statement is one of admonishment and not an exhortation for Job to muster up his integrity to curse God. However, the author of the dialogues, unlike the author of the prologue, specifically takes up and addresses the latter interpretation of the wife's question beginning in ch. 3 (see below).

nullify his sense of loss and agony. If release from life is not the answer for Job, then is it consolation? This is the question with which the prologue ends.

The prologue presents a Job who in the face of unrelenting misery remains the ideal representative of conventional wisdom. In its wider context, the prologue powerfully recalls traditional values and their broad appeal, values that quickly become a source of contention, however, once the reader moves beyond the story-world setting of the prologue into the turgid, tension-filled discourse of the dialogues that follow.

II. THE DISCOURSE: INTEGRITY RE-PROFILED

Job's character unites the prose and poetry of his story as well as provides for the story's literary tension.[23] From ch. 3 onward, the reader encounters a different Job from the one profiled in the prologue. Job's inner life is starkly revealed; he is no longer a stock character that stoically accepts what God has allotted him. Job is enfleshed with ambiguity and complexity as he begins to detail and assess his life. As Meir Sternberg observes, "The clash between Job's epithetic and dramatic characterizations threatens the unity of his character and lends some color to the friends' (and Satan's) insinuation that the upright Job is little more than the public image exposed by adversity."[24] Yet what holds the prose and poetic characterizations of Job together is Job's claim that he is able to maintain his hold on integrity throughout his passionate outbursts (27:6). In the poetry, Job's integrity is never jettisoned; it is reformulated, although the patient endurance that so characterized him in the prologue is subsequently overturned.[25] Job the silent has become Job the verbose, full of bitter complaints.[26] Indeed, the verbal excess with which Job complains gives expression to what is essentially unspeakable in the prose. It is no coincidence, then, that the Testament of Job, a later revision of the biblical

---

23. As Moore points out, the center of the thematic tension between the prose and poetry is Job himself (21). See also Claus Westermann, "The Two Faces of Job"; Meir Sternberg, *The Poetics of Biblical Narrative*, 345-46.

24. Sternberg, 345.

25. Moore, 31.

26. See Bruce Zuckerman, *Job, the Silent.*

story, by and large passes over Job's outbursts against God and the friends, preferring rather the clear and unambiguous portrait of Job presented in the prologue/epilogue.[27] Yet enmeshed in the unorthodox words of his poetic discourse in the biblical account, Job is somehow still able to lay claim to his integrity, an integrity that is defamed by his friends, deconstructed by the poet, and reformed by Yahweh.

Job's Birthday Curse

As is often noted, the words Job utters in ch. 3 profile a very different Job from the one introduced in the prologue. In fact, the warning flag is raised even before Job begins to speak: The narrator marks the following discourse as Job's birthday *curse* (3:1), acknowledging that Job's lament is fraught with tension. In the prologue, Job categorically rejected the curse as an appropriate response. Now his lips are filled with cursing.

Since Job's initial speech lays the groundwork for almost forty chapters' worth of discourse, it is helpful to treat Job's curse in some detail. A general movement from Job's past to the present, from his inception to his personal distress, is clearly evident within the structure of Job's initial lament in ch. 3. The multi-level network of metaphors sets in relief the two foci of life and death.

With death are associated the cosmological images of impenetrable darkness, gloom, cloud, sea, night, and the underworld. Together they represent the powers of chaos invoked by Job to overcome the light of his life. By calling for a reversal of creation, Job curses not only a particular day on the calendar, his birthday, but by extension all of creation itself, signified by light, the first act of creation (Gen. 1:3). Job cannot but help perceive the world through the prism of his tormented life. His curse begins with a structural and theological antithesis to Gen. 1 (Job 3:4a).[28] "Let that day be darkness!" as opposed to "Let there be light" (Gen. 1:3). Moreover, the reference to the seven days during which Job's friends dare not speak is a counterecho to the Priestly Creation account, in which all creation is brought about and structured by divine speech (Gen. 1:1–2:4a).

---

27. Judith R. Baskin, "Rabbinic Interpretations of Job," 104.

28. E.g., Norman C. Habel, *The Book of Job*, 104; Leo G. Perdue, *Wisdom in Revolt*, 97-98.

Job's lament is a veritable assault on creation.[29] Job curses his birth and, by extension, all of creation. The inception of Job's life functions *pars pro toto* for the moment of cosmic creation. Although Job has not cursed God, Job's self-curse is only a technical distinction. In fact, God is mentioned by Job in his curse. In Job 3:4, Job commands God not to seek the day, since it is to be overcome by darkness. Such darkness stands sharply at odds with God's creative purposes. Furthermore, Job accuses God of having "fenced" him in (3:23). The identical expression is found in 1:10, in which the satan accuses Yahweh of protecting Job at the expense of his character. From Job's mouth, however, a much different accusation is leveled. God has not only hidden Job's "way"; the deity has made it inaccessible to him. Job is kept in the dark as to the particular fate God has in store for him. Yet there is an ethical dimension as well. The "way" *(derek)*, as noted in Proverbs, is a root metaphor of wisdom, and thus of correct character. Job complains that God has blocked all access to wisdom, and thus all means of continuing in integrity. All in all, by cursing his life and creation, Job pushes the envelope of his integrity.

In Job's curse of birth and life, death is in turn cloaked with positive images. Job's assault on creation is not an assault for its own sake, as if Job himself were the embodiment of chaos. The cosmic language highlights Job's desire to find permanent rest, even at the expense of creation and God. The rest that Job seeks through death is cast in terms of *communion* with the dead, both great and small, an indiscriminate, egalitarian bonding that erases all oppressive relations (3:18-19). Furthermore, Job casts himself in solidarity with those who long for death (3:21-22). Death presents a radically different configuration of social relations for Job compared to that of his present life, which can only offer torment in isolation. Bereft of family, Job now looks through the threshold of death toward a new establishment of social ties that knows no boundaries.

Job is ready to join the peaceful community of the dead, where even the "raging" *(rōgez)*[30] of the wicked ceases (3:17). Yet such "raging" has come to disturb his longed-for peace:

---

29. See Leo G. Perdue, "Job's Assault on Creation."

30. The nominal (participial) form *rōgez* in 3:17 finds its antithesis in the parallel colon in the verb "to rest" *(nwḥ)* and most likely refers to the quarrelsome rantings of the wicked (cf. Gen. 45:24), a common stereotype of the wicked in biblical and Egyptian wisdom literature (cf. Job 37:2). In death, even the wicked are quieted.

> "I am not at ease, and I am not quiet;
> I cannot find rest, for 'raging' has arrived." (3:26)[31]

Job dreads this *rōgez*, whatever it is. The term has usually been taken to refer either to Job's personal agony[32] or to divine wrath.[33] The immediate context, however, suggests a more specific focus. In 3:17, it is connected with the divisive, disquieting behavior of the wicked. In the prologue, what arrived, thereby setting the stage for the discourse that is to follow, is Job's three friends (2:11b). Job's final words in his lament appropriately anticipate the verbal onslaught he is about to suffer from his friends. Whereas Job fervently seeks the solitude necessary for him to die and thereby find rest, Job's friends rudely interrupt the process. The peaceful communion for which Job desperately yearns among the dead is about to be displaced by strife among the living.

In short, Job's lament cracks open the confident assessment of his character found in the prologue. Instead of the patriarch of patient endurance, the Job of the lament is filled with bitter angst and determined to make a quick end of it all by cursing his life and in so doing dragging all of creation down with him. With a masterful control of rhetoric, Job reverses the images of life and death as he rejects what little is left of his own life. Unconditional acceptance of his situation is replaced by bitter complaint. Job's lament begins to give credence to the satan's charges. Indeed, the next natural step for Job would be to curse God and end it all. But, for better or for worse, his friends unwittingly interrupt Job's inexorable slide into cursed oblivion, the comfort he seeks.

Job's Character in Relation to His Friends: The Clash of Wisdom Models

In the dialogues that follow his lament, Job is among peers in a debate first and foremost over his character, and by extension over the moral coherence of the world in which they all live. Any *formal* hierarchy typical of the pedagogy of proverbial wisdom is lacking. Gone are the

---

31. Author's translation.
32. So Habel, *The Book of Job*, 112; Marvin H. Pope, *Job*, 33.
33. So Perdue, *Wisdom in Revolt*, 94.

formal categories of teacher and pupil, parent and child. Now only the teachers, the sages, have their say among themselves. In sharp contrast, however, to the proverbial guidelines for civil discussion, the rebukes from Job's friends do not elicit much collegial appreciation (cf. Prov. 9:8-9) on the part of Job. Unlike the silent son, Job is not reluctant to talk back. However, despite the *apparent* egalitarian relationship between Job and his friends, much of the tension that erupts within the deliberations is rooted in the friends' strained attempts to press the dynamics of the discourse back into the traditional hierarchical setting of conventional wisdom teaching, which Job regards as nothing else than a pedagogy for the oppressed. Indeed, at one point Job sarcastically plays upon his friends' attempt to force him into the role of student: "Teach me, and I will be *silent;* make me understand how I have gone wrong" (Job 6:24).

So Job's friends, missing the sarcasm, attempt to teach him. Praise of traditional wisdom is most pronounced in Bildad's speeches. His appeal to the unbroken chain of inherited tradition presents the classic testimony to the veracity of sagacious tradition:

> "Inquire now of bygone generations,
>   and consider what their ancestors have ascertained. . . .
> Will they not teach you and tell you
>   and utter words out of their understanding?" (8:8, 10)

Bildad urges Job to hearken to the univocal voice of the ancient past, the very ethos and vehicle of traditional wisdom.[34] As the father figure in Proverbs imparts the wisdom of his own father (Prov. 4), the past generations, the *'ābôt,* are given a single voice that requires attention from the inquiring heart.

Intermixed with such appeals to tradition is the language of character. Eliphaz's initial appeal to Job's character in Job 4:6 illustrates the inextricable connection between wisdom and character. Eliphaz appeals to an essential incompatibility between integrity and the impatience exhibited by Job in his lament. Indeed, such impatience is nothing less than a character flaw for a master teacher and comforter like Job. You have instructed and supported others in the past, so reasons Eliphaz; but now

---

34. See James L. Crenshaw's discussion of the three major rhetorical strategies present in wisdom literature, namely ethos, pathos, and logos ("Wisdom and Authority").

that the roles instructor and victim are reversed, your situation has forced you out of character. Eliphaz presses such reasoning further by raising up for the first time in the poetic deliberations the issue of guilt and innocence (4:7), thereby setting the direction for the remainder of the dialogue.

Eliphaz's "comfort" is both a subtle indictment and an attempt to diffuse the issue of just desert. The upright and the innocent are not cut off (4:7), but all mortals are unrighteous before God (4:17-21; 5:7). Eliphaz's argument then turns to an appeal for Job to seek God, who saves the needy and the poor as well as foils the wise in their craftiness (5:8-16). Which category of character has been reserved for Job is deliberately left open ended or is altogether evaded by Eliphaz, particularly given his brief treatise on the necessity of God's discipline in 5:17-18. The lines of demarcation between victim and wrongdoer with respect to Job are blurred by Eliphaz. Yet any insinuation against Job's character is in Eliphaz's mind outweighed by the prospect of restoration for Job (5:19-27). All Job needs to do is gratefully accept his condition as discipline. Eliphaz's collegial rebuke, which is meant to evoke a response of grateful consideration on the part of Job, is an exemplar of sagacious discourse (cf. Prov. 9:8).

The dialogic exchanges between Job and his friends, however, degenerate from there. Within the dynamics of the debate, the connection between wisdom and character forces Job into the unenviable position of having to defend his integrity in order to convince his friends of the veracity of his new-found wisdom. The close association of wisdom and character accounts for how the friends' discussion frequently reverts to verbal discharges of accusation against Job. From the friends' perspective, recourse to blaming is a legitimate mode of instruction. Job's defense is that such blame has been cast against an *innocent* victim (see below). The most strident example of the slippery relation between instruction and blame is found in Eliphaz's second speech in ch. 15. Eliphaz denounces Job's "windy knowledge" (15:1) and accuses Job of undermining wisdom (the fear of God) in v. 4, attributing Job's subversive speech to moral failure (v. 5). Rather than a student of wisdom, Job has been all along a student of iniquity, charges Eliphaz.

The friends find Job's defense a matter of arrogant pretension and condescension. Bildad regards such condescension particularly offensive: "Why are we counted as cattle [by you]? Why are we stupid in your sight?" (18:3). In addition, Eliphaz sarcastically asks Job: "Are you the firstborn of the human race? Were you brought forth before the hills? . . . Do you limit wisdom to yourself?" (15:7-8). The implication is that

Job has pretentiously identified himself with the ageless voice of wisdom herself (see Prov. 8:22-27), the height of arrogance and the next step to blasphemy. The severity of Eliphaz's charge is reflected in the fact that Job has refused to assume a subordinate position within the traditional pedagogy of wisdom (Job 13:2).

In short, the tenor of such dialogue is anything but one of collegial mutuality. The wise reader, who might well expect a constructive, civil dialogue among the Joban sages, will find only a parody of sagacious discourse in the book of Job. The friends condescendingly try to force Job back into the role of the silent son, the unquestioning recipient of wisdom. Job needs to be re-educated, and the first step is for him to acknowledge his inferior status before his consoling elders. By invoking the traditional pedagogy of hierarchy, Eliphaz suggests that Job must in some sense regress back to the family of his childhood in order to reappropriate the values of traditional wisdom.

Job, however, refuses to assume such a position: "No doubt you are the people, / and wisdom will die with you. / But I have understanding as well as you; I am not inferior to you" (12:2-3; see also 13:2). Job questions the very foundation of wisdom: "Is wisdom with the aged, / and understanding in length of days?" (12:12). The traditional tenet that age and wisdom intersect is overturned. Conversely, long life and prosperity, the by-products of wisdom, are available to the wicked as well as to the wise: "Why do the wicked live on, reach old age, and grow mighty in power?" (21:7). The qualitative and quantitative distinctions so firmly established in proverbial wisdom between the wise and foolish, the righteous and the wicked, can either reverse, as in Job's case, or even merge, a more frightening prospect (see 9:22).

Eliphaz presents the most blistering attack against Job's integrity in ch. 22. He accuses Job of inhumane treatment of his family and of those marginalized by society (22:6-11). But more grievous are the theological offenses: Eliphaz blasts Job for claiming that God is limited in knowledge (22:13-14) and, in a masterful twist of words, accuses Job of mimicking the discourse of the wicked:

"They said to God, 'Leave us alone,'
And 'What can the Almighty do to us?'" (22:17)[35]

---

35. Reading with the Greek and Syriac. The Masoretic text casts the object in the third person *(lāmô)*.

Eliphaz's portrayal of the wicked is marked by an attitude of confident defiance against God. The irony behind Eliphaz's words, however, lies in the fact that Job has uttered similar words to 22:17a (7:16a, 19b; 10:20b). Whereas Eliphaz reads the demand of the wicked as a mark of defiance, Job's words are in fact desperate pleas for respite from suffering.[36]

From Job's perspective, the friends have sorely failed in their responsibility to comfort him in his pain. He accuses them of treachery (6:15), of withholding kindness (v. 14a), of forsaking the fear of God (v. 14b), and of abandoning him in his moment of dire need (vv. 17-18). Such accusations are rife with the language of betrayal. Indeed, Job makes the generalization that such behavior is akin to pure, unadulterated greed:

> "You would even cast lots over the orphan,
>   and bargain over your friend." (6:27)

Equally damning is Job's charge that his condition has put his friends to shame and even inspired fear (6:20-21). Job perceives behind the vehemence with which his friends accuse him of all manner of misdeeds an underlying sense of fear and failure of nerve. Job's observation in effect answers the question he poses in 16:3b: "What afflicts you to argue (as such)?" The answer is the fear of the incomprehensible. Job had hoped to receive from his friends encouragement and consolation that would assuage his pain (16:5). Instead, they see Job as a monstrous anomaly within their restrictive moral world, a lived world in which sin and divine retribution are rigidly correlated.

The anomaly that Job presents to his friends requires a fundamental change in the cultural framework in which traditional wisdom has had its home. In defending his character to his friends, Job refuses to be the listening heart, despite the urgings and protestations of his friends. That wisdom is inextricably linked to Job's character is confirmed by the simple observation that Job constantly accuses his friends with defamation of character while his friends are only trying to be consoling and instructive (15:11). To them, Job embodies anti-wisdom by rejecting the wisdom's traditional ethos and relying instead on the veracity of his personal experience of suffering.

---

36. Any common ground between Job and the wicked, however, is erased in the second colon of Eliphaz's accusation (22:17b). Nowhere does Job entertain the possibility that God is *not* in control over his livelihood. Indeed, quite the opposite: Job accuses God of having singled him out for unwarranted abuse (see below).

Job is nothing less than a monstrosity in the eyes of his friends. His situation and his character do not fit within any schema of moral and theological coherence with which they are familiar. In their eyes, Job's consistent protestations of innocence cannot be tolerated in light of his suffering condition. Hence, their language becomes increasingly strident: Job is accused of uttering blasphemy (15:4, 13; 22:13-14, 17) and of destroying himself and seeking the collapse of the cosmic order. Bildad pointedly asks: "You who tear yourself in your anger — / shall the earth be forsaken because of you, / or the rock be removed out of its place?" (18:4). While echoing Job's lament in ch. 3, Bildad's reference to the disruption of creation is rooted in the moral inversion Job represents in a seemingly coherent universe (see Prov. 30:21-23). Job is a threat to both himself and the world order, living in a realm of betwixt and between by refusing to repent and be restored, to the dismay and disdain of his friends. To the friends Job represents nothing less than moral and cosmic *disorder*.[37] His liminal character confuses the boundaries of ethical behavior.

The friends' assessment of Job as threat is also shared by his family and closest friends. With his patriarchal position undermined (Job 19:13-17), young children despise him (v. 18) and youth "make sport" (*śḥq*) of him (30:1). In surely one of the most poignant protests in his discourse, Job laments:

> "[God] has put my family far from me,
>   and my acquaintances are wholly estranged *(zārû)* from me.
> My relatives and my close friends have failed me;
>   the guests in my house have forgotten me;
> my serving girls count me as a stranger *(zār)*;
>   I have become an alien *(nokrî)* in their eyes.
> My breath is repulsive *(zārâ)* to my wife;
>   I am loathsome to my own family." (19:13-15, 17)

It is significant that the words for "alien" and "strange," found also in Prov. 1–9 (Prov. 2:16; 5:20; 7:5) to refer to the "strange woman," are employed here to refer to Job in relation to his household. Abhorred as an "alien" by his own family and closest friends, Job is the object of

---

37. See Mary Douglas's ground-breaking discussion on disorder in *Purity and Danger*.

social castigation of a magnitude that is matched only by the harsh rhetoric that targets the female outsider profiled in Prov. 1–9.[38] As a stranger Job threatens the collapse of the moral world order as it has been traditionally construed. Thus, it is perhaps with an affirmative nod from his friends that Job plaintively cries out to God: "Am I the Sea, or the Dragon, / that you set a guard over me?" (Job 7:12). To his friends, Job embodies moral and thus cosmic chaos. Like the God who has prescribed bounds for the sea, like the parental figures in Proverbs who warn the son of the alien woman, Job's friends are compelled to contain his iconoclastic words, which threaten to shatter the coherence of their cleanly structured worldview.[39] But unlike Proverbs, with the discourse of the strange woman, the book of Job affirms Job's dissenting voice of pathos, a voice that conventional wisdom would rather muffle.

Job 28: Wisdom's "Inaccessibility"

Another, yet related view concerning the relation of wisdom to Job and his friends comes from the self-contained passage in Job 28, the poem on wisdom. The poem begins with a declarative statement concerning the existence of a mine for silver and proceeds to describe the methodical yet daring enterprise of mineral extraction. Such activity is appropriately described with verbs denoting perception and discernment (Job 28:3, 7, 10b, 11) as well as construction (vv. 4a, 9, 10a) and retrieval (v. 2a). The subsection comprising vv. 7-8 tugs at such imagery by employing the new image of the unknown path, suggesting that something more than underground mining activity is meant. The poem then abruptly redirects its focus in v. 12 by posing the question of the location of wisdom. As a result of this shift in subjects, from the lodes of precious metals to those of wisdom, the surface-level description of mining in the first section is unveiled to reveal multi-layered metaphors that describe the topography of the quest for wisdom (cf. Prov. 25:2). Whereas the animals do not know the way of the miner, human beings (Job 28:13), indeed all living things (v. 21), know not the way of wisdom. Wisdom is inaccessible to even the best and most daring of sages. Only

38. See Chapter 2.
39. Indeed, the chaos invoked by Job in ch. 3 resonates with the chaos Job's friends perceive vis-à-vis his character.

God knows the way of wisdom, having discovered and established it (v. 27).

As is often noted, the poem of wisdom functions as a "veiled judgement" on the dialogues.[40] The circles of discourse that seem to go nowhere between Job and his friends illustrate well the poet's point that wisdom is by nature unfathomable. This wisdom is not out pounding the pavement and calling out from the city gates, vying for everyone's attention, as portrayed in Prov. 1–9. To the contrary, the wisdom celebrated in Job 28 is as inscrutable as proverbial wisdom is accessible. In short, a new characterization of wisdom is forged out of a perceived lack of progress within the in-house dialogue between fellow sages in the story of Job. The poem in effect highlights the failed attempts on the part of both Job and his friends to account for his suffering. On the one hand, the friends espouse ad nauseam a traditional yet ultimately inadequate model of wisdom that ends up obfuscating rather than illuminating Job's situation. Job, on the other hand, is incapable of giving account of his predicament. Any humble admission of failure on his part to penetrate the veil of ignorance that shrouds him from above is displaced by caustic attacks against his friends and God — certainly not the model of restraint and sagacity. Indeed, Job is accused of doing away with the fear of God, and not without justification (15:4; see also 6:14; 22:4).

The last line of the poem, in which God proclaims to humankind that the "fear of the LORD" is wisdom (28:28), appears to be in tension with the previous material, for it is clearly not meant to imply that holy reverence is as inaccessible to human beings as wisdom has just been described. Indeed, the discourse identifies the only window of access to wisdom available to humankind, namely the appropriate posture of reverence before God and dissociation from evil.

Regardless of the literary-historical relationship between the final verse and the body of the poem, the divine proclamation introduces a new dimension to the model of wisdom espoused in Job 28. Wisdom is not simply some entity of inestimable worth, placed forever out of reach of human grasp, of which only God can lay claim. Wisdom, unfathomable as it may be, becomes accessible only in practice. Wisdom, as unreachable as it may be, does not sever its ties from character. There is an ethical component to inscrutable wisdom that cannot be discarded, even if

---

40. So Habel, *The Book of Job*, 392. See also John F. A. Sawyer, "The Authorship and Structure of the Book of Job," 255.

ignorance is lamentably the ultimate end of the sagacious quest. This final testimony to the nature of wisdom offers a caveat, for it warns against all attempts to separate wisdom from its essential ethical moorings, that is, to disembody or *decharacterize* wisdom. Carole R. Fontaine is correct in noting that this final verse, suspicious as it may seem from a literary-critical perspective, represents the heart of the book of Job in its final form.[41] Cloaked in ignorance, cut off from true knowledge of his situation, Job can still lay claim to wisdom because of his adamant insistence upon holding fast to his righteous integrity (27:5-6; cf. 1:8). As will be seen, it is in and through Job's character that the fear of the Lord, the foundation of wisdom, is fundamentally redefined.

Job's Character *in situ:* The Transformation of Integrity

It is precisely Job's integrity that motivates his iconoclastic words in dialogue with his friends.[42] Indeed, for Job to concede the arguments of his friends would not reinstate but rather surrender his integrity. In defiance of his friends and God, Job protests (27:5-6):

> "Far be it from me to say that you are right;
>   until I die, I will not put away my integrity from me.
> I hold fast my righteousness, and will not let it go;
>   my heart does not reproach me for any of my days."

Such a statement marks a culmination in the development of Job's character, which begins in bitter lament and ends in radical revision.

Job's self-characterization initially is that of a victim who yearns for death, his only consolation (6:3-10). Yet interrelated to Job's death wish is the newly emerging posture of self-defense. Job's defense takes root in the soil of defenselessness. Bereft of strength, Job musters enough stamina to accuse his friends of betrayal and defend his righteousness (*ṣedeq;* 6:29). For the first time, the issue of honesty comes to the fore in Job's defense. Job drives a wedge between his honest words and the reproving words of his friends (6:25-26). Honest words, particularly of a desperate person, are not inconsequential, contrary to the perspective

---

41. Fontaine, "Wounded Hero on a Shaman's Quest," 79.
42. See Newsom, "Job," 132.

of his friends (6:26b). As Job's words begin to reshape the contours of integrity, an uncompromising, even strident, honesty comes to possess Job, breaking the shackles that have suppressed all previous discourse (7:11). Contrary to the ideal of the quiet sage, Job's integrity loosens his tongue rather than restrains it.

As Job's integrity comes to be redefined, so also Job's relationship with God is recast. Job dramatically portrays God as his oppressor in a scathing parody of Ps. 8:4-6 in Job 7:17-18. God is mindful of humanity only as tester and tormenter rather than as a majestic benefactor (*contra* Ps. 8:4).[43] Whereas the prologue suggests that Yahweh's testing is prompted by an unyielding trust in Job's character before the satan's challenge, Job himself attributes divine testing to God's relentless desire to torture human beings. Ruthless in pursuit, God is constantly targeting human beings for oppression. Hence, Job's initial appeals to God consist of pleas for respite (e.g., 7:16b; 10:20). Notably lacking is any reference to God's silence or absence from Job. Indeed, quite the opposite: God is omnipresent in abusing Job, whose purpose, however, Job cannot comprehend (9:11). Though elusive in character, God is ever-present in torture.

Not only a ruthless terminator, God is found by Job to be utterly capricious. How then can Job, the innocent victim, justify himself before Almighty God in court? Job's answer is one of resignation when he realizes that it makes utterly no difference whether he is innocent or guilty, for God's wrathful strength undermines any rational adjudication of Job's case (9:22). Job discovers there is no basis to which he can appeal to call God to account, since justice bears no compelling force over an arbitrary God (9:19). The perceived contradiction between the character of God and the nature of justice is internalized by Job to the point that he himself suffers an epistemological split:

> "Though I am innocent, my own mouth would condemn me;
>   though I am blameless *(tām)*, he would prove me perverse.
> I am blameless *(tām);* I do not know myself;
>   I loathe my life." (9:20-21)

Job knows, yet senses some doubt about his innocence, given the incontestable certitude of God's intention to declare him guilty (cf.

---

43. See Michael Fishbane's discussion in "The Book of Job and Inner-Biblical Discourse."

9:35b).[44] The insurmountable theological contradictions are mirrored in contradictions of self-knowledge. By questioning God's character, Job casts his own character into question, and so drives himself deeper into despair. The verb that describes Job's self-loathing *(m's)* in 9:21 denotes a decisive rejection of his own life, in preference for death. Not only do Job's physical afflictions, the castigations of his friends, and abuse by God provide more than sufficient reason for Job to yearn for death; now self-doubt appears to be the final straw that can break Job's will to pursue his case.

Yet somehow against all odds, Job does not give up his life but heroically presses his case. In the end Job is able to identify and conquer what prevents him from presenting his case, namely his fear of divine intimidation (9:33-35). For the first time Job makes reference to an outside party, namely an "arbitrator" *(môkîah)*.[45] This third party is invoked twice more (16:19; 19:25) as Job's discourse gains momentum and focus. Job appeals to this enigmatic figure in order to guarantee a hearing before a God who by all appearances has thrown Job's case out of court. Tentatively at first, Job allows himself to speak without the "fear of [God]" (9:35a). As Eliphaz correctly notes, Job has in his new-found courage undermined the very fear of God that is foundational to all wisdom (15:4). From Job's perspective, the requisite reverence of piety, stripped of all its pedagogical trappings, is nothing more than divinely inspired terror.

Job's speech in ch. 10 marks a turning point in the direction of his discourse, for Job now freely gives voice to his complaint without fear of recrimination. The charges are prefaced in 10:1 by the revulsion Job feels toward his life. Such loathing occasioned by his suffering (9:28) provides the basis by which Job receives the courage to prepare and articulate his case. The enormity of his suffering has overcome his concern for life and terror before God. In short, Job's suffering has *empowered* him.

Job, once among the powerful, now among the disenfranchised, publicly declares his desire to engage God directly, regardless of the

---

44. Attempts to explain away this epistemological contradiction are unconvincing, such as the translation "I do not care about myself" (Clines, 237) or reference to loss of consciousness in an Akkadian medical text (Shalom M. Paul, "An Unrecognized Medical Idiom in Canticles 6,12 and Job 9,21").

45. See Habel's discussion of *môkîah* in *The Book of Job*, 196-97.

repercussions (13:13). Such courage is expressed in the formulaic saying of putting one's life in one's hands (13:14; see Judg. 12:3; 1 Sam. 19:5). However, unlike the English cliché, Job's declaration operates in a profoundly ironic way. Job assumes control of his life with the full knowledge that God will kill him (Job 13:15). Life is no longer a concern for Job; his vindication has become all-consuming (13:18). Job is ready to risk all. Two obstacles, however, remain before Job can directly engage God. Job requests that God's hand be removed from him so that terror will not incapacitate him from preventing his case, and that God provide the proper forum for a hearing (13:21-22; cf. 14:15). Neither, however, is fulfilled, and Job is forced to ask why God's face remains hidden and whether God will frighten a dried-up leaf like himself (13:24-25). The theme of God's absence, which is only now beginning to emerge, is rooted in the language of jurisprudence: Though God's heavy-handed treatment of Job is immediately felt, God refuses to be arraigned in court.

Job makes another perhaps more daring petition in ch. 14. He requests that God provide him temporary asylum in Sheol until God's anger has subsided so that a proper appointment can be established for a juridical accounting (14:13-17). With such a hope, Job could patiently wait, even indefinitely (14:14).[46] Job's willingness to wait out the transient emotions of God betrays a defiant confidence that ironically confirms Zophar's prediction in 11:18-19a:

> "You will have confidence, because there is hope;
>   you will be protected and take your rest in safety.
> You will lie down, and no one will make you afraid."

The crucial difference, however, between Zophar's remedy and Job's hope is that Job seeks vindication, not repentance, to effect such restoration. Job's public declaration is worlds apart from his initial plea for mercy from his divine accuser (9:15).

Job's character has changed remarkably from the one presented in his initial discourse. The rhetoric of victimization has become Job's impervious defense. Job repeatedly points out that he has done nothing to provoke such unwarranted action by God. Indeed, in concluding the most graphically violent description of the divine warrior in all of

---

46. Such a statement provides a stark contrast to Job's earlier statements regarding his inability to wait.

biblical literature, Job offers an abruptly simple statement about his integrity in 16:17:

> "There is no violence in my hands; my prayer is pure."

At base, Job's recharacterization of God as a divine terminator is intended to drive a deep wedge between God and himself. Job, the "pacifist," will have nothing to do with this violent tyrant. Job's defense is as much a personal vindication of his character as it is a scathing condemnation of God's integrity. Contrary to the prologue's claim that Job never charged God with wrong-doing (1:22), the poetic Job accuses God of deliberately undermining justice (9:24). Without an appeal to a just God, Job becomes aware that there is no option except to appeal to a third party, one who can guarantee due process for Job (16:19-21). Job is through with pleading to God;[47] his only avenue of redress now is to bypass God by appealing to another member of the divine council, his arbitrator/vindicator/redeemer[48] (9:33; 16:19; 19:25).

It is precisely in developing his case that Job takes another radical step in mustering self-support for his cause: Job renounces death, which he formerly had been so eager to embrace. He comes to the realization that there is no hope in death (17:13-16). After death, vindication is a *non sequitur.* From this point on, Job becomes unflinching in his pursuit and wholehearted in his commitment to prove himself innocent in the face of divinely inflicted punishment. Job charges God of having put him in the wrong with violence (19:6-12) in the same way his friends have done to him with their destructive words (19:2-3). In a protestation of faith, Job bears witness one final time to his vindicator (19:25). Job has come full circle in mustering support for the exclusive aim of holding God accountable. With no lack of courage, Job confidently contends that God would give heed to him in the presentation of his case rather than overwhelm him, if God could only be found (23:6, 8-9; cf. 9:19). But God appears missing within the governance of human affairs as the wicked run roughshod over the poor of the earth (24:2-12).[49] For Job any preferential option for the oppressed does not exist.

47. Dale Patrick has perceptively noted the marked decrease in Job's direct appeals to God after ch. 14 ("Job's Address of God").

48. See Habel's discussion of 16:20 in *The Book of Job,* 265-66, 275.

49. Given the theological tension, it is assumed that 24:1-17 are Job's words, whereas vv. 18-25 represent one of Job's friends.

So out of defenselessness, Job constructs a powerful defense. Before God and his friends, Job defiantly wages a battle over his integrity. His arsenal consists of words of powerlessness and vulnerability that in the end overcome the authoritative words of his friends. His friends, however, see only misdirected anger bent on self-destruction, Job's weapon turned against the bearer (18:4). Within the arena of human intercourse, words can assuage and empower (16:5) or exacerbate and oppress. Discourse can be consoling or destructive. Job plaintively asks:

> "How long will you torment me,
>   and break me in pieces with words?
> These ten times you have cast reproach upon me;
>   are you not ashamed to wrong me?" (19:2-3)

Stripped of its initially guarded protocol, such "sagacious" discourse has degenerated into a crossfire of contention and conflict. It is in such a context that Job can speak with the heaviest of sarcasm in exhorting his friends to attend carefully to *his* words of consolation (21:2). Whereas a credible debate focuses on articulating arguments and marshalling evidence for support, rarely does the rhetoric of sapiential discourse stoop to such a level of *ad hominem* attacks and outright defamation of character (e.g., 22:5-6). But then it is precisely Job's character that is the primary topic of discussion, around which the issues of morality, God, theodicy, and creation revolve. It is Job's integrity that inexorably diverts the course of the discussion to the level of casting aspersions on Job's character.

Our Joban poet has dramatically illustrated the depth to which human discourse can stoop. What initially was meant to be a pastorally sagacious conversation among friends quickly retrogresses to mud-slinging. If an important measurement of a community is the quality of its discourse, then the community portrayed by our poet has failed miserably. Probing and insightful words have been replaced with slings and arrows. The dialogues are not only a parody of pastoral counseling; they serve as an indictment of the wise community as a whole. The language of comfort is displaced by the language of betrayal and brutal victimization, and Job must also bear some responsibility in this downward spiral of verbal cacophony. Job does not say, "Father, forgive them, for they know not what they do," but rather "God, damn them, for they know very well what they are doing!"

Job 27:1-12 represents a high-water mark in Job's self-defense. With vitriolic flair, Job utters an oath that is meant to guarantee, at his own risk, the credibility of his discourse, while at the same time indicting God for having violated his right to redress (27:2). Job's oath lifts the level of discourse to a new height (27:1). No longer is he locked in rhetorical combat with his friends; rather, Job attempts to elicit a response from God, *not* in the form of a prayer or plea, but in an oath, a veritable self-curse (27:2). His oath marks the height of his discursive power, the trump card of his lamentations: In swearing by God, Job can compel God to act.[50] As Habel rightly points out, Job's oath provides a counterbalance to the curse that Job's wife had proposed for the purpose of provoking God to kill him.[51] Yet the oath also echoes the satan's self-imprecation, which had incited God to act against Job in the first place (1:11; 2:5).

With Job's declaration of his integrity in 27:6, an overarching inclusio is established with the prologue (2:3), a literary envelope that also closes the cycle of discourse with Job's friends. From here on out, Job's discourse will be directed primarily at God,[52] but in a manner very different from that of the bitter prayers and supplications of mercy Job had employed earlier.

Job's Final Defense

Continuing the momentum established in ch. 27, Job's final defense in chs. 29–31 constitutes the crowning mark of his discursive power. The first part of his final defense (ch. 29) consists of recollections of the past, in which Job was considered the paragon of righteousness. The movement of the unit begins with Job's personal relationship with God but gradually extends to encompass his family and ultimately his community. At each step, Job depicts himself as above reproach. Similar to the prologue,

---

50. Habel, *The Book of Job*, 380.

51. *Ibid.*, 380.

52. If one assumes that 27:7-12 was originally part of the Joban discourse (vv. 13-23 are more doubtful), then the discourse in chs. 29–31 is meant not only to provoke God to action, but also to serve as the final and decisive demonstration of Job's integrity to his friends.

evidence from Job's involvement in family and community life is marshalled in order to confirm his unassailable character. Perhaps faintly echoing the satan's charges against God's beneficence toward him, Job contends that God used to watch over him, guiding and protecting him through the darkness. What the satan identifies as a point of contention concerning Job's character, namely the nexus between Job's character and God's beneficence, Job recasts as a seamless whole. Indeed, the transition from divine initiative to human initiative is both gradual and subtle:

I.	Divine initiative	29:2-5a
	A. Protection	29:2b
	B. Guidance	29:3
	C. Companionship	29:4-5a
II.	Results for Job	29:5b-6
	A. Family companionship	29:5b
	B. Material provision	29:6
III.	Job's initiative	29:7-20
	A. Social esteem	29:7-11
	B. Social service	29:12-17
	C. Social security	29:18-20

Job was once a leader of his community, commanding respect from young and old alike. As his circle of influence widens to include even the fringes of society,[53] Job's self-declared status rises to that of royalty as he himself declares in conclusion: "I lived like a king among his troops, / like one who comforts mourners" (29:25). Job boasts of his beneficence to the disenfranchised (29:12-16), of vanquishing the power of the wicked (29:17), of being clothed with justice (29:14), and of dispensing advice like spring rain (29:22-23). As the final jewel in his crown, Job refers to the light of his countenance in encouraging the downcast (29:24). All in all, ch. 29 describes the apotheosis of Job's character *that once was.*

Job's final defense is also important from the satan's perspective. The movement from divine blessing to right conduct and high esteem is unapologetically natural in ch. 29. Thus, the satan's charge that God has made it worth Job's while to act according to right character seems to be left unaddressed. However, Job's defense makes quite clear that his righteous acts are free of ulterior motives. It begins with the simple

---

53. E.g., the poor, orphan, and the widow in 29:12-13.

fact that God has graciously provided for Job, without any mention made concerning warrant or desert. The natural movement from divine provision to righteous behavior suggests that God consistently remains in the background, guaranteeing the efficacy of Job's behavior. Ultimately it is God who provides the means for Job to "break the fangs of the unrighteous" (29:17), to become eyes to the blind (29:15), and to put on justice like a robe (29:14b). Job's defense unpolemically makes the claim that righteousness is the result of, not the means for, divine blessing. Implied is that gratitude has directed Job to act in these ways. Explicit is the denial that self-interest has been the underlying motive behind Job's integrity. In short, Job's rehearsal of the past clearly acknowledges God's role in the formation of character, which leads to a life of gratitude and opportunity, but one in which self-interest plays no discernible role. Thus, the *telic* twist with which the satan questioned Job's conduct (1:9) is in Job's defense redirected into a *causal* one: Job explains his conduct as a *response to* rather than *an occasion for* divine beneficence. Regardless of whether this would clear Job vis-à-vis the satan's accusation, the relationships between divine blessing and human conduct is sufficiently nuanced to release Job from direct blame.

All the evidence that Job has marshalled in ch. 29 to confirm his indisputable character is, however, overthrown in ch. 30. All the blessing, honor, and prosperity, the by-products of wisdom, that had for so long confirmed his character have now vanished. Social disconfirmation has forced Job into the position of victim, analogous to those whom he once helped (30:24-26). As one whose bitter mourning has alienated him from civilization, Job regards himself exiled among the wild jackals and ostriches (30:29). In the light of traditional wisdom, which claims an inextricable link between inward character and outward success (cf. Prov. 31:10-31), Job's once estimable character appears to have betrayed itself.

Consequently, the long chain of oaths presented in the last chapter of Job's defense follows upon the heels of his poignant description of present misery in ch. 30 in order to lay to rest any doubt regarding his integrity. The series marks the grand finale of Job's defense and summation of his character. Together, the oaths offer a personal confession of innocence that is designed to inflict divine punishment if Job is found to have violated any one of them. These self-imprecations are fundamentally intended to compel God to come and measure Job's integrity:

"Let me be weighed in a just balance,
   and let God know my integrity!" (31:6)

The oaths cover a wide-ranging catalogue of vices that Job denies outright.

I. General ethical violation (false way)	31:5-7
II. Adultery	31:9
III. Violation of slave rights	31:13
IV. Inhumanity toward the needy	31:16-21
V. Avarice	31:24-25
VI. Idolatry	31:26-27
VII. Vindictiveness	31:29-30
VIII. Inhospitality	31:32
IX. Hypocrisy	31:33-34
X. Land Violation	31:38-39

The catalogue of vices is not structured in any particular way, except in that the first oath is cast in the most general of terms, hence an appropriate formal introduction to the series. In addition, appropriately near the end of the list is the sin of hypocrisy, of withholding confession of any moral indiscretions (vv. 33-34). Job's final oath denies any violation of the land, which begins with the conditional clause: "If my land has cried out against me, / and its furrows have wept together . . ." (v. 38). In antiquity, the land was considered a mirror of ethical conduct. When Israel sinned, the land mourned or reacted adversely.[54] As Job had appealed to his own actions throughout the series of oaths, he now appeals to the reaction of the land as witness to his integrity. Also of note is the oath on maintaining the right of the slave (v. 13). On the surface, Job maintains his innocence against the charge of negligence in preserving the legal rights of his slaves. Job claims that he has never dismissed any just complaint submitted by his slaves. Yet, ironically, this is precisely Job's charge against God: God has thrown out Job's case by refusing to appear and hold court.

Job's negative confession is typical of ancient Near Eastern legal or oath lists, particularly Egyptian and Babylonian,[55] yet it is far more

54. See Hos. 4:3; Jer. 12:4; 14:1-8; cf. Gen. 3:18; 4:10-12.
55. See Georg Fohrer, "The Righteous Man in Job 31," 9-10.

comprehensive and specific than any comparable piece of Hebrew Scripture, such as the psalmic protestations of innocence (e.g., Ps. 17:3-5; 26:4-7).[56] Given the predominance of the theme of Job's integrity, such an extensive list is by no means surprising. The fact that the confession is cast in a series of oaths invites comparison with the two oaths uttered by the satan in the prologue (Job 1:11b; 2:5b). Both Job's and the satan's self-curses serve to challenge, indeed compel, God to act. The satan incites God to wreak havoc upon Job with the hope of exposing Job's integrity as a facade. Job challenges God to examine his character so that he might be vindicated. In the prologue Job did not need to be tested for vindication's sake. Now Job pleads for such a test. Job's negative confession is meant to provoke a written indictment from God (31:35), which Job would then wear as a badge or part of his crown, his ticket of admission to approach God with fearless confidence "like a prince" (31:37).

As the climax of Job's discourse, Job's bold words in chs. 29–31 are unequaled in their persuasive power: They silence friends and ultimately provoke God. Far from pleading for a quick death to relieve himself from the unbearable pain of continued living (ch. 3), Job has turned full circle, renouncing death and seeking at all costs a hearing with God. As the direction of Job's rhetoric has shifted, so has Job's character. The cycles of discourse that seemed to go around in circles, seemingly progressing nowhere, in actuality trace the journey of Job's character, reshaping the contours of his integrity. Committing himself to the unflinching pursuit of seeking redress, Job has found the courage to call God to account, regardless of the consequences. Ostracized with the jackals and ostriches, Job has found strength in his character far surpassing the passive patience embodied by the Job of the prologue. The final series of oaths in ch. 31 reaffirms Job's own sense of integrity and equips him for the impending confrontation with Yahweh.[57]

Job's words are iconoclastic words. Yet his final defense returns to the world of the prologue. The hallmark qualities set forth in 1:1 appear again in different language in ch. 29. The debate between Job and his friends that culminates in Job's final defense is a battle over Job's past, including the story world of the prologue. By reshaping Job's character, the poet cracks open the flat characterization of Job *as well as* confirms

56. Habel, *The Book of Job,* 429.
57. So also Fontaine, "Wounded Hero on a Shaman's Quest," 79.

it. The friends' attempt to discredit the thesis of Job's integrity set forth in the prologue ends in failure. The poet transforms or re-profiles Job's character without undermining the basic thesis: Job persists in his integrity while seeking to challenge God face to face.

Such a re-profile of integrity breaks the traditional mold that is cast in the prologue. The more Job challenges his friends and God, the more Job gives expression to his sense of moral outrage against God, the more Job widens the gulf between his integrity and the kind of righteousness that requires unquestioning submission before God. Such righteousness can generate words of praise; Job's words, however, are the stuff of censorious blame. The words that scandalize the theological sensibilities of his friends reflect a Job whose integrity is anchored not so much in the traditional categories of moral virtue as in Job's newly found autonomy and courage.[58] Job justifiably embodies an ethos of grievance and victimization that is necessary for his transformation. The road to "moral perfection no longer subsumes but opposes unquestioning acceptance."[59] Yet it is in his protest that Job in the end commends himself to God.[60]

---

58. Langdon Gilkey is correct in noting the striking shift in the dialogues from Job's "innocence or virtue" to his courage and autonomy in the discourse ("Power, Order, Justice, and Redemption," 164). However, the basis of Job's reconstructed integrity is to be found precisely in his innocence (rather than at its expense), without which Job's unorthodox discourse would have no credibility.

59. Sternberg, 346.

60. See Chapter 4.

4 The Reformation of Character: Job 32–42

The building momentum of Job's protest reaches its culmination and focus in chs. 29–31, wherein Job's case for vindication is finalized in his oaths of innocence (ch. 31). Job now rests his case, but he rests it with a slightly different emphasis than earlier envisaged. His unflinching quest for vindication has reached a point at which he begins to commend himself to God rather than level another protest. "Let me be weighed in a just balance, / and let God know my integrity!" (31:6). Job's passionate conviction to vindicate himself at the expense of God's integrity is redirected, and a deeper conviction begins to emerge. Job no longer resorts to censorious blame to press his case. He does not say, "May my vindicator take my case to prove God wrong!" (cf. 16:19; 19:25). In assessing his life *in toto,* Job has come to identify a deeper longing, a longing to reestablish communion with God, and in so doing attain a knowledge that is born of intimacy. "Let God know my integrity," Job utters, not so much out of the self-righteous grievance that characterized his earlier laments, as of raw yearning. Job's desire for vindication is still present, but it is now coupled with the deeper longing to establish relational ties with a God who has been only oblivious to the pathos of Job's character. It is at this point of poignant self-disclosure that the stage is set for Yahweh to enter.

I. ELIHU: THE UNTAMED, WISE YOUTH

Yet Yahweh does not appear. An unannounced figure interrupts the movement of the plot as it strains toward resolution, thereby postponing the expected theophany. Indeed, the introduction of this new character marks the one last-ditch effort to "save" Job. It is no accident, then, that this spoiler who appears out of nowhere is named Elihu, "He is my God." Elihu's character has recently been disparaged by some scholars with almost unmatched vehemence. Variously described as a "fool, albeit a brilliant young fool,"[1] "a bore,"[2] and unintelligible,[3] Elihu is imputed a seemingly pompous and convoluted style that lends itself to many a modern caricature. Such judgments, however, constitute nothing less than character assassinations done under the guise of scholarly objectivity. From a historical literary perspective, Elihu in all likelihood was intended to be a commendable figure who spoke to a generation of readers who regarded him as offering a viable solution to Job's protestations and embodying estimable character.[4] In short, Elihu was written into the book of Job in order to salvage the friends' argument from a radically new perspective, one that emerges from a new generation of Joban readers.

Regardless of how one reads the literary history of the book of Job and Elihu's place in it, it is significant that Elihu's character is depicted much differently from that of Job's friends. Elihu is the literary antithesis of the friends in the arena of wisdom: He is young and yet learned in

1. Norman C. Habel, "The Role of Elihu in the Design of the Book of Job," 88.
2. Edwin M. Good, "Job," 429.
3. *Ibid.,* 429.
4. It is important to note, e.g., that Elihu's seemingly verbose style is evident only against the relatively succinct speeches of Job's three friends, in contrast to Job, whose verbosity is matched only by Elihu! Redactionally, Elihu is a foreigner to the text of Job; his character is inserted at a later stage in the literary development of the book. For the literary placement of the speeches, see David Noel Freedman, "The Elihu Speeches in the Book of Job"; Bruce Zuckerman, *Job the Silent,* 88, 238 n. 230. Although it is often assumed that Elihu serves as a foil for God, whose appearance follows upon the heels of Elihu's discourse, much of what Elihu says coheres in content to the speeches of Yahweh in chs. 38–41. Indeed, Elihu concludes with a fitting introduction to the theophany in ch. 37. If Elihu is a foil at all, he is a foil for Job's friends. As Zuckerman points out, Elihu fills a hole in the friends' argumentation brought about by their unwillingness to address Job in the legal language that Job himself employs to provoke an encounter with God (147, 150-55).

the ways of wisdom, but of a wisdom granted solely by God (32:6-14). Elihu chides the friends by overturning the long-held tenet that associates wisdom with age: "It is not the old[5] that are wise, / nor the aged that understand what is right" (v. 9). Although humility does not become Elihu, his sweeping statement is not without justification, for Elihu himself had once given deference to his elders: "I thought, 'Let days speak, / and many years teach wisdom'" (v. 7). But no more. Age and experience have proved to be sapientially bankrupt. Rather, "it is . . . the breath of the Almighty that makes for understanding" (v. 8b).

Elihu rejects the traditional picture of the sage, whose head is hoary and back is bent, and comes close to a prophetic understanding of wisdom, whose source is unmediated revelation.[6] As a result, Elihu overturns the developmental model of traditional wisdom. The process of sapiential appropriation is jettisoned.[7] As his name suggests, Elihu fancies himself as the veritable mouthpiece of God, and his very youthfulness undergirds, rather than undermines, his self-declared status. He is a *tabula rasa*. Age corrupts, but the purity of youth remains untouched. Unlike Prov. 1–9, the book of Job does not define the ideal of youth represented by Elihu in terms of receptivity within the framework of a social human hierarchy. Wisdom is not inherited from the preceding generations; rather it is received immediately and directly as inspiration. Youth is the empty vessel of divine wisdom.

Elihu, the self-declared prodigy of sagacity, develops the ideal of youth in his discourse on the human condition in Job 33:15-28. God chastens with fear and pain in order to compel mortals to repent (vv. 15-22). If there is one who is righteous, there is deliverance (vv. 23-24), and it comes in the form of *rejuvenation:* "Let his flesh become fresh with youth; / let him return to the days of his youthful vigor" (33:25). Elihu's sermon is clearly meant to reorient Job in his plight, to call him back to his youth. Job is beckoned to place himself in the subject position of Elihu, the ideal youth,[8] and relearn from God's mouthpiece what age

---

5. Reading the Greek, Peshitta, and Vulgate. The MT is haplographic.

6. Leo G. Perdue, *Wisdom in Revolt,* 249.

7. Elihu nowhere mentions the classical expression "the fear of the Lᴏʀᴅ," which the friends accuse Job of rejecting (15:4), for the phrase implies a developmental model of wisdom in proverbial wisdom (e.g., Prov. 1:7; 2:1-5; 9:10; see Chapter 2).

8. Technically, Elihu summons Job to "interpellate" himself in Elihu's character, that is, to identify with Elihu and embody his particularly ideology. Similarly, the reader of Prov.

has inexorably corrupted (33:31, 33). In short, the traditional model in which age and experience are placed at the apex of sapiential authority is turned on its head.

The Character of Wisdom in Elihu's Discourse

Wisdom assumes a secondary status in Elihu's discourse. Indeed, there is a dearth of references to wisdom in his speeches, the majority of which are either sarcastic (34:1) or directed polemically against Job and his friends (32:7, 9, 13; 34:35). Elihu confesses that he is full of words of wisdom, but they are not gained through age and experience. Wisdom is rather paralleled with "breath" and "the inspiration from the Almighty" (32:8). Elihu spiritualizes, or more accurately, "theocentrizes" wisdom. Consequently, Elihu's discourse attests to God's *direct* role in human affairs. It is not wisdom who reminds "a man where his duty lies," but a divine messenger or interpreter (33:23).

How then is it possible to teach such wisdom? Given Elihu's perspective, it seems ironic that he casts himself as a teacher of wisdom (33:33), particularly when he stresses the fact that he is not divine but a figure of clay like Job (33:6). Such talk reveals the tension inherent in casting wisdom in strictly revelatory terms without entirely abandoning the sapiential enterprise. From Elihu's perspective, wisdom cannot ultimately be imparted horizontally from human to human. Only God is the true teacher (36:22). Nevertheless, the human capacity to receive wisdom is inherent in the creation of life: "The spirit of God has made me, / and the breath of the Almighty gives me life" (33:4; see 32:8). Elihu sees himself as the instrument of God who is able to clear the cobwebs of age for inspired wisdom to be apprehended directly from the divine source.

> "Listen, listen to the thunder of his voice
> and the rumbling that comes from his mouth." (37:2)

Elihu's task is to fine-tune the reception.

1–9 is compelled to take up the subject position of the son (see Chapter 2; Carol A. Newsom, "Woman and Discourse of Patriarchal Wisdom," 143; see Louis Althusser, *Lenin and Philosophy,* for the meaning and function of "interpellation" [174-75]).

The Character of Elihu's God

Elihu's discourse empties wisdom of all self-sustaining content and, in turn, refills it with divine revelation. The motifs of journey and pursuit, of development and accumulation are replaced with the dynamics of reception and discharge (32:19-20; cf. Jer. 20:9), in effect a prophetic paradigm. Since the element of human initiative has been all but eliminated, wisdom is completely subsumed by the divine. Any examination concerning wisdom's character (or lack thereof) must point directly to the character of the divine. God is depicted as an immediately perceivable, vigorous force that is directly in charge of earthly affairs. Indeed, the cosmos is entirely transparent of divine presence, hence the frequent use of theophanic language in Elihu's discourse. Much like Elihu himself, Elihu's God shows no partiality to those who are on top of the cultural hierarchy, including the nobles and the rich (Job 34:19), Job not excluded. In fact, earthly royal figures are the frequent object of Elihu's disdain (34:17-20). Conversely, God is depicted as a divine warrior and mighty sovereign, whose actions are described with potent verbs (34:20-30). The theology of retributive justice as espoused by traditional wisdom is replaced by a theology of retributive terror (34:20).[9] All creation hangs precariously by the thread of divine favor.[10]

In sum, Elihu's character is presented as an ideal, as one who perceives the world in revolutionary and dynamic modes and behaves accordingly by submitting to no one except God. Although Elihu presents himself as a sage of sorts, he is quick to point out that only God is the true "teacher" (36:22). Elihu's brand of wisdom depends entirely upon divine inspiration and favor, as opposed to accumulated appropriation. Elihu's posture is clearly that of anti-establishment assertion. His style, therefore, is not so much pompous as it is unapologetically reckless. His unwillingness to refrain from stepping on the toes of his elders is by no means a character *flaw* meant to undermine the young sage's words and credibility. To the contrary, Elihu's unabashed and persistent self-reference is more an indication of what he is up against, namely the lumbering inertia of traditional wisdom, which has all but discounted the voice of youth. Elihu feels compelled to make his voice count among a group of elders rendered silent by Job's bitter complaints.

9. Perdue, *Wisdom in Revolt*, 252.
10. *Ibid.*, 251.

By championing the voice of youth and inspired wisdom, Elihu is a reckless rebel within the ethos of wisdom. He is a rebel *with* a cause; no silent son is he.[11]

As for the virtues that Elihu's character exhibits, his unabashed confidence, courage, defiant assertiveness, and passionate zeal are traits that, paradoxically, have come to be shared by Job. Such qualities Job eventually embodies as his character progresses from stoic resignation and surrender (chs. 2–3) to defiance against God and humanity. But Elihu's character traits are marshalled for a different aim, namely to defend God *against* Job. In a way, Elihu is the youthful counterpart of Job who espouses a wisdom that seeks to put Job in the wrong as much as Job's friends have sought in kind. Elihu is a rejuvenated Job turned against Job.

Among the early readers of the book of Job, Elihu's character is one that would have elicited endorsement from an audience later than the original readers of the book of Job, a later generation that espoused a prophetic understanding of wisdom over and against the traditional model of human observation and gradual appropriation.[12] Elihu's addition into the dialogic fray injects a new dimension into the Joban conflict. He introduces a level of contention between the aged and the young over the issue of who truly possesses the lion's share of wisdom. Elihu reflects a rebellious, new model of the sage, who not only talks back to his elders, but has the audacity to expose their folly. Indeed, Elihu as the gifted, rhetorically adept youth provides a prototype of the young Daniel depicted in the Story of Susanna and the Elders in the Septuagint text, who successfully undermines the machinations and alibis of the two lascivious elders in a trial of sexual misconduct.[13]

Lamentably, Elihu vanishes as quickly as he appears, but not without an appropriate exit by effectively setting the stage for Yahweh's appearance and discourse: "Listen, listen to the thunder of his voice /

11. The contrast is perhaps most sharply drawn in comparison to the figure of the deferential son in Prov. 1–9.

12. See Chapter 2.

13. The tale is usually dated near the end of the second century B.C.E. See Helmut Engel, *Die Susanna-Erzählung,* 180. As Engel points out, Daniel is the "the spiritually gifted youth," the paradigmatic opponent of the religious authorities represented by the two lascivious elders. Daniel's charge that the elders have grown old in wickedness counters the ethos of traditional wisdom, as found in Proverbs. The Theodotian text of the story, on the other hand, softens the contrast between the aged and youth.

and the rumbling that comes from his mouth. . . . Hear this, O Job; / stop and consider the wondrous works of God. . . . The Almighty — we cannot find him; / he is great in power and justice" (37:2, 14, 23). Elihu reveals as much as he tries to conceal what is about to transpire.[14]

II. YAHWEH'S DISCOURSE

As quickly as Elihu takes his exit bow, Yahweh appears to "answer" Job (38:1). Yet what Yahweh has to say does not appear to address Job's particular situation, as has been often noted. Job has desperately appealed for a hearing before God in order to vindicate himself and call God to account. Yet in his confrontation with Yahweh, Job is scarcely given a chance to present his case, as he had done to his friends. Furthermore, Yahweh talks almost *ad nauseam* of cosmic structures, wild animals, and mythological beasts through a rapid series of rhetorical questions. Is this merely an evasive tactic or "snow job" on the part of God? On the surface, Yahweh appears to play the role of tyrant, who intimidates Job into submission through a dazzling display of creation that seems to diffuse rather than resolve Job's case.

Within the dynamics of the plot, Yahweh must compel Job to recant his charge that Yahweh has committed a travesty of justice, not only against Job but against all humankind. "Shall a faultfinder (*rōḇ*) contend with the Almighty?" Yahweh presses Job (40:2; cf. vv. 8-9). This question lies at the heart of Yahweh's rebuttal, and it never lets up until Job can only haltingly muster a response in the end. In short, Yahweh's discourse appears to miss the mark. Indeed, the speeches of God have understandably been regarded as "poor theology,"[15] neutralizing "the subversive force of Job's speech."[16]

Given the elusive nature of the speeches and the negative assessment of some interpreters, it is tempting to be satisfied with the simple fact that God appears to Job, thereby establishing some kind of communion with Job, and to leave it at that. But clearly the Joban poet found

14. The placement of Elihu's speeches between Job's forceful defense and Yahweh's response is also theologically strategic, for it softens the incisive aim of Job's defense to compel God to act, thereby safeguarding God's sovereign freedom.

15. James G. Williams, "Job and the God of Victims," 222.

16. René Girard, *Job, The Victim of His People,* 141.

the content of the divine speeches, along with the epilogue, sufficient in providing a climactic resolution to Job's situation. Indeed, all along the content and form of deliberated speech in the book of Job have played the all-important role of revealing the worldview and character of each participant. God essentially enters into the debate between Job and his friends over Job's character, and what God says to Job is crucial, not only on Job's behalf, but also God's, for it is equally God's character that is at stake. Like Job's friends, Yahweh "answers" Job (38:1), but unlike them, Yahweh responds with rebuke rather than blame, a reproof grounded in love rather than in fear or hatred.[17] Yahweh's answer to Job is in the end an empowering one (cf. Zech. 10:6b-7!).

The Rhetoric of the Yahweh Speeches

It is important to note at the outset that the divine discourse is framed with rhetorical questions concerning Job's identity,[18] knowledge,[19] and ability.[20] As Job has consistently appealed to the veracity and scope of his personal experience and integrity against the traditional wisdom espoused by his friends, so also Yahweh appeals to Job's experience and character. Job defends the veracity of his perception; Yahweh reveals the limitations of his experience. Yahweh does not, however, admonish Job for questioning the ethos of traditional wisdom as represented by his friends. Far from it. What Yahweh has to say to Job also breaks with the long-held principles and boundaries set by traditional wisdom.

Contrary to Norman C. Habel's claim, Yahweh's questions are far removed from the kind of questions intended to pique intellectual curiosity.[21] No "Eureka!" ever comes from Job's lips. Yahweh's rhetorical

17. The discursive function of the "loving rebuke" is discussed in Chapter 2 in connection with Prov. 9:8.

18. E.g., 38:2, 5, 6b, 8, 25, 29, 36, 37, 41; 39:5; 41:2b(Eng. 41:10b); 42:3(41:11), 5(41:13), 6(41:14).

19. E.g., 38:4, 6a, 19, 24; 39:1; 38:18, 21, 33a.

20. E.g., 38:12, 16, 17, 22, 31, 32, 33b, 34, 35, 39; 39:2, 10, 19, 20, 26 (wisdom); 40:9, 10-14 (imperatives), 25(Eng. 41:1), 26(41:2), 27-28(41:3-4), 29(41:5), 31(41:7), 32(41:8). Yahweh's questions are essentially moral questions that deal with Job's vocation and identity (J. Gerald Janzen, *Job.* Interpretation [Atlanta: John Knox, 1985], 225-28; Carol A. Newsom, "The Moral Sense of Nature," 16).

21. See Norman C. Habel, "In Defense of God the Sage," 33. Habel is undeniably correct in noting the significance of the style of questioning. However, I differ with his

questions are designed, rather, to challenge Job in his creaturely status and finite experience as well as broaden the horizons of his moral worldview. Job had charged Yahweh with injustice (Job 9:21-24; cf. 40:8), compelling Yahweh to offer a defense (31:35-37). In response, Yahweh meets Job's challenge with a challenge that culminates in a barrage of imperatives in 40:10-14. At stake in the divine speeches are *both* Yahweh's and Job's integrity. Divine integrity is profiled by the way in which Yahweh is related to creation. Similarly, the contours of Job's character in the divine discourse are also prescribed in the way Job is positioned in relation to the cosmos. Inseparably tied, both Yahweh's and Job's characters require probing in order to unlock the enigma of the divine speeches.

The Character of Yahweh in Creation

The poetic discourse of the book of Job began with Job's curse on his birthday, and by extension, all of creation (ch. 3). It is no surprise then that the poetic climax of the work, the divine discourse, should also address the theme of creation.[22] Yahweh's incessant reference to creation throughout chs. 38–41 marks a return to the initial theme that had initiated the dialogues.[23] The divine speeches begin with the cosmos and move to Job's own character. As in ch. 3, the discursive movement in chs. 38–41 weaves back and forth between the individual and the cosmos. Job deconstructs creation through the prism of his personal chaos; God, conversely, must reform Job's character by reconstructing for him creation's majestic goodness.

---

final conclusion that God's character is modeled after the sage. Yahweh's questions are *not* those of a "shrewd sage who confronts Job with . . . tantalizing clues that will exercise the mind and test the spirit of all those who would be wise" (38). The answers to these questions are either banally obvious (it is God alone who can do such-and-such) or unfathomable to human apprehension ("Do you know the ordinances of the heavens?"; 38:33). These are not exam questions; rather, they serve to defend Yahweh's character in response to Job's indictment within the discourse of legal jurisprudence.

22. See Robert Alter, *The Art of Biblical Poetry,* 85-110; James G. Williams, "Job's Vision," 261.

23. Edwin M. Good suggests that after ch. 3 the whole discussion takes on a new direction with Eliphaz when he injects the issues of justice and deserved suffering into the discussion. From this perspective the Yahweh speeches integrate both issues, justice and creation (*In Turns of Tempest,* 212-13).

Yahweh's opening challenge in 38:2 is an ingenious wordplay on 3:4-7. Job had invoked darkness to invade the day of his birth, indeed, creation itself. God now accuses Job of "darkening counsel." The reference to "counsel" (*'ēṣâ*) is a *double entendre* of sorts. The word is a common wisdom term that refers to a well-conceived and executed plan; however, in context, it refers specifically to Yahweh's plan of creation, the design of the cosmos.[24] Implicit in Yahweh's charge is the claim that Job has obfuscated that design, indeed, revoked the created order.[25] Thus, God's defense must respond specifically to this curse of Job. In fact, Yahweh's response in ch. 38 treats the same cosmic domains of earth, sea, heavens, and underworld,[26] covered in Job's curse. But unlike Job, Yahweh reconstructs these domains in order to counter Job's devaluation of creation. And it doesn't end there. Not satisfied with broad cosmic categories, Yahweh pushes the language of reconstructive cosmology into other realms, to which Job had been oblivious. With increasing specificity, the divine speeches even touch upon the infinitely variegated realms of animal and myth, worlds chock-full of strange and fascinating species that revel in their independence and free play. As will be shown, Yahweh's world is an *inductive* world of rugged nominalism,[27] which revels in the individuality and intrinsic worth of every created being, in contrast to Job's (and the friends') social world of *deductive* hierarchy and dependence.

The Cosmological Realm

Yahweh begins the litany of creation with a description of the earth (38:4-7). Meticulously planned and executed, the earth is likened to the structure of a temple. In the Old Testament, as well as in ancient Near Eastern literature,[28] the temple was commonly regarded as a microcos-

---

24. See also Job 12:13; Prov. 8:14; Isa. 5:19; 46:10; Perdue, *Wisdom in Revolt*, 203; Habel, "In Defense of God the Sage," 34.

25. As noted earlier in 3:4-10, Job's curse is an attempt to revoke God's creative command.

26. For a structural breakdown of these domains, see Perdue, *Wisdom in Revolt*, 204-5.

27. "Nominalism" is used here in the philosophical sense à la William of Ockham, who countered Medieval scholasticism by claiming that the universe was essentially an aggregate of autonomous individual beings rather than a hierarchy of ideal forms (see below).

28. E.g., *Enuma elish*, in which Marduk constructs the Esharra over the Apsu in

mos. Conversely, the world described here is a cosmic temple that elicits worshipful praise from the heavenly creatures.[29] References to measurements, lines, pillar bases,[30] and the cornerstone[31] depict a world characterized by precision and stability, and God as its supreme and celebrated artisan, not unlike Gen. 1 and Plato's depiction of the demiurge in the *Timaeus*.[32] Whereas Job invoked the amorphous domains of gloom and darkness in his birthday curse, Yahweh speaks of exacting measurements and solid pedestals. Job spoke of the darkening and silencing of the morning stars (Job 3:7, 9); Yahweh defers to their joyous accolades.

Creation, however, does not end with the erection of this cosmic temple. Next comes the sea, which introduces a dissonant note into the univocal symphony of the cosmos (38:8-11). In contrast to the immovable bedrock of earthly creation, the sea (*yām*) is alive and livid with rage. Its destructive waves are stopped only at the bolted doors of the earth-temple. Chaos is contained, and the boundaries of its "proud waves" are prescribed.[33] Yet containment is not the only metaphor to describe divine action. Yahweh as a caring mother or midwife wraps chaos with a cumulus swaddling band (38:9b). Leo G. Perdue correctly notes the stunning language of individual creation.[34] Moreover, such unusual language has a specific purpose: to provide a direct counterpart to Job's account of his own birth in ch. 3. Job laments that the doors of his mother's womb had opened to allow his birth (3:10). Ironically, *yām*, as a cosmic *enfant terrible*, also has its birth from the womb and is

---

the same way the earth is constructed (*ANET*, 67). For an intriguing discussion of both the inner and extrabiblical parallels, see Jon D. Levenson, *Creation and the Persistence of Evil*, 78-130.

29. The completion of the temple's foundation is occasioned by festive praise (Ps. 148; Ezra 3:10-12; Zech. 4:7). Praise is also given at the time of Marduk's completion of the cosmos and the temple (*ANET*, 68-72), as well as after the construction of Baal's temple (*ANET*, 134).

30. The architectural term *'eden* is found frequently with reference to the tabernacle in Exod. 26–27 and 35–40. The word refers to the base or pedestal upon which the pillars of the tabernacle or earth are supported.

31. The well-known cornerstone references are found in Ps. 118:22 (*pinnâ*) and Isa. 28:16 (*pinnat yiqrat*), both of which draw from temple language to describe restoration and salvation.

32. See William P. Brown, "Divine Act and the Art of Persuasion in Genesis 1."

33. The motif of containment is paralleled in Ps. 104:9; Prov. 8:29; Jer. 5:22.

34. *Wisdom in Revolt*, 207.

nurtured. The dark clouds for which Job had yearned (3:4-10, 20-21) provide the seas' protective swaddling wrap. Caring sustenance and firm restraint are woven together. Yahweh nurtures as well as sets limits to chaos and conflict. Chaos is not an inimical force that must be annihilated.

Whereas the figure of the exacting architect who works with solid, inanimate materials is the predominant image in the first section, the description of the sea's *dynamis* in the second section elicits, in turn, a livelier depiction of divine agency, one of nurturing and restraining. Thus a tension is built into creation that chips away at the corners of the cosmic temple, a tension set within its proper context. Chaos is controlled neither by a dramatic display of brute force and destruction, so common among the ancient Near Eastern cosmogonies, nor by a rationalistic program of demythologization, as in Gen. 1, but by playful parody. Chaos has its own rightful, albeit confined, place in which to exist. The powerfully destructive waves of the sea are likened to a rambunctious infant with an attitude.

The pageant of creation presents another cosmic character to Job, namely the dawn, whose restorative powers are highlighted (Job 38:12-15). Divine help in the morning is a powerful motif that runs deeply throughout the Old Testament as well as in ancient Near Eastern literature.[35] The action of the morning sun is particularly vivid: It seizes *('ḥz)* the corners of the earth, shaking the wicked out *(h'r)*, molds and gives color to the earth, and withholds light from the wicked. Indeed, nowhere else in the Old Testament does the dawn assume such an active role in the restorative maintenance of the cosmos. Carol A. Newsom appropriately likens it to turning on the kitchen light in the early hours of the morning, sending the cockroaches scurrying into the dark corners and cracks.[36] What is more remarkable concerning dawn's role is that there is no talk of direct divine intervention. God is one step removed. While the dazzling rays of the morning sun re-create the world from its dark and turgid state at night, divine agency is relegated to that of initial command and assignment of the dawn's function. It is the sun that plays the active role. A celestial being has assumed the role of divine inter-

---

35. E.g., Isa. 17:14; Ps. 46:6(Eng. 5); 88:14(13); 90:14; 143:8. See J. Ziegler, "Die Hilfe Gottes am Morgen"; Bernd Janowski, *Rettungsgewissheit und Epiphanie des Heils.*
36. "The Moral Sense of Nature," 20.

vention in the art of cosmic maintenance.[37] The preservation of the cosmos is a delegated task.

The following two sections (38:16-18 and 19-21) explore further the motifs of light and darkness: the watery depths, the gates of deep darkness and death, the dwelling places of light and darkness, and the ends of the earth. Darkness, death, sea, and light are all portrayed as entities that dwell in remote areas. God assigns and leads them along their respective paths. From Job's perspective, the deep darkness for which he had longed in his birthday curse reemerges (vv. 16-17). Yahweh rhetorically asks Job whether he's been to the gates of death and deep darkness. Job, of course, must say no; his experience has not touched upon such realms, since his impassioned plea for death remains unfulfilled. Implied in God's question is that Job would have been all the wiser if his curse had actually been fulfilled. Such is the height of irony.

The Meteorological Realm

Following the paired constituents of the cosmos (earth and sea, dawn and darkness, life and death), another host of characters is introduced to Job: the meteorological phenomena of snow, hail, light, wind, rain, dew, hoarfrost, ice, constellations, and clouds (38:22-28). Each element has its active role in the grand pageant of creation, while Yahweh's role is that of constraining, assigning, storing, planning, and directing, in short, as the Toscanini of a cosmological symphony of movement, with each element having its assigned task and vector path.

The cosmos is presented as something overwhelmingly larger and more complex than the world to which Job is accustomed. Job's *perceived* world is provincially Newtonian, as it were, and anthropocentric: for every action there is an equal and opposite reaction, a world full of direct interventions, of dependencies, and of hierarchies. God is depicted as directly intervening in human affairs, wreaking, for the most part, irreparable havoc, as described, for instance, in ch. 12. In Job 38, however, God's self-portrayal is of a deity one step removed who allows aspects of creation to run their course, while achieving an intricate cosmic coherence. The language of direct intervention has no home in this kind of cosmological scheme, contrary to Job's own accounting, in which everything is thrown

37. As has been often noted, the dawn resembles the sun-god Shamash, who traverses the heavens discovering and judging evil (e.g., Perdue, *Wisdom in Revolt*, 208).

directly upon God's shoulders. From the divine perspective, the delicate but lively balance of cosmic and natural powers constitutes the warp and woof of the world's dynamic structure.[38]

The Animal "Kingdom"

Following the remedial course on meteorology, the animal realm then marches by Job two by two: the lion and the raven, the mountain goat and deer, the onager and wild ox, the ostrich and the war horse, the hawk and the vulture. They are by and large undomesticated beasts that are characterized by their special strengths and needs. The lion and the raven testify to Yahweh's role of sustainer and provider. The mountain goats revel in their God-given independence. The same goes for the onager, whose bonds are loosed (cf. 38:31) and who scorns the domestic life of the city. Like the mountain goat, the untamed ox will never return to serve a master (39:12). All of these animals are affirmed in their wildness and independence. Not one is subject to another; all have equal standing in the animal kingdom. Indeed, the animal kingdom is no kingdom at all; it is an ordered anarchy.

The ostrich in 39:13-18 stands out from the other animals described because of the critical tone the discourse adopts.[39] Fierce independence, which has so far *positively* characterized the animals, is pushed to extremes, spilling over into an ignorant recklessness (v. 13) that even endangers the ostrich's young. The ostrich laughs at the sight of danger and even death, but to its own harm. Unlike the other animals, this one lives without direction. The example of the ostrich attests to the negative side of fierce freedom. Yet, like the other animals, the ostrich assumes its rightful place in the wild kingdom. At the very least, it serves as a telling example of a stubborn independence untouched by wisdom.

---

38. Perdue also notes this, but unduly simplifies the issue by reducing it to the persistence of chaos in the world (*ibid.*, 211). Rather, it is the *interconnected balance of relative forces* that brings about cosmic order (see below).

39. There is some question concerning the textual status of the ostrich passage within the litany of creation, since it is entirely absent in the Septuagint. Content-wise, this section provides an exception to the otherwise positive assessment of the vitality of nature. The passage was probably introduced later into the litany of nature in order to maintain some critical distancing from Job's character and relation to creation (see below). For the purposes of interpretation, however, it will be assumed that the passage has an appropriate hermeneutical place within the divine speeches.

As the ostrich laughs at the war horse, the war horse laughs at fear itself. But unlike its predecessor, the horse's fearlessness is built on courage rather than stubbornness. Though it is the only domesticated animal listed, the distinction of the war horse lies not in its "tameness." No one can make it "leap like the locust." Rather, unwavering courage and strength are the hallmarks of this beast of war. Indeed, this animal is paradigmatic: control, courage, and brawn are impressively combined in this animal figure. It exhibits a focused fierceness that resists mechanical subservience. Any human master remains in the remote background (39:25b).

The hawk and the vulture attest to the heights as well as to the violence of the created order. Like the hail and snow, the vulture has its home in the remotest of places, from which it can easily discern its food. The livelihood of the vulture depends entirely upon the death of its victims. Again, like the other animals, these raptors serve no one, yet have carved out an existence within the created order that depends upon a balance of powers in the struggle for life.

Throughout this litany of nature, God revels in the wildness of creation. This is no static world governed by fixed laws. Boldness, courage (stubbornness in one case), conflict, and restoration characterize God's world. This is no orderly world of the Priestly Creation account, which methodically unfolds hierarchically and culminates with the establishment of human authority over creation. To the contrary, Yahweh's world is a messy one, populated with individual characters passionate about their existence, a "disordered" kingdom that is for the most part oblivious to human authority or natural hierarchy. It is a nominal world without dominance and subservience, filled with unique identities and intrinsic worth. Each species is an indispensable thread woven into the colorful fabric of life. And Yahweh proudly points to each of them in order to recontextualize the provincial world of Job and his friends. In other words, Yahweh *denaturalizes* the world in which human beings have considered themselves the pinnacle of creation and lords of the world.[40] Rather, it is the non-human forms of life, partic-

---

40. The term "denaturalize" is preferable to Matitiahu Tsevat's claim that Yahweh "de-moralizes" the world, which overstates the case at best, and at worst misrepresents Yahweh's positive valuation of the cosmos ("The Meaning of the Book of Job," 102). Yahweh presents a world that exhibits moral coherence, but a coherence much different from the one presupposed by Job and his friends, one that values and finds intrinsic worth in every form of life.

ularly the wild animals that roam and play on the margins of civilization, that receive Yahweh's special attention. Their worth is not grounded in service to a higher, human order. They are the objects of God's gratuitous attention. Indeed, Yahweh does not refrain from sending refreshing rain on the uninhabitable wastelands (38:25-27). For Yahweh, it is not a waste of resources but a labor of love.

In his opening rebuttal to Job's birth curse, Eliphaz constructs a world wherein God overcomes and destroys the wild kingdom to illustrate the demise of the wicked (4:7-11):

> "The roar of the lion, the voice of the fierce lion,
>   and the teeth of the young lions are broken.
> The strong lion perishes for lack of prey,
>   and the whelps of the lioness are scattered." (vv. 10-11)

In contrast, Yahweh's providential care of such animals is highlighted in divine discourse. No conflict between God and the wild kingdom is implied. Yahweh is both director and caretaker of the animals, allowing them no small degree of free rein. Eliphaz goes on to state that when Job is redeemed by God, the wild beasts will be at peace with him (5:23), that is, domesticated, a sort of restoration of the Priestly ideal (Gen. 1). Nowhere is this implied in Yahweh's discourse in Job 39. Indeed, their untamability is precisely what is to be affirmed rather than quashed.

The divine discourse radically revises Job's worldview in another significant way. Job had at one point likened the outcasts of human society to the wild animals:

> "Like wild asses in the desert
>   they go out to their toil,
> scavenging in the wasteland
>   food for their young.
> They lie all night naked, without clothing,
>   and have no covering in the cold.
> They are wet with the rain of the mountains,
>   and cling to the rock for want of shelter." (24:5, 7-8)

Job views life in the wild animal kingdom as impoverished and fragile, a drab wasteland of subsistence. But whereas Job disparages such marginal existence, Yahweh invests it with strength and nobility. Fragility is replaced by resilience, impotence with power, enslavement with fierce independence. To be a brother of jackals and a companion to ostriches is to keep honorable company indeed, Yahweh in effect says to Job (cf. 30:29). Job has landed in a place where humans fear to tread, a place where the trappings of patriarchy and human control are entirely absent.[41] Job is *literally* in a no-man's-land.

Through this overwhelming visual litany of undomesticated characters, Yahweh seeks to elicit praise from Job. But Job is only capable of a muted response, for he has come to perceive his role, indeed his very species, demoted to a vanishing breed. Job correctly perceives himself of "small account" (40:4). What is perceived from the human point of view as threatening and chaotic is unveiled as misguided specieism, a sense of superiority over creation. Yahweh has established certain flexible structures, domains, directions, and roles to preserve and sustain the frontiers that extend far beyond "civilized" life. From the divine field of vision, chaos is not the inimical state of betwixt and between that must be overcome; rather, the dark and dangerous forces are nurtured in their rightful place within the creative order. Chaos is, properly speaking, no longer chaos, but simply part of the tensive balance of powers in creation.

Yahweh launches into a second speech that opens with specific reference to Job's case. Yahweh's initial question in 40:8 severs all connection that Job had hoped to establish between his acquittal and his condemnation of God.

> "Will you even put me in the wrong?
> Will you condemn me that you may be justified?"

Adopting the language of divine combat, Yahweh then challenges Job to assume the position of divine ruler over creation by vanquishing the wicked and the proud (vv. 12-14). If Job is victorious, then Yahweh will acknowledge Job in praise *(ydh)*, as Yahweh had hoped to elicit from Job in the first speech. Surprisingly, Yahweh adopts the language of Job's friends in describing the maintenance of cosmic justice: certain and decisive victory over the wicked. Yet this runs absolutely contrary to Job's own observations: God has given the earth into the hand of the wicked (9:24a).

Both assertions cannot be true. Most commentators have taken Yahweh's challenge to Job as depicting what Yahweh is actually doing in

---

41. Newsom, "The Moral Sense of Nature."

the world, namely, maintaining justice, or more accurately eliminating the need for it (40:12).[42] Again, this does not cohere with Job's observations. Athalya Brenner, on the other hand, views this passage as an admission of divine *failure*.[43] In other words, God challenges Job to do a *better* job than God. However, it is important to note that the rhetorical intent of the passage need not imply incapacity on the part of God, though it does describe a certain kind of divine action. Yahweh challenges Job to act in a deified fashion by eliminating the wicked, but is it a divinely *dignified* fashion from God's point of view? Not according to the overall tenor of Yahweh's discourse. The arrogant ostrich, for example, is left on its own to carve out its existence in the face of danger. Yahweh does not destroy the mythological monsters of chaos (see below). Yahweh's ways are those of nurture and restraint rather than reaction and intervention.[44] Yahweh essentially challenges Job's *conception* of divine sovereignty, namely, one of direct and decisive intervention in the course of earthly affairs. The theological point of Yahweh's challenge to Job to take the reins of sovereignty is that God does not rule with an iron fist, grinding the wicked into the dust and coercing obedience from earthly subjects. Rather, Yahweh governs with an open hand, sustaining creation in all of its variegated forms, leaving both good and bad characters to weave their existence into the complex network of life.

Such is the case with Behemoth and Leviathan, the last two animals in the creation litany. Yahweh takes delight in describing and praising every detail of these mythological beasts. Behemoth is the first of God's creation,[45] made just as Job (40:15).[46] Verse 19 is curious in that God

---

42. E.g., "What Job is *unable* to do God *is* doing in his dealings with these beasts" (Tryggve N. D. Mettinger, "The God of Job," 45). Perdue maintains that although the passage does not claim that God is vanquishing the proud, it is implied (*Wisdom in Revolt,* 221).

43. "God's Answer to Job," 133.

44. See Habel, "In Defense of God the Sage."

45. Many suggestions have been made as to what precisely is Behemoth, ranging from the red hippopotamus to the "Bull of Heaven" in the Gilgamesh Epic (see Perdue, *Wisdom in Revolt,* 224), but no identification is certain. Regardless of its specific identification, it takes on mythological proportions as a fearsome amphibious creature, similar to Leviathan.

46. The only explicit reference to Job in the divine litany of creation is found here.

is proclaimed as the beast's creator yet is also portrayed as approaching it "with the sword." Although some mythological vestige of cosmic battle between a god and chaos is presupposed in the imagery, as has been often noted, what is *not* said in the text speaks louder than faded allusions. No battle, no life-and-death struggle, is anywhere mentioned. Within the wider rhetorical context of the speeches, the reference to the sword makes the point that only God, and not Job, could ever think about engaging in battle with Behemoth on occasion. At most, the statement illustrates the necessity to restrain Behemoth. But any reference to a life-and-death struggle with the beast, as between Marduk and Tiamat or Baal and Yam is suggestively lacking.[47] The saber may rattle, but Yahweh does not engage Behemoth in mortal conflict. To the contrary, as in the case of the sea in 38:8-11, there is a playful rambunctiousness between Behemoth and God's creation. Behemoth is left where all the wild beasts play, lazily sleeping under the lotus plants (40:20-21). The language of battle is replaced with the language of praise and admiration.[48]

At the apex of the litany, Leviathan represents the pinnacle of creation. Indeed, Behemoth, whose bones are "tubes of bronze" and "limbs like bars of iron" (40:18), is no match for Leviathan, who "counts iron as straw, and bronze as rotten wood" (41:19[Eng. 27]). Not surprisingly, of all the animals described, this sea dragon is given the most attention. Meticulously described are its frame, its breath of fire, invincibility before weapons, and its home. The last verse proclaims him king over all the "sons of pride." All attempts to domesticate this animal are doomed from the start.[49] Indeed, the predominant metaphor that characterizes Yahweh's relationship with the Leviathan is found in 40:29(41:5), a reference that echoes the playful imagery found in Ps. 104:26: "Will you play with it as with a bird, or will you put it on leash

47. Gisela Fuchs refers to this transformation of the *Chaoskampf* myth as a thoroughly ironic move on the part of the poet (*Mythos und Hiobdictung,* 288-90).

48. Perdue's attempt to find ancient Near Eastern analogies of praise language prior to or at the beginning of engagement in battle is suspect. The description of Yam's resistance to Baal's attack by Kothar-wa-ḫasis is not praise language by any stretch of the imagination (*Wisdom in Revolt,* 226 n. 1). Rather, such language serves only to heighten the suspense of battle.

49. Any opposition between this beast and Yahweh is only vaguely alluded to in the textually corrupt passage in 41:2-3(10-11). The NRSV translates the verses correctly, with the subject consistently being Leviathan, not God.

for your girls?" Yet the Leviathan is without equal. Much is made of its destructive, overpowering strength, but it is its royal role that is stressed in the end. Leviathan's regal role ensures that the proud and lofty do not overrun the world, a cosmic "chaos" against moral chaos. Leviathan's nature is transformed from a fearsome to majestic character.

Conclusion

The character of Yahweh in this complex creation is not the God Job had envisioned throughout the debate with his friends. God is not the exacting or arbitrary judge and warrior Job had envisaged. Yahweh presents a new profile of the world, and hence a new characterization of the divine self. Yahweh is one who balances and directs the powers and needs of all creatures, cherishing their freedom and delighting in their fierceness and respective talents. Subservience and utility do not characterize them; rather, every living being is appreciated for the way it exercises both its freedom and interdependence.[50]

Like a young parent who proudly displays the pictures of her children, God presents the grand sweep of creation, from the lion to Leviathan, in order to elicit praise from Job. Each creature is part of God's lively creation, a child that is to be nurtured and, if necessary, restrained on occasion. In short, Yahweh has *recharacterized* creation for Job. Every aspect of creation is transformed into a fully living entity, including even the basic elements of the cosmos such as water, land, light, and darkness, which have their respective "homes" and paths to follow. There are no inert objects in this world. There are no puppets or tools employed by a capricious god. Each entity is invested with a relative degree of self-initiative and character. Indeed, the signs of character already begin to appear in the litany of cosmological phenomena: the impulsive, rambunctious sea, which, if left un-checked, can wreak havoc like a child in a temper tantrum. In contrast, the sturdy temple/earth connotes solid security and consistency. To-gether, they represent the basic balance of forces. Indeed, a whole myriad of forces comes into play: the dawn forcefully tugging at the corners of the earth to shake out the wicked; the life-giving quality of rain described as God's children; the wayward constellations that

---

50. See the similar conclusions of J. Gerald Janzen, "Creation and the Human Predicament in Job 1:9-11 and 38-41," 51-53.

continually need guidance; the ever-ready lightning bolts that stand in attention, ready to assist God. All the animals have their own integral character, but what binds them together, ironically, is the capacity to play (Job 40:20) and the admiring attention they receive from Yahweh.

In short, Yahweh is praised not for directly intervening to subjugate the chaotic forces inherent in creation and eliminate conflict, though that potential is always there. Rather, Yahweh is characterized ultimately by creativity, self-restraint, and gratuitous pride. Yahweh allows the host of characters not only to exist but also to develop and exercise their endowed qualities, both positive and negative. Unlike the Egyptian and Mesopotamian kings, who hunted down the wild animals as a way to assert their sovereign authority,[51] Yahweh cares for them and allows them to develop true to their nature. To use an analogy from Dorothy Sayers and Iris Murdoch, good dramatic literature contains characters whose defining traits and personalities are neither mere extensions of the author nor foils; they are rather allowed to develop their own, independent characteristics. In the art of writing, the author must exercise restraint and care in creating authentic characters.[52] Such an act involves a "step back" on the part of the author.[53] It is out of gratuitous delight that Yahweh steps back and lets creation run its course, allowing the citizens of the cosmos the freedom to maneuver and negotiate their respective domains and lives. Far from being a divine tyrant, Yahweh is the gentle parent whose care extends beyond the maintenance of order and structure. Yahweh's love embraces each creature's individuality and unique role within the wonderfully complex network of life. Yahweh has countered Job's chaos and curse of creation (ch. 3) with blessing and balance.[54]

---

51. See Othmar Keel, *Jahwes Entgegnung an Ijob*, 65-81.

52. Diogenes Allen, *The Traces of God*, 35. Allen mentions modern authors Dorothy Sayers and Iris Murdoch, but without citation.

53. See Langdon Gilkey, "Power, Order, Justice, and Redemption," 166-67, who draws from Kierkegaard.

54. See below, note 69.

The Character of Job in Yahweh's Speeches

It is curious that nowhere in Yahweh's speeches do human beings receive even a modicum of attention. The litany altogether bypasses humanity, considered the pinnacle of creation in Gen. 1 and Ps. 8. Instead, the culmination is reached in the twin creatures of chaos, Behemoth and Leviathan. What is humanity's place, specifically Job's place, in this new order of creation? On the surface, only one clue is offered, and it is found in Job 40:15:

> "Look at Behemoth,
>   which I made just as I made you."

Clearly Job's creation has something in common with Behemoth, but what could it possibly be? Habel suggests a common destiny, namely that of subjugation.[55] However, subjugation is not at all the issue here, as noted above. Where one might expect a discussion of humanity's place and role in the order of creation, one finds instead effusive descriptions of the two mighty beasts, as if these two monsters have displaced humanity's traditional position at the top of the created order.

In a highly suggestive essay, John G. Gammie discerned certain connections between Job and the two beasts. Gammie claims that Behemoth and Leviathan are "intended by the author as caricatures of Job himself, images put forth not only to put him down, but also to instruct and console."[56] For example, Behemoth, when oppressed, "neither fled in fear nor abandoned trust (40:23)." Although he never says this directly, Gammie begins to discern certain *character* links between the figures of Job and Behemoth. Such connections, however, are even more evident when one looks beyond those limited to linguistic correspondence.

In fact, such a comparison between Job and Behemoth is established much earlier in Job's dialogue with his friends. In 6:12-13, Job ironically refers to his lack of strength:

> "Is my strength the strength of stones?
>   or is my flesh bronze?"

---

55. Norman C. Habel, *The Book of Job*, 565.
56. John G. Gammie, "Behemoth and Leviathan," 218, 222.

Such language is not alien to the detailed description of Behemoth's strength.

> "Its strength is in its loins. . . .
> Its bones are tubes of bronze,
>   its limbs like bars of iron." (40:16a, 18)

The connection is undoubtedly ironic: Job finds himself bereft of strength (see 16:15b), quite the opposite of the character of Behemoth. Yet Job claims that God is treating him as if he were a mythological beast that has rebelled against God and needs to be soundly destroyed (e.g., 3:8; 7:12). Indeed, Job's vulnerability resonates with the restraints placed upon the sea. In 13:27, one finds Job lamenting:

> "You put my feet in the stocks,
>   and watch all my paths;
>   you set a bound *(tithaqqeh)* to the soles of my feet.

In 38:10, the sea is described in the following fashion:

> "[When] I prescribed my bounds *(ḥuqqî)* for it,
>   and set bars and doors. . . ."

Yet Job's continuous reference to his vulnerable state eventually turns in his favor in his quest to engage God in disputation.[57] Job's laments of powerlessness and suffering are transformed into powerful weapons of protest. Job's words have become his weapons in his battle for recognition with his unwavering confidence securely anchored in his integrity. By the time he presents his final defense and, in turn, silences his friends, Job has developed a hide as tough as bronze.

Similarly, the last words concerning Behemoth's strength focus on its confidence.

> "Even if the river is turbulent, it is not frightened;
>   it is confident though Jordan rushes against its mouth." (40:23)

The reference to Behemoth's mouth is curious and suggests a specific allusion to Job's verbal battle with his friends. Despite the onslaught he must suffer at the *mouths* of his friends, Job emerges victorious in the end,

---

57. See above.

rendering his three friends silent. But is Job, at the height of his confidence and power, to be subjugated, taken "with hooks" and "pierced" by the nose? That remains to be seen. Nowhere is Behemoth given such an ignominious end. Rather, its strength is praised, and, vicariously, so is Job's.

As for Leviathan, the allusions to Job's character are even more plentiful. It is not fortuitous that in his first discourse, his lament over his birthday, Job likens himself at birth to Leviathan (3:8).[58] As Gammie points out, the extensive references to what comes out of the mouth of the monster resonates with Job's "verbal defenses."[59] This is clear from the very start of Yahweh's description of Leviathan, in which speech comes immediately into the foreground:

> "Will it make many supplications to you?
> Will it speak soft words to you?" (40:27[41:3])

Certainly to his friends, Job was not known for gentle speech. What comes out of Leviathan's mouth is flaming torches, sparks of fire, smoke, and flames (41:11-13[19-21]). The speech of Leviathan incinerates everything in its path; hence no one would ever want to be the object of this monster's "discourse." Likewise, Job's discourse has reduced his friends' deliberations to ashes (13:12).

> "Your maxims are proverbs of ashes,
> your defenses are defenses of clay."

In his inflammatory deliberations, Job the verbose relentlessly pursues his vindication against the onrush and torrents of baseless claims. Job defends his "tongue" as honest, a sure defense and weapon against the reproof of his friends (6:25-27). Yet it is precisely his tongue that gets him into trouble.

> "Therefore I will not restrain my mouth;
> I will speak in the anguish of my spirit;
> I will complain in the bitterness of my soul.
> Am I the Sea, or the Dragon,
> that you place a [muzzle][60] over me?" (7:11-12)

58. Gammie, "Behemoth and Leviathan," 224.
59. *Ibid.*, 225.
60. See Mitchell Dahood's analysis of *mišmār* ("*Mišmār* 'Muzzle' in Job 7_{12}"), and Habel, *The Book of Job*, 153.

The pairing of the theme of bitter speech with the image of the sea monster is deliberate. Who is that sea monster? None other than Leviathan, whose speech spares no one. Both Job and Leviathan are linked together by their overpowering discourse.

Before Job's masterful display of rhetoric and honesty, all counter-arguments are exposed for what they are, emptied of all rhetorical force and burned to a crisp. Indeed, more than morning breath is implied when Job laments, "My breath *(rûaḥ)* is repulsive to my wife, / loathsome to the sons of my own mother" (19:17). The statement is charged with irony when one compares it to the description of Leviathan's searing exhalation (41:12-13[20-21]).

As Job gains confidence through his discourse, he comes to the point where he is able to speak boldly, without fear. Job has reached the status of the invincible sea monster, whose mouth is its most fearsome weapon. Similarly, what makes Leviathan unique among all the creatures is its lack of fear (41:25[33]). Iconoclastic words that break down orthodox piety and character can only be uttered by one equally fearless.

One can also discern parallels between Job and the creatures with which God has populated the world of nature. As noted above, potency and strength also characterize the animal realm, from the lion to the vulture. Earlier, Job had lamented that he had become "a brother of jackals, / and a companion of ostriches" (30:29), cast out from the human community. Yahweh now proudly presents to Job his new companions, who have more in common with Job than his peers and family. Through an unwelcomed solidarity with these denizens of the margins, Job is compelled to acknowledge the estimable qualities embodied by these untamed figures by recognizing a bit of himself in each. Like the animals, Job remains undefeated and untamed within the arena of human disputation. In every case, from lion to Leviathan, Job is presented with a mirror of himself that reflects his tenacity, fearlessness, courage, as well as vulnerability (cf. the raven [38:41]) and stubbornness (cf. the ostrich [39:13-18]). Though Job complains that he is treated like the sea, confined and muzzled, in the battle over his integrity, he comes to realize that, like the sea, he receives nurture and praise from Yahweh. Yahweh does indeed know Job's integrity (cf. 31:6) and proves it by demonstrating Job's solidarity with all of creation. In short, Job finds himself mysteriously mirrored in creation and creation mysteriously mirrored in himself. Yahweh has turned Job's declaration of independence into one of interdependence.

Job's Response: 42:1-6

Job's response in ch. 42 presents a major crux for interpreting his transformed character, and hence interpreting the book as a whole. Job begins by acknowledging Yahweh's supreme strength, conceding that nothing can stand in the way of divine purpose, and utters two approximate quotations of Yahweh's challenge to him in 38:2 and 3b (see also 40:7b). Together, Job's final words constitute Yahweh's opening words. Job's ostensible failure to meet Yahweh's challenge is indicated in the way in which Job responds not by pressing the case he had so passionately prepared, but by haltingly imitating divine speech. Job assumes divine discourse, establishing common ground with God. By citing his own version of divine discourse, Job admits defeat and gives assent to Yahweh's own defense of the cosmic design. Job has gained a new foundation for his knowledge of God, namely, a vibrant, visual, direct knowledge, before which all means of traditional wisdom are simply "hand-me-downs" by comparison.

Abruptly shifting from imitating divine discourse, Job's response in 42:6 profiles his own position in relation to Yahweh. Job utters his summary statement, revealing something of his posture and integrity before God. But what appears on the surface as simple and brief is fraught with much background, even ambiguity, as indicated by the wealth of interpretations the verse has generated among interpreters. The traditional rendering is:

> "I despise myself,
>   and repent in dust and ashes." (NRSV)

To the large pool of interpretations,[61] I offer my own rendering of this contested verse:

> "I hereby reject [my life],
>   and am comforted concerning dust and ashes."

---

61. One cannot even begin to cover the variety of suggestions offered. See Habel, *The Book of Job*, 576, for the suggestions from commentators; Marvin H. Pope, *Job*, 348-350, for the textual versions, particularly 11QtgJob; John Briggs Curtis, "On Job's Response to Yahweh"; Dale Patrick, "The Translation of Job XLII 6," 369-370; L. J. Kaplan, "Maimonides, Dale Patrick, and Job XLII 6"; Luis Alonzo-Schöckel and J. L. Sicre Diaz, *Job*, 592-93. Others will be mentioned below.

The verb of the first clause (from *m's*), whose basic meaning is "to reject" or "despise," appears twice elsewhere in the book of Job in the first person: 7:16 and 9:21. In the first instance, the verb, as in 42:6,[62] stands without an immediate object; however, in context it is clear that the implied object is "life."[63] Job proclaims his preference for death by rejecting his own existence. The second use of the verb is set in Job's protestation over the futility of initiating litigation against God (chs. 9 and 10). Job is in complete despair over the fact that God destroys both the guiltless and the guilty (9:22). The theological contradiction of divine integrity is internalized by Job (9:21-22);[66] consequently, Job laments that he has no other option than to give up *(m's)* his life (9:21b). Yet the fact that Job no longer values his existence is what ultimately enables him to formulate his charges against God, regardless of the consequences to himself.[65] Job's rejection of life is initially an act of surrender and despair that turns to defiance in the later stages of Job's dialogue with his friends.

In the case of Job's final response to Yahweh, the context is more nuanced. Job has just acknowledged seeing God with his own eyes, and thus expects death. Indeed, Job already anticipated such an expectation in 9:16-17a.

> "If I summoned him and he answered me,
>   I do not believe that he would hear my voice.
> For he [would crush] me with a tempest."

Job's rejection of his life reflects his anticipation of certain death, now that he has directly beheld God in creation.[66] It is important, however, to note that Job formulates his expectation of death in active terms, "*I reject*," not something like "Woe is me" or "I'm as good as dead."[67] By using active self-referential language so typical of the dialogues, Job takes the initiative once again to seize the opportunity, in this case to declare

---

62. The theory that the direct object of the verb in 42:6 is "dust and ashes" in the second colon is awkward syntactically (contra Patrick, "The Translation of Job XLII 6," 370; cf. Perdue, *Wisdom in Revolt*, 237 n. 1).

63. See NRSV translation and the discussion in Habel, *The Book of Job*, 153.

64. See previous section.

65. See previous section.

66. Cf. Exod. 33:20.

67. Cf. Isa. 6:5.

his release from life, beating death and perhaps even God to the punch. Job has received his "hearing"; there is no longer any reason to continue his quest. Job can now embrace death.

The meaning of the second clause in Job's "confession" is in essence a *double entendre,* since the Hebrew verb "to repent" *(nḥm)* actually has a range of meanings from "being sorry" to "being comforted."[68] In the book of Job, this verb occurs six other times and always with the sense of "comfort" (2:11; 7:13; 16:2; 21:34; 29:25; 42:11). Furthermore, the theme of consolation is a prominent feature in Job. Job's friends come "to console and comfort him." But it is God's "gentle rebuke" that has, in the end, assuaged Job's pain. Two striking parallels can be discerned in the literary development of the poetic dialogues: Job's final rejection of life in 42:6 corresponds to his initial death wish in ch. 3, and the final achievement of consolation correlates with the friends' failed attempt to console him. In Job's last words the themes of comfort and death are once again joined together.[69]

Upon the ash heap and before the grand sweep of the cosmos, Job has found comfort over his state of utter destitution.[70] His rejection of

68. Many interpreters have looked toward the following preposition *('al)* for help in discerning the precise nuance. One influential suggestion is the meaning "to change one's mind *about* something planned," as in Exod. 32:12, 14; Jer. 18:8, 10 (see Patrick, "The Translation of Job XLII 6," 370). Hence, Job forsakes his position of mourning and lament, indicated by the reference to dust and ashes. See also Habel, *The Book of Job,* 576. Perdue, on the other hand, correctly notes that the preposition can equally be rendered to mean "to be comforted over" (2 Sam. 13:39; Jer. 16:17 [*sic*]; Ezek. 14:22; 32:31), and notes that the meaning of repentance is evident only when the verb is followed by a term denoting "evil" (Perdue, *Wisdom in Revolt,* 237 n. 2). See also William Morrow, who suggests an inherent ambiguity in the phraseology ("Consolation, Rejection, and Repentance in Job 42:6").

69. By the end of Yahweh's discourse a literary symmetry emerges among the themes of comfort, character, creation, and community.

A Comfort attempted: Job's friends (2:11-13)
  B Creation: curse and chaos: death affirmed (ch. 3)
    C Job's character: the victim (chs. 3–10)
    C′ Job's character: the strong (chs. 12–31)
  B′ Creation: blessing and balance: life affirmed (chs. 38–41)
A′ Comfort achieved: Job's new "friends," the wild animals (chs. 39–41)

70. As is often noted, the pairing of "dust and ashes" in 42:6b is also attested in Gen. 18:27, in which Abraham abases himself while challenging God's justice in connection with the fate of Sodom and Gomorrah. The phrase clearly conveys diplomatic

life is paralleled by the comfort achieved by Yahweh's revealing creation's inherent goodness, a radically expansive goodness that deconstructs and reforms Job's previously restricted worldview and, thus, ultimately his character. In *mysterium tremendum*, Job finds resolution in his quest. Conversely, in his very human and toilsome search, without which no answer could come, Job encounters awe and a new-found knowledge about God, creation, and himself. In revelation, Job's deepest human longings are fulfilled. In his final defense, Job began to sense a deeper desire than winning his case and exacting concessions from his Opponent. Job seeks the prospect of communion, inviting God to know his integrity and to permit him passage through the threshold that separates heaven and earth (31:6, 37). Human search and divine granting find their intersection in Job, whose only possible response to God's full disclosure is to offer his life back to God.

III. THE EPILOGUE: JOB RESTORED

What Job expected, even welcomed, however, did not transpire. Quite the opposite: Job was restored! The poet masterfully establishes a creative tension between poetry and prose similar to the initial juncture in chs. 1–3. Job does not expire as expected; he is not in the end released from a life that has been consumed by the pursuit of a resolution to his suffering. Consolation and restoration now become partners in the epilogue, replacing the former's old partner, death.

Many modern interpreters have regarded the epilogue to the book of Job as a "covenantal counterpoint,"[71] at best, to the disturbing dis-

---

humility before Yahweh. The pairing of "dust and ashes" finds its only other parallel in Job 30:19.

> "[God] has cast me into the mire,
> and I have become like dust and ashes."

The verse tangibly conveys the certain reality of defeat and death. Here, God is depicted as Job's relentless persecutor, who will unfailingly bring about his death (30:23). The reference to "dust and ashes" connotes the evanescence of Job's fragile life before a ruthless god. In Job 42:6, the phrase connotes Job's overwhelming sense of fragility before an awe-inspiring God who, in the end, *affirms* Job in his quest.

71. To borrow Levenson's phrase in *Creation and the Persistence of Evil*, 156.

course or, at worst, a theological cop-out.[72] However, the primary frame of reference from which to discern the epilogue's significance must come from within Job's character, where the reader has been all along. The reader of the dialogues has experienced firsthand Job's turmoil and distress, witnessing the voice of pathos discounted by his friends, knowing all along that Job is innocent. Such an empathetic and privileged position of the reader is not meant to be abruptly jettisoned in the epilogue. The literary movement begs the question of what Job must have felt in the transition to restoration, of what it meant *for Job* to be restored.

In the prologue, the reader viewed Job from the outside: Job's actions and responses outlined the external contours of his character. In dialogues, however, Job's inner life was unapologetically laid bare; his character shifted from the stoically flat to the passionately complex. And now there is no going back. While the epilogue undoubtedly recalls the story-world naiveté of the prologue, it cannot beat a path back to Job's flatly depicted character. The dialogues have made sure of that. Job now reenters his *story* fleshed out and fully human, and the reader, having experienced the depths of his travail, is beckoned to fill in his inner life as the character of Job is restored in narrative. In short, the epilogue is overwhelmingly fraught with background.[73]

At the outset, Job is vindicated in God's address to Eliphaz. That Job has spoken rightly instead of his friends is repeated twice in the epilogue (42:7, 8). Such vindication affirms that Job's relentless quest and protestations have been legitimate and acceptable, at least provisionally. Throughout the dialogues, Job's character has progressed from resignation to protest to deep yearning, acceptance, and finally surrender, a veritable *reformation* of character.

The epilogue adds a new virtue to Job's developing character, compassion for the other. Job prays on behalf of his opponents, setting in motion the process of restoration (42:8-10). As in the Yahweh speeches, the shackles of correlative justice are broken, a form of justice that feeds itself on vindication and punishment. Logically, Job's vindica-

---

72. One avenue of interpretation is to highlight the ironic undertone that proves the friends correct in the end, since their whole case against Job was to prove that there is retributive order in creation, and Job, after all, was vindicated.

73. Erich Auerbach's analysis of Gen. 22 as a deceptively simple story "fraught with background" applies equally to the epilogue of Job (*Mimesis*, 5-10).

tion must be asserted at the expense of his friends. They were wrong and consequently must be condemned, as they have tried to condemn Job and as Job wanted to condemn God. Now the tables have turned. But Job's prayer on their behalf, in conjunction with the prescribed sacrifices, overcomes such necessity of reversal, as much as Yahweh's presentation of the cosmos overcomes the necessity of condemning God in light of Job's vindication (40:2, 8). The friends are restored as surely as Job is restored. The act of prayer reveals something new about Job, a streak of compassion, specifically a *gratuitous* compassion that could only be found in the discovery of the God who takes gratuitous delight in all of creation. A suggestive counterpoint to Job's prayer is Job's sacrificial actions on behalf of his children in the prologue (Job 1:4-5). There, Job's actions were motivated by fear and honor as head of the household. Job's prayer on behalf of his friends, on the other hand, is motivated by compassion.

What happens next in the epilogue poignantly conjoins consolation and restoration. Job's siblings and acquaintances succeed finally in what Job's friends had failed to do, namely to offer effective consolation. Edwin M. Good has appropriately focused attention on the action of Job's family as providing a solution, perhaps the only solution, to the problem of evil.[74] Their response to Job's suffering is part and parcel of Job's restoration; it constitutes the very beginning of the reversal of his misfortune.

The epilogue does indeed have something new to say regarding Job's character. Job is not the flat character that is often assumed in this Hollywood-like ending. The way in which Job is restored tugs at the stereotypical image of the patriarch. Job, to be sure, is doubly restored, but with the same number of children: seven sons and three daughters. This time, however, his daughters are specifically named: Dove, Cinnamon, and Horn-of-Antimony, titles that highlight their striking beauty. As Yahweh took an almost parental pride in the wondrous beauty of creation in all of its variegated form, there is a concomitant sense of pride that is focused uniquely on Job's daughters.

What is perhaps more striking is that Job's last act is his giving his daughters an inheritance along with their brothers, an unprecedented act in Israel's legal traditions. As Num. 27 and 36 suggest in the case of the daughters of Zelophehad, females can receive an inheritance if, and

---

74. "The Problem of Evil in the Book of Job," 69.

only if, there are no male siblings to carry on the father's lineage.[75] Though Job is restored as head of the household, he and his new family are cut from a different cloth. As his poetic words broke the norms of orthodox perspectives in the dialogues, Job breaks traditional social norms by granting his three daughters an equal share of the inheritance. Like Behemoth and Leviathan, Job displays a certain bold confidence, an "untamed" recklessness, that is not suppressed but affirmed. Job, patriarch that he is, breaks with traditional family values by dispensing material equality to his daughters, thereby severing the bonds of patriarchal dependency and allowing them a degree of autonomy in a world steeped in hierarchy.

More suggestive, perhaps, is the abrupt transition from Job's plight to restoration. Literarily, it seems particularly abrupt, perhaps even artificial, as many have noted. But in light of the continuity of Job's character, the prospect of restoration takes on a different, realistic dimension. From Job's angle, the epilogue is a portrait of tenacious faith.[76] Far from a mechanical reversal of fate, restoration for Job entails returning to the fold of civilized life, after having spent time in the wilderness with the jackals and the ostriches. It is crucial that Job does not remain in the wilderness, meditating upon God's awesome beneficence in creation. Job is not a mystic. Just as he was thrown into the margins of life, where the periphery suddenly replaced the center, Job is now thrown back into the community with a new sense of purpose and moral vision. On the one hand, Job's restoration requires nothing short of a bold reinvestment in family and communal life, along with the accompanying responsibilities and risks in a world that lacks all security and guarantees and is ever potent with unpredictable mishap. On the other hand, Job's restoration requires a bold reinvestment on the part of his family and community in him to welcome him back and begin the process of healing and restoration. If there is any unpardonable sin that is more clearly identified in the book of Job, it is the sin of communal neglect of the sufferer. To suffer and die in isolation is nothing short of an indictment against community and family. In short, Job's refashioned integrity is met with a reconfiguration of the community's integrity.

75. See also 1 Chr. 2:34-36; Ezra 2:61; Neh. 7:63.
76. Ellen F. Davis is the only one I am aware of who has articulated this point, and it is from her discussion that I draw these final conclusions ("Job and Jacob," 219-220).

Restoration requires risk, the risk to give and receive love in an ever-threatening world. For Job, such risk is evinced in raising a new family vis-à-vis such a world, in reintroducing into his own life the "chaos" of raising children with all of its accompanying risks, challenges, and joys (cf. 38:8-11). Without condition Job has accepted and mirrored God's world on its own terms, a world of flux and conflict, of demise and restoration, a world of vicissitudes that subvert all attempts at constructing a hierarchical, self-contained model of cosmic and moral coherence. In the end, the book of Job is not only a book about tenacious faith amid trial and tribulation; it is also a book about the tenacious acceptance of blessing. Life is in the giving and receiving, passionate investment and risky reception. It is about finding the blessings in the barrenness and the duties in the blessings.

IV. CONCLUSION: THE ECOLOGY OF CHARACTER

The book of Job is essentially about Job. Such an observation may appear trivial at first glance, but it is crucial to keep in mind that all other issues commonly associated with the book, including those of creation, theodicy, and the nature of God, are of secondary importance before the central issue of the Joban character and its transformation. The satan's challenge to Yahweh remains a constant query throughout the story (1:9), for what the satan raises is in essence the issue of Job's character: "Does Job fear God for nothing?" And bound up with Job's character is the nature of integrity, posed by Job's wife: "Do you still hold fast to your integrity?"

Character in Transition

Job is a character in transition. The poet highlights the initial stage in Job's "formation" by setting in tension the Job of the prologue with the poetic Job. Job the Patient becomes Job the Complainer. And for some forty chapters the poet renders in turgid discourse what is essentially unspeakable in the prologue. Yet what binds the two vastly different characterizations of Job together is Job's integrity *(tummâ)*. Both the silent and the verbose "Jobs" lay claim and hold fast to integrity. Integrity is presented as a dynamic component of character that can oscillate between complete adherence to moral norms and unorthodox honesty and tenacity. The poet's purpose consists by and large of reshaping the contours of Job's integrity. Character as depicted in the prologue typifies the root values of traditional wisdom: self-restraint in speech and emotion, a near stoic acceptance of one's fate, an all-consuming concern with personal honor within the family and community, and submissive reverence of God.

The dialogues, on the other hand, deconstruct every traditional virtue, yet claiming to retain some vestige of their underlying integrity. Job's reconfigured integrity is marked by bold tenacity, brutal honesty, righteous anger, and flagrant self-assertion. An ethos of grievance and victimization replaces one of restraint and self-sacrifice as Job's discourse gains momentum and focus in the dialogues. It is these unorthodox traits, not the traditional virtues, that constitute the raw material out of which God reforms Job's worldview and character. Job dares to persist in claiming that his hold on integrity is secure (27:6), and he does it in defiance of all the traditional means of measuring and confirming good character: esteem, prosperity, health, position of authority, large family, etc. Despite all appearances to the contrary, Job asserts himself as righteous, and from the poet's perspective, Job can say this with all sincerity, contrary to the friends, who see only the hallmarks of wickedness.

Divine Reverence in Transition

At one point Eliphaz indicts Job for undermining the "fear of God" (15:4). As Job's discourse recontextualizes his integrity, so it also refashions reverence of God. The "fear of God" in proverbial wisdom profiles a relationship of openness and receptivity to divine authority.[77] However, Job initially reconstrues the traditional notion of the "fear of God" as divinely inspired terror in light of his situation. Rooted in divine capriciousness, such terror overwhelms and incapacitates Job, suppressing his speech and prompting him to seek shelter in Sheol. However, this dark dimension of divine reverence Job eventually overcomes and rejects. Yet he still reveres God in some sense. His reverence is now

77. See Chapter 2.

rooted in a freedom to come before God "like a prince" (31:37), in the confident hope that God will respond with equity to his case. Job does not reject God; he does not in the end curse God. To the contrary, God remains the end and goal of his quest.

Job's reverence is evinced in his courage and yearning to engage God. According to Job's friends, godly fear should inspire timidity, surrender, and repentance. If that is the proper stance before God, Job would have aborted his quest for justice before he ever began. What generates Job's unflinching pursuit of his case is not a terror-inspiring fear but a radical trust in God, born out of a hope against hope, of a trust that God will indeed hear him out and respond in kind, a defiant trust.[78] Instead of the kind of fear that requires unquestioning submission, godly reverence is imbued with a far-reaching trust that is rooted not in God the Terminator, but in God the Just. It is a reverence born out of a yearning for deeper communion and out of trust that God's creation is indeed good, despite all appearances to the contrary. Equally significant is Job's self-trust. Job never gives up in his trust in the veracity of his experience whose truth intones a dissonant note to the univocal voice of past tradition. Without such trust, Job would never have gone beyond his birthday curse.

The divine discourse in chs. 38–41 adds another dimension to this reformulation of fear before God. Whereas Job recasts the issue of fear as a matter of defiant trust, Yahweh's discourse, to which Job in the end gives assent, recaptures the awe-inspiring dimension of reverence. The litany of the cosmos was not meant to terrify Job into submission, but to broaden Job's moral worldview, to bring about a "spiritual Copernican revolution."[79] Indeed, the divine rebuke functions to affirm Job and identify his rightful place within the created order. Yahweh unveils common ground, more specifically common character, between Job and the beasts of the wild and even the elements of the cosmos. By proudly displaying the variegated forms of life on the margin where Job finds himself, Yahweh indirectly affirms Job's character in his quest for mean-

---

78. It is this trust in God's justice that inspires Job to declare:

"Would he contend with me in the greatness of his power?
　　No; but he would give heed to me.
There an upright person could reason with him,
　　and I should be acquitted forever by my judge." (23:6-7)

79. Carole R. Fontaine, "Wounded Hero on a Shaman's Quest," 83.

ing. Such affirmation turns explicit in the epilogue: Job has spoken what is right (42:7). Job's development is now complete: He has attained a reverential trust in God that is equal to the trust he places in himself. Job's character, indeed, his very integrity, is marked above all by self-honesty and courage to counter the impersonal march of traditional wisdom that would suppress the threatening truth behind his experience. It is in his passionate protest that Job has found the will to live. And it is in his protest that God restores Job to a new moral vision, one that takes Job out of himself and back into the community with a new sense of compassion that supersedes the patriarchal parameters of honor and esteem.

Beyond Transformation

As the silent son in Prov. 1–9 successfully made the passage from the cloistered walls of hearth and home to the larger community as an adult, so, too, Job abandons the confines of his safe, restrictive worldview as a patriarch and finds a global community revealed to him by God. Like the son-turned-family man at the conclusion of Proverbs, Job, the patriarch-turned-citizen of the cosmos, returns to his domicile and community with renewed vision.

How did Job spend the rest of his life, all 140 years worth? Still upright and blameless, Job, I suspect, exhibited a passionate investment in the life of the community, one that was no longer obsessive, but took gratuitous delight in the created order that extends into the very margins of life. To be sure, Job never again roused himself early in the morning to offer sacrifices for fear his children had sinned the night before. In fact, he may have occasionally crashed the party, much to the delight of his children. If Job got up at all in the early morning hours, he did it to see the sun rise and marvel at it, as he began his day of work and play. Job no longer needed the gestures of deference from youth and old alike to sustain his moral vision of the community and himself. Job came to see beauty in the barrenness and dignity in the dispossessed. He no longer saw the social outcasts as objects, whether of charity or of contempt. Rather he viewed them as partners, for it took a procession of wild animals and a boastful God to reveal to Job the common bond of life that embraces both ostriches and kings, the foolish and the wise, the stranger and the elite.

As Job found both reorientation and solace in the presence of God awesomely displayed in creation at the fringes, Christians see the radical presence of God in one more place, on the cross. In the cross, one beholds the next and final move of God, whose very self becomes marginalized, experiencing contempt as an outsider, rejected by humanity, and in death unleashes new life and vision to those who can say with Job, "I had heard of you by the hearing of the ear, / but now my eye sees you; / therefore I reject my life and find restoration."

5 Character Reconstructed: Ecclesiastes

The book of Ecclesiastes profiles a character whose approach to wisdom is unique within the larger framework of wisdom literature. Unlike Proverbs and Job, Ecclesiastes lacks any definably prescriptive view of the community in its role in the formation of character. Indeed, if the community plays any role, it plays one that is largely negative, if not indifferent. Consequently, Qoheleth — the speaker throughout most of Ecclesiastes[1] — models a different type of character, one that deconstructs the center of traditional wisdom from within rather than from the outside, as in the case of Job.

I. QOHELETH'S SELF-CHARACTERIZATION

Unique to the Hebrew Scriptures, Ecclesiastes is essentially a self-presentation. What gives the book its literary coherence is the fact that it is by and large a series of confessions. As Walther Zimmerli has observed, the most characteristic speech form of Qoheleth is the "confessional or self-referential style."[2] Only near the end of Ecclesiastes does the second person address occur in a way that formally echoes the

---

1. The exception is the epilogue in 12:9-14, the product of the final editor.
2. My translation of *Bekenntnisstil* and *Ich-Stil* (Walther Zimmerli, *Die Weisheit des Predigers Salomo*, 26; see Kurt Galling, "Kohelet-Studien," 280; James G. Williams, "What Does it Profit a Man?" 179 [repr. 375]).

patriarch's address to his son in Prov. 1–9 (see below). The bulk of the book, however, consists of a person who, like Job, shares his personal discoveries and bares his soul, but without dialogic partners.[3] Qoheleth revels in a confession of failure as he recounts his pursuit to understand the world and himself through wisdom.[4] Yet it is precisely in this apparent weakness that Qoheleth attains his greatest authoritative status.

Qoheleth's Hebrew title can conceivably refer to his role either as a teacher who assembles students or as a collector of wisdom sayings. In either case, the title is equally apt, for Qoheleth is depicted as a sage who teaches as well as collates proverbs (12:9). Crucial to understanding Qoheleth's character is his self-designation as king, particularly in his self-introduction in 1:12–2:26. The reasons behind the use of the royal metaphor are no doubt drawn from Solomon's legendary status as the wise king par excellence, but within Qoheleth's self-presentation the rationale is found in ch. 2. There Qoheleth reports on a series of grand experiments to test pleasure and its relationship to the pursuit of wisdom. Owing to his regal status, nothing is withheld and all means are at his disposal. Moreover, it is the very duty of the king to pursue wisdom: "I, Qoheleth, when king over Israel in Jerusalem, applied my mind to seek and to search out by wisdom all that is done under heaven" (1:12-13a; cf. Prov. 25:2).

Qoheleth's self-declared status gives him royal recourse and the means to search out everything. As king, Qoheleth does not need to rely solely upon past tradition, the corpus of conventional wisdom. Rather, he is in the relatively unique position to test and confirm the veracity of traditional wisdom and, if need be, modify it. So Qoheleth embarks on an ambitious series of experiments that are designed to do just that, test the efficacy of wisdom. What follows is a veritable litany of accomplishments: "I made great," "I built" (Eccl. 2:4), "I planted" (vv. 4-5), "I made" (vv. 5, 6), "I acquired" (v. 7), "I gathered" (v. 8). In social means and stature, Qoheleth is one step beyond the biblical Job in the business of wisdom.[5]

---

3. Contrary to the claim that Ecclesiastes is a diatribe or disputation. See Michael V. Fox's discussion in *Qohelet and His Contradictions*, 20-28 and 28 n. 11.

4. A telling contrast is the flat, parental figure featured in Prov. 1–9 and Qoheleth. On one occasion, the father recounts his life as a boy, but never at any point does he adopt a confessional tone (Prov. 4:3-9).

5. This escalation in the authoritative status of the subject or protagonist in

Choon-Leong Seow has ably demonstrated that Qoheleth's self-introduction is based on the widespread genre of royal inscriptions "in a way that is contrary to the intent of the typical royal inscription."[6] Essential to the genre is a listing of the king's grand achievements, from success in battle to erecting monumental edifices, all for the purpose of immortalizing the king, at least in memory.[7] By adopting this form of self-presentation, Qoheleth also intends to immortalize himself through his accomplishments, not in order to highlight his successes, but to point out his failures.

> I considered all that my hands had done and the toil I had spent in doing it, and again, all was vanity (heḇel) and a chasing after wind, and there was nothing to be gained under the sun. (2:11)

All of the king's accomplishments amount to nothing in the royal quest for wisdom. Qoheleth generalizes his failure at other points in his confession:

> All this I have tested by wisdom; I said, "I will be wise," but it was far from me. That which is, is far off, and deep, very deep; who can find it out? (7:23-24)

> When I applied my mind to know wisdom, and to see the business that is done on earth . . . I saw all the work of God, that no one can find out what is happening under the sun. However much they may toil in seeking, they will not find it out; even though those who are wise claim to know, they cannot find it out. (8:16-17)

In short, all the king's horses and all the king's men could not put wisdom together again.

Qoheleth's grand experiment reveals an important part of his self-characterization, namely his unchallenged, authoritative position of power and understanding. Elsewhere, Qoheleth casts himself as an elder

---

wisdom literature continues in the figure of Job presented in the Testament of Job. In this pseudepigraphical work, Job ("Jobab") receives the title "the king of all Egypt" (T. Job 28:7; see Russell P. Spittler's translation in *Old Testament Pseudepigrapha,* ed. James H. Charlesworth, 1:852). Cf. Job 29:25.

6. "The Farce of the Wise King."

7. E.g., West Semitic royal inscriptions such as the Mesha Inscription (*ANET,* 320-21) and the Kilamuwa Inscription (*ANET,* 654-55).

sage. He has seen "everything," including the multitude of life's contradictions (7:15). He claims to have "acquired great wisdom," surpassing
all before him (1:16a). Indeed, Qoheleth has personally experienced
wisdom and knowledge in all of its manifold forms and fathomless
depth (1:16b). No neophyte can talk like this. In stark contrast to Elihu,
Qoheleth exploits all the traditional motifs of journey, pursuit, search
for wisdom, and hierarchy to cement his position as the elder royal sage
at the top of his form, as the one who has been at the business the
longest and with the most means at his disposal. With the poignant
treatise on the ravaging effects of old age concluding his discourse to
the "young man" in 12:1-8, Qoheleth presents himself not as the parental
figure of Prov. 1–9, or as the inspired youth in the character of Elihu,
but as the king and grandfather of wisdom, who in the end comes up
empty-handed.[8]

II. THE SHAKING OF THE FOUNDATIONS

Qoheleth undermines the traditional ethos of wisdom in a number of
ways, from exalting the value of youth to depreciating the cosmos.

The Positive Image of Youth

Qoheleth's implied age constitutes a central element of his character.
His senior status enables him to assume the highest position of authority
in the pursuit of wisdom. This is particularly clear when Qoheleth wields
his authority in his address to the young man in Eccl. 11:9. Qoheleth's
advice formally resembles the parental advice of Proverbs. However,
what is similar in form cannot be more dissimilar in content. Instead
of warning the youth of the dangers of "strange" women (Prov. 7:4-27)
or the thrill of highway robbery (Prov. 1:8-20), the first words old man
Qoheleth utters to the youth is "rejoice while you are young, and let

8. Given Qoheleth's self-presentation as the royal sage who uses all sagacious
means at his disposal to understand the world and the human condition, it is erroneous
to claim that Qoheleth in principle undermines the sagacious enterprise per se. See Fox,
Qohelet and His Contradictions, 79-120; *idem,* "Wisdom in Qoheleth."

your heart cheer you in the days of your youth" (Eccl. 11:9). Youth is idealized, but unlike Elihu, Qoheleth does not press the point that youth is the perfect receptacle of uncorrupted, divinely inspired wisdom. Rather, youth is the ideal embodiment of what is joyful and vital about life. Wisdom, whether divine or appropriated, does not have much to do with youth except to highlight its transient nature. For Qoheleth, enjoyment is what makes life worth living amid the vanities of life, even though it is as fleeting and unplanned as the wind.[9] Thus, the idea of youth does not connote the negative values of immaturity, naiveté, and uncontrolled passion, vices targeted in the rhetoric of traditional wisdom. To the contrary, youth for Qoheleth embodies joy and fulfillment within the fragile and evanescent structures of life.

Qoheleth looks positively at youth in other ways that strain the traditional cultural model of wisdom. He entertains the possibility that a youth can be wise, even of royal material: "Better is a poor but wise youth than an old but foolish king, who will no longer take advice" (4:13). As seen in the case of Elihu, the ideal of youth points to the bankruptcy of inherited, traditional wisdom. For Elihu, the seamless chain of appropriated tradition is the bearer of false, ineffective wisdom. Qoheleth presses this negative assessment further by claiming that even the past generations cannot be recalled. The past simply cannot be remembered: "The people of long ago are not remembered, nor will there be any remembrance of people yet to come by those who come after them" (1:11; cf. v. 4).

The Static Cosmos

By citing the endless cycle of generations, Qoheleth effectively undercuts all possibility of accumulated, inherited knowledge and progress. All social and cosmological structures are locked in a static, self-contained movement without direction and progress. Locked in an endless cycle of sameness, the cosmos is stripped of all vitality and majesty. As the sea

---

9. See the insightful study of R. N. Whybray, "Qoheleth, Preacher of Joy." Though overstated, Whybray's argument uncovers a crucially important dimension of Qoheleth's discourse on the meaning and worth of life. See also Diethelm Michel's salient point that joy, as a part of toil, is radically distinguished by Qoheleth from profit gained through toil ("Vom Gott, der im Himmel ist," 279 [repr. 91]).

always remains unfulfilled (1:7), the quest for knowledge is ever without fulfillment. By analogy, the pursuit of wisdom is no journey at all; wisdom is a destination that dissipates like mist once the first steps are taken toward it. Qoheleth finds inherited tradition, the wisdom of the ages, to be a *fata morgana:* progress, growth, and fulfillment are all mirages of the same illusion. The workings of the cosmos, in which no real purpose or direction can be discerned, only confirm the ephemerality of wisdom.

The Family

The traditional cultural unit in which wisdom is at home, the family, is undermined by Qoheleth. In 4:8 Qoheleth observes lone individuals enduring unending toil without progeny or siblings. Although Qoheleth gives credence to the practical advantages of solidarity, that two are better than one in toil (4:9-12), nowhere does he mention the work of the family. One gets the impression that the family, the once stable unit and basis of culture in proverbial wisdom, has disintegrated in Qoheleth's social world. Qoheleth addresses a world filled with individuals, like himself, who are without associations and can find only meager utilitarian value in common labor.

The collapse of the family is also viewed from the inside out. Qoheleth tells the tale of a man who begat a hundred children and lived many years, but was unable to enjoy life's blessings, and concludes that a stillborn child is better off than he (6:3). In addition, Qoheleth focuses on that permanent threat to the family, the "stranger" (*nokrî*; 6:2). In Prov. 1–9, this threat is cast in gender-specific terms and given a dramatic role. In Job, the "stranger" is Job himself, estranged from his community and embodying moral ambiguity (Job 19:13-17). As for Qoheleth, the stranger is simply an anonymous character that is given the role of receiving and controlling profits gained by another's work (Eccl. 2:18-19, 21). Stripped of all fear-inspiring qualities, this "stranger" is reduced to a cog in the absurd wheel of fate. Despite God's gracious granting of wealth, possessions, and honor, deserving recipients cannot enjoy them; instead, only a stranger does (6:2). The reference to the "stranger" is simply one instance out of many that illustrate the transient nature of profit: All for which one has labored must be left for another who did not earn it (2:21), and what kind of profit is that (v. 22)? The disillusionment Qoheleth feels does not target the figure of the anonymous "someone" so much as the absurd vicissitudes of time and history, for which only God can be held accountable (see below).

In short, Qoheleth calls up instances that shatter the efficacy of the family's traditional reputation for guaranteeing security, well-being, and order, the hallmarks of wisdom. The family's demise is symptomatic of the sweeping contradictions Qoheleth perceives and to which he resigns himself: the righteous perishing in righteousness; the wicked prolonging their lives (7:15); slaves on horseback and princes on foot (10:7); the same wretched fate for both the wise and the foolish (2:14), much less animals (3:18-20); the pervasiveness of oppression (4:1; 5:8); and the advantage of death over life (4:2). Such contradictions, along with the demise of the family, reflect an implosion of wisdom.

III. WISDOM RECHARACTERIZED

Although Qoheleth incorporates a variety of forms of wisdom, the tenor of his confessions does much to undermine in part or at least set in tension many tenets of traditional wisdom.[10] Thus, the ways in which Qoheleth characterizes wisdom require primary attention on his reflectional or testimonial statements. It must be noted at the outset that Qoheleth's treatment of wisdom is remarkably diverse. Wisdom is characterized as vulnerable (e.g., 9:12-16),[11] inaccessible (7:23b-24), as both a method and a goal (e.g., 2:3, 9; 7:23a, 25; 8:17),[12] and perhaps even

---

10. Fox makes the valid point that Qoheleth revels in contradictions without eliminating or resolving them; instead, Qoheleth duly notes them to illustrate the absurdity of life (Fox, *Qohelet and His Contradictions*, 21-22). However, Qoheleth adopts a critical stance against the more ambitious claims that conventional wisdom holds concerning the rewards for the wise. Whether or not Qoheleth's critical stance constitutes an actual *crisis* in wisdom goes beyond the scope of this study (see Roland E. Murphy, "Qoheleth's 'Quarrel' with the Fathers," 235-245; Fox, 120, 144). Nevertheless, it is clear that by severing the causal connection between ethical conduct and outcome, Qoheleth presents a radical reconstrual of the limits of wisdom and hence of normative character. Even Murphy admits that Qoheleth "rejects traditional wisdom for the security it offers," but in so doing "purifies and extends it" (*Ecclesiastes*, lxiii, lxiv).

11. Fox, *Qohelet and His Contradictions*, 117; Murphy, *Ecclesiastes*, lxii.

12. For a fuller discussion of Qoheleth's treatment of wisdom as a methodology, see Fox, *Qohelet and His Contradictions*, 80-89.

as a fickle woman (7:26-29).[13] Indeed, one scholar has described wisdom in Ecclesiastes as *der unheimliche Gast* ("the eerie guest").[14] However, there is another aspect to wisdom that is quite decisive for Qoheleth and dominates his discourse.

Qoheleth charges at the very outset in his confession that the pursuit of wisdom is an "unhappy business" (*'inyan rā'*) that has no payoff (1:13-14; cf. v. 3). With such low commendation, Qoheleth likens the quest for wisdom to a failed business venture. In so doing, Qoheleth gives wisdom a distinctive materialistic slant.[15] Such a construal is not unprecedented in traditional wisdom; material prosperity had long been considered a natural result of the successful appropriation of wisdom. However, Qoheleth's narrow focus merges the material by-products of wisdom with wisdom's source.[16] Wisdom, in short, is materialized. It is tied to the question of material gain (1:3). The question of what kind of *yitrôn* ("net gain from an economic transaction"[17]) results from labor is not simply a matter of objective curiosity by which wisdom is employed as a methodological tool. To the contrary, the very nature of wisdom is bound up with how one answers the question of material gain. Both wisdom and the pursuit of profit are depicted as business ventures: "When I applied my mind to know wisdom, and to see the business *(ha'inyān)* that is done on earth . . ." (8:16). The pursuit of wisdom and the affairs of business go hand in hand (2:19-20).

Wisdom is not simply a means to pursue an economic net gain; it is indeed the end of all pursuit. Qoheleth even correlates wisdom with economic gain, construing it as a personal possession (see 2:19: "*my* wisdom").[18] "The protection of wisdom is like the protection of money" (7:12), so Qoheleth intones. In short, wisdom is given a quantitative character that is tied to Qoheleth's concern to find some sign of permanence in gain amid the vicissitudes of living.

Why does Qoheleth profile such a materialistic view of wisdom? To be sure, Qoheleth's view of wisdom reflects the social climate of the

---

13. Fox in conversation.

14. Hans-Peter Müller, "Der unheimliche Gast."

15. See Frank Crüsemann, "The Unchangeable World," 65-66.

16. Compare Solomon's prayer, which makes the distinction clear (1 Kgs. 3:9-14).

17. Kurt Galling, *Der Prediger*, 69.

18. Related to Qoheleth's material treatment of wisdom is his use of wisdom as a methodology to discern the absurd nature of life (see above, n. 10).

aristocratic class in Judah, which evidently shared in both the risk and gain of heavy taxation under Ptolemaic rule.[19] Encouraged by aggressive international trade and tight financial control imposed by a central bureaucracy, money rose to an unprecedented importance under the Ptolemies.[20] There were great fortunes to be made and lost. Given such conditions, Qoheleth says something quite significant about the nature of wisdom. Qoheleth's answer to the question of gain, namely that there is none and that the pursuit of it is like striving after wind, points to a radical reconstrual of wisdom. As gain can be unwillingly handed over at a moment's notice to the "stranger," to one undeserving of the fruits of one's labors, wisdom, too, can slip easily through one's fingers. Wisdom is unfathomably elusive:

> All this I have tested by wisdom; I said, "I will be wise," but it was far from me. That which is, is far off, and deep, very deep; who can find it out? (7:23-24)

Wisdom is the irretrievably lost coin. Like the meditation on wisdom in Job 28, what is described by Qoheleth is a sort of *sapientia abscondita*, a hidden wisdom. But even this does not entirely hit the mark for Qoheleth. Wisdom essentially has no character. On the one hand, it is reduced to a material possession, a tangible means by which Qoheleth hoped to gain security and profit, but to no avail. Wisdom is an investment that guarantees no return. On the other hand, wisdom is so abstracted and disembodied that it remains forever beyond the reach of Qoheleth's grasp. In either case, wisdom is devoid of personhood comparable to her character in Proverbs.[21] Such wisdom cannot be embodied.

Qoheleth depicts the business of wisdom as one that carries with it much vexation, pain, and sorrow (Eccl. 1:18), striking contrasts to the inherent benefits acquired through wisdom described in Proverbs and 1 Kgs. 3. The journey of wisdom is in the end an exercise in futility, a striving after wind, for wisdom remains forever ahead and beyond the

---

19. See Crüsemann, "The Unchangeable World," 66; Martin Hengel, *Judaism and Hellenism*, 1:18-23, 126-27. Hengel erroneously suggests, however, that although Qoheleth "sees through the nihilism of this 'bourgeois' existence," he provides no ethical alternative (127).

20. See R. N. Whybray, *Ecclesiastes*, 10-11.

21. See Fox, who arrives at a similar, though not identical conclusion from his treatment of wisdom in Qoheleth as a methodology (*Qohelet and His Contradictions*, 95).

reach of the inquirer. Like currency that has lost its value, the wisdom of past generations depreciates to nothing. Like tarnished coins, wisdom deteriorates with age (cf. Eccl. 4:13-16). Even the value of wisdom's call to serve the poor plummets in a sea of bureaucratic diffusion:

> If you see in a province the oppression of the poor and the violation of justice and right, do not be amazed at the matter; for the high official is watched by a higher, and there are yet higher ones over them. (5:7[Eng. v. 8])

Qoheleth attributes the ubiquitous oppression of the poor to an interminable social hierarchy that diffuses communal responsibility for the poor. Either everyone's hands are tied or nobody cares in this bureaucracy of indifference. This is a highly stratified society in which wealth gan be gained only laboriously and then easily lost; indeed, the pursuit of economic gain is all-consuming. At the same time, the diffusion of societal responsibility constitutes a debilitating social milieu that inexorably undermines the efficacy of wisdom. Is there any room for formation of character amid such lamentable conditions? All appearances would suggest not.

Nevertheless, Qoheleth does model a new form of character, one that is rooted squarely in how he positions himself with respect to his world; that is to say, in how he perceives himself and his environment. Like pennies from heaven, only snippets of the contours of right character can be discerned from wisdom so remote and abstract.

IV. QOHELETH'S RELATION TO THE WORLD: THE ABSURD

Harmut Gese has perceptively noted that Qoheleth's wisdom is the product of a unique "mutation of structure" that stems from the author's relationship to his world.[22] By this Gese means that in the role of the observing subject Qoheleth has totally removed himself from his world. Qoheleth's perspective is that of a stranger to the world.[23] Gese's

---

22. "The Crisis of Wisdom in Koheleth," 142-43.
23. *Ibid.*, 143.

observation is still relevant: The individual's reputation no longer constitutes any relationship to the self's essence.[24] Qoheleth effectively drives a deep wedge between the self and character.[25]

Such a bifurcation of the individual is reflected in Qoheleth's views on cosmology. From the very outset, Qoheleth focuses on the unwavering, wearisome repetition of the cosmos: the unfilled sea, the static cycles of the generations, the sun, the wind, the insatiable thirst for knowledge, the illusion of memory, and the rhythm of life. The monotony of the cosmos is summed up in two succinct expressions: "All is vanity" (*hebel*; 1:2b), and "There is nothing new under the sun" (v. 9b). Such observations come from an epistemological posture that views the cosmos as a totality from the outside, a position of absolute detachment. The universe has in effect become a stranger to Qoheleth.[26] He has taken a step backward and come to view the world in its indifferent, meaningless whole. Such a move carries with it an ethical as well as epistemological component, but both lead to the same outcome: the apprehension of the absurd or *hebel*.[27]

The material meaning of the term *hebel*, usually translated "vanity," is found in the phenomenon of vapor or mist.[28] Qoheleth frequently pairs the term with the expression "chasing after wind" *(reʿût rûaḥ)*.[29] Both expressions connote the idea of futility and meaninglessness. To pursue wind is tantamount to folly in traditional wisdom as well as in prophetic literature.[30] However, Qoheleth's rather wide-ranging use of

24. *Ibid.,* 144.

25. Harold Fisch rightly notes that the existence of such self-division or self-duplication is the "mark of the ironic mode of existence" (*Poetry with a Purpose,* 169). Fisch cites Paul de Man's definition: The act of self-duplication "sets apart a reflective activity, such as that of the philosopher, from the activity of the ordinary self caught in everyday concerns . . . [and] designates the activity of a consciousness by which a man [*sic*] differentiates himself from the non-human world" (Paul de Man, "The Rhetoric of Temporality," 194-95). Clearly, such an act of self-consciousness finds much resonance in the way in which Qoheleth arrives at the notion of the absurd.

26. Fisch, 166.

27. See Michael V. Fox, "The Meaning of *Hebel* for Qohelet"; *Qohelet and His Contradictions,* 29-47.

28. E.g., Isa. 57:13 and Prov. 21:6. See Oswald Loretz's definition in *Qohelet und der alte Orient,* 223.

29. See Eccl. 2:11, 17, 26; 4:4, 6; 6:9. The synonymous expression *rʿayôn rûaḥ* is paralleled by *hebel* in 4:16.

30. See Prov. 30:4 and Hos. 14:10(Eng. v. 9); Choon-Leong Seow, "Hosea 14:10 and the Foolish People Motif," 212-224.

he̲bel is by no means limited to the term's physical denotation. Taking his cue from Albert Camus's classic essay *The Myth of Sisyphus,* Michael Fox best captures the comprehensive meaning of *he̲bel* by connecting it with the modern sense of the absurd.[31] The notion of the absurd reflects an understanding of the world that is in tension with the framework of human expectations and hopes.[32] For Qoheleth, it is downright absurd that "there are righteous people who are treated according to the conduct of the wicked" (8:14). It is absurd that wealth gained by one's own hands will be left to someone else (2:18-19). It is an utter travesty that humans must suffer the same fate as the animals (3:19). The brevity of youth is absurd (11:10). Indeed, the transient nature of life itself is absurd.[33] All in all, *everything* is *he̲bel* or absurd (1:2; 12:8).

The force of "everything" in Qoheleth's thesis statements, however, is open to interpretation. For Fox, Qoheleth does not mean the "entirety of reality, but only of what happens in the realm of human existence, 'under the sun.'"[34] According to Fox, "everything" is limited to life events "taken as a whole."[35] Fox's restriction of the semantic application of the "absurd" in Qoheleth's thought, however, belies Qoheleth's cosmological observations that open the book (1:2-11).[36] *He̲bel* is as much a description of the absurdity of the cosmic and human condition as it is an indication of *how the self is positioned in relation to the world in its totality.*[37] Absurdity acknowledges both the incomprehensible na-

31. See also Diethelm Michel, who arrives at the same conclusion (*Untersuchungen zur Eigenart des Buches Qoheleth,* 40-51).

32. Fox, "The Meaning of *Hebel* for Qohelet," 409; *idem, Qohelet and His Contradictions,* 31-32.

33. Many have noted the intertextual connection between *he̲bel* and the proper name Abel in Gen. 4. In the story, the name of Abel is associated with a tragic, yet righteous life, a life of nothingness (Jacques Ellul, *The Reason for Being,* 58-59; cf. Duncan B. MacDonald, *The Hebrew Literary Genius,* 207). If indeed Qoheleth is deliberately alluding to the fate of Abel, which is not altogether clear, the story of Gen. 4 would be an archetypal example of the absurd demise of familial relations.

34. Fox, "The Meaning of *Hebel* for Qohelet," 423.

35. *Ibid.,* 424.

36. Fox's assertion that the natural phenomena described in 1:4-8 simply illustrate "the futility of human efforts" misses the point (*ibid.,* 423).

37. Fox alludes to this dimension of the absurd only briefly when discussing the unique role wisdom plays in Qoheleth's thought: "Qoheleth alone tries to think about life in its totality," which results in a "global judgment" (*Qohelet and His Contradictions,* 111).

ture of the world and the individual's relationship to it, which can only be recognized by the individual's capacity to "step back" and view both the world and the self as a meaningless whole.[38] Thus, the absurd is integrally a matter of character. Qoheleth's notion of the absurd is forged not only from a collision between his expectations and the world, but also from a collision within himself.[39] Philosopher Thomas Nagel takes Camus's definition of the absurd one step further:

> Humans have the special capacity to step back and survey themselves, and the lives to which they are committed, with that detached amazement which comes from watching an ant struggle up a heap of sand.[40]

Similarly, Qoheleth is able to remove himself from self and thereby question the point of all human activity. By stepping back from the purposes of his life and effort, Qoheleth can also step back from the progress of human and cosmic history. Once the seed of personal doubt about the point of all activity has taken root, there is nothing stopping it until it has reached the very frontiers of human knowledge. Qoheleth never says that the cosmos is incomprehensible. To the contrary, he claims to understand it fully. Only God remains inscrutable (8:17; 11:5).

This dynamic of stepping back from a situation or context constitutes an indispensable part of the ethical discipline.

> Nothing about character in itself implies that in the presence of a complex situation we cannot "step back" and ask ourselves what we should do in order that we might do the morally right thing.[41]

---

38. See Thomas Nagel, "The Absurd."

39. See *ibid.*, 722. It must be noted, however, that Nagel's notion of the absurd does not entirely fit Qoheleth's use of *hebel*. Nagel criticizes, perhaps justifiably so, Albert Camus's definition that the absurd arises from the world's failure to meet our demands, implying that if the world were any different, the sense of the absurd would not persist. Nagel's point is that the sense of the absurd would necessarily arise within *any* conceivable world (722). However, Qoheleth does seem to envision a world that could by nature be non-absurd, namely a world in which the causal nexus between deed and consequence were tightly forged, in which death and hardship were relegated only to the wicked, and in which some progress could be discerned in the motions of the cosmos and human history. For Qoheleth, the absurdity of the world reflects the absurdity of the self and vice versa.

40. *Ibid.*, 720.

41. Stanley Hauerwas, *Character and the Christian Life*, 124.

Stanley Hauerwas claims that stepping back enables the moral subject to understand better what he or she is doing in the context of past endeavors.[42] Is this the case with Qoheleth? Yes and no. By stepping back, by exercising the inherently human capacity to transcend the self, Qoheleth no doubt arrives at a new and profound knowledge of the world and his relationship to it. He perceives himself estranged from the world, which dispassionately runs like clockwork, recording only an eternal sameness. That may not be much of a context for enlightened ethical discernment. What Qoheleth does goes far beyond what most modern ethicists have in mind in "stepping back." Qoheleth steps *out of character*[43] and assumes the role of detached spectator of himself and the lived world. If Prov. 1–9 is about the makings of a man, Ecclesiastes is about the makings of a "ghost."

Not only is the world a stranger to Qoheleth; he is a foreigner unto himself. He sees himself consumed with the vocation of seeking out wisdom while knowing in retrospect that he is doing nothing more than chasing after wind. Yet he can do no other. Qoheleth knows he toils for no one, let alone himself; yet driven by insatiable ambition, he finds himself unable to stop.[44] This catch-22 reflects the larger tension in which Qoheleth finds the human race to be trapped:[45] While seeking to understand the transcendent Will that governs the universe, human beings are caught in a vicious circle of limitation and ignorance.[46] By stepping back, Qoheleth nullifies the notion of traditional character and undermines the business of character formation, at least in terms of how character relates to the consequences of fortune and misfortune

---

42. *A Community of Character*, 144-45.

43. Cf. Hauerwas: "What the experience of being able to 'step back' from ourselves discloses is not that we have a self above our character, but that even our ability to 'step back' is actually dependent upon and limited by what we have become through our past" (*Character and the Christian Life*, 124).

44. Fox, "The Meaning of *Hebel* for Qohelet," 426; *idem, Qohelet and His Contradictions*, 47.

45. Perhaps it is this dynamic of self-transcendence and contradiction that can best account for — without resolving — the many tensions one finds in the book. Qoheleth repeatedly contradicts himself on the journey toward self-transcendence through his use of the term *hebel* in a variety of contexts (e.g., 2:24-26). For a thorough discussion, see Fox, *Qohelet and His Contradictions*, 19-28, in which he reviews how the contradictions of the text have been interpreted and erroneously resolved through harmonization and positing additions and quotations in the history of interpretation.

46. Kathleen M. O'Connor, *The Wisdom Literature*, 122.

(7:15-16).[47] What traditional wisdom assumed were inextricably tied together, namely right character and prosperity, Qoheleth, like Job, has split asunder.

V. CHARACTER RECONSTRUCTED

Qoheleth has deconstructed the traditional notion of character that links one's destiny to one's behavior, but in so doing arrives at a new notion of character that is distinctly individual. Like Job, who comes close to cursing God, Qoheleth does not destroy character altogether. Indeed, underlying Qoheleth's reflections is an explicit awareness that the formation of personal character is a primary goal of wisdom.[48] The movement and structure of Ecclesiastes confirm this. Qoheleth begins with certain reflections on cosmology (1:1-11) as well as a confession of his own life and pursuit of wisdom (1:12–2:26). Then he effortlessly slides into further observations about life that are increasingly replete with proverbial maxims (3:1-8; 4:5-6, 13; 5:3[4]; 5:10-12[11-13]; 7:1-13; 8:1-2; 9:17-18; 10:1-4, 8-20; 11:1-4) and instructions (4:17–5:1[5:1-2]; 5:4-6[5-6]; 9:7-10; 11:5-10; 12:1-8, 13-14). Overall, the latter half of Qoheleth's treatise is clearly weighted toward instruction and concludes with a formal address to the "young man" in 11:9–12:8. The address to the youth at the end of Qoheleth's discourse, as noted earlier, appropriately concludes the treatise by approximating the same social setting as that envisioned in Prov. 1–9. As in the proverb that vilifies the old king for not taking advice (Eccl. 4:13), Qoheleth's rhetorical aim is to impart advice required for a reconstruction of character. In short, Qoheleth is no nihilist when it comes to the business of character formation.

Qoheleth's reconstruction of character is achieved by a dynamic movement in perspective similar to that in Job. Both Job and Qoheleth are afforded the opportunity to step back and see the world in its entirety. But, unlike Job, whose character is refashioned by the external dramatics of plot, dialogue, and divine confrontation, Qoheleth has no God to point

---

47. See below.

48. Ronald E. Clements, *Wisdom in Theology*, 35. Clements, however, erroneously claims that the predominant theme of character formation in Qoheleth is what makes the book *distinct* among the wisdom books.

out creation's majestic vitality. Rather, Qoheleth by sheer intellectual force steps back and observes life and the cosmos in their meaningless, self-contained whole and returns in resignation. Qoheleth moves from hating his toilsome life (2:18) toward a resigned acceptance of its mundanity. Ecclesiastes is in some sense, like Job, a treatise of protest, a protest that all life is contaminated with *hebel*. On the other hand, Qoheleth's protest is infused not with caustic blame and passionate investment in life, but with tragic resignation. "Do not be amazed at oppression," Qoheleth despairingly intones (5:7a[8a]). After concluding that nothing is to be gained from toil (2:2-23), Qoheleth solemnly states, perhaps with a twinge of irony, "there is nothing better for mortals than to eat and drink, and find enjoyment in their toil" (2:24). Inflated and ambitious goals, pretentious claims of knowledge, obsessive concerns for getting ahead are all exposed for what they are in the face of the absurdity of life, mere delusions of grandeur. Life's grand purposes are whittled down to simple, fleeting pleasures. With such a minimalist orientation, Qoheleth offers his own list of cardinal virtues.

Quietude

Paradoxically, Qoheleth's stance toward life enables him to echo some of the traditional values of wisdom, particularly the ideal of silence. For instance, Qoheleth locates the root of all obsessive toil in "envy" *(qin'at)* and prefers quietude *(nāhat)* over toil (4:4-6). Indeed, it is precisely this quiet rest that prompts Qoheleth at one point to prefer the fate of a stillborn child over the life of an adult (6:3). Other examples of the virtue of quietude include:

> The quiet words of the wise are more to be heeded
>> than the shouting of a ruler among fools. (9:17)

> To draw near to listen is better than
>> the sacrifice offered by fools. (4:17b[5:1b])

> Never be rash with your mouth,
>> nor let your heart be quick to utter a word before God,
> for God is in heaven, and you upon earth;
>> therefore let your words be few. (5:1[2])

Do not let your mouth lead you into sin,
  and do not say before the messenger that it was a mistake;
why should God be angry at your words,
  and destroy the work of your hands? (5:5[6])

Simplicity

Qoheleth's preference for the life of few words, the ideal within traditional wisdom, also serves to impart many related values such as caution, self-restraint, and an acceptance of less (5:9[10]) — that is, a life of simplicity and simple pleasures, which are all too often taken for granted. What a powerfully ironic image Qoheleth has set up: the Solomonic king unmatched in accomplishment and unsurpassed in glory finding himself envious of the common laborer, whose sleep is far more blissful than that of the wealthy (5:11[12])! The simple life, without great and glorious ambitions, however noble, is Qoheleth's ideal, a life of simple sufficiency in which constructive work, sufficient food, and fellowship are all that is needed to live fully.[49]

In one of his most profound statements concerning the human condition, Qoheleth invests a different nuance in a common virtue:

See, this alone I found, that God made human beings straightforward (yāšār), but they have devised many schemes. (7:29)

Within traditional wisdom, the Hebrew term yāšār is synonymous with "righteous" and "blameless" (Job 1:1). Qoheleth sharply delineates between yāšār and the multitude of schemes or devices (ḥiššᵉḇōnôt). Clearly, a predominant component that functions critically in Qoheleth's sense of "uprightness" is simplicity. God created human beings both simple and just; corruption, however, emerges through the proliferation of self-serving machinations.

Enjoyment

Related to Qoheleth's endorsement of the simple life is his exhortation to appreciate such simple pleasures as eating, drinking, and finding

49. O'Connor, 130-31.

enjoyment in one's work.[50] Qoheleth's exhortation is given seven times throughout the book: Eccl. 2:24-26; 3:12-13, 22; 5:17-19(18-20); 8:15; 9:7-10; 11:7–12:1a. Throughout his discourse, enjoyment is considered a gift rather than an achievement, and thus is to be received in gratitude. Indeed, enjoyment is God's gift to human beings, whose lives are brief and whose ignorance of the future is insurmountable; hence, it cannot be earned. Such depressingly realistic assessments of the human condition highlight the serendipitous nature of enjoyment. Enjoyment, Qoheleth observes, has a mysteriously incidental quality to it, since it lies outside the domain of human achievement and design. Its source lies exclusively within the sphere of divine providence. Thus, when and to whom the refreshing breezes of enjoyment blow, no human being can determine. All the more reason to enjoy it.[51]

Qoheleth presses the enigmatic nature of enjoyment to its limit when he avers that pleasure can even be found amid one's toils. Given his predominant assessment of toil as oppressive, Qoheleth's insistence on the presence of enjoyment in one's labor is paradoxical.

> There is nothing better for mortals than to eat and drink, and find enjoyment in their toil. (2:24)

> Moreover, it is God's gift that all should eat and drink and take pleasure in all their toil. (3:13)

> So I saw that there is nothing better than that all should enjoy their work. (3:22a)

> This is what I have seen to be good: it is fitting to eat and drink and find enjoyment in all the toil with which one toils under the sun. (5:17[18])

> So I commend enjoyment, for there is nothing better for people under the sun than to eat, and drink, and enjoy themselves, for this will go with them in their toil through the days of life. (8:15)

In five out of the seven commendations, Qoheleth discerns an inextricable connection between enjoyment and toil. Regardless of how this connection is to be construed, it is to be sharply contrasted with the

---

50. The most significant study is Whybray, "Qoheleth, Preacher of Joy."
51. *Ibid.*, 88.

lack of relation between gain and toil (e.g., 1:3).[52] Enjoyment has nothing to do with earned gain or profit. That does not mean that Qoheleth gives up on work. To the contrary, he places surprisingly high value on it. He enjoins:

> Whatever your hand finds to do, do with your might; for there is no work or thought or knowledge or wisdom in Sheol, to which you are going. (9:10)

Rather than urging divestment from work, Qoheleth urges a total, personal investment in one's effort. The reason he provides is remarkably simple and realistic: There is no work or even consciousness after death. Conversely, nothing less than the vitality of life breathes through the strain and rigor of everyday work, providing in the end sustenance and enjoyment. At base, Qoheleth's view of work is essentially nonutilitarian; work conducted as a secure means to a gainful end will inevitably lead to frustration and despair. However, viewed as an end in itself, work does have its rewards, first and foremost enjoyment. Indeed, enjoyment can accompany one's toil at every step (8:15).[53]

Qoheleth's view on the relation of joy to work provides an intriguing revisionist alternative to Camus's interpretation of the Greek myth of Sisyphus. To be sure, both Qoheleth and Camus find much common ground with regard to their views about the absurd life. The metaphor of Sisyphus's pointless labor finds striking resonance with Qoheleth's view of toil. But Camus and Qoheleth philosophically part company at the moment in the story when Sisyphus, condemned by the gods to futile and hopeless labor, observes the boulder that he has slavishly pushed up to the pinnacle of the mountain hurtle down back into the valley below. Camus states:

---

52. Michel, "Vom Gott, der im Himmel ist," 279.

53. *Contra* Fox, who suggests that Qoheleth's use of *ʿāmāl* ("toil") in his reflections on pleasure implies that pleasure is "toil's product," which places it on a similar level to that of wealth (*Qohelet and His Contradictions,* 56). Fox is correct in pointing out that Qoheleth is not preaching the intrinsic "joy of labor." However, the relationship between enjoyment and toil for Qoheleth is nuanced. Qoheleth certainly does not equate enjoyment with the gain that is produced through toil; rather, pleasure *accompanies* a person in toil (8:15; Fox, 57). In so doing, Qoheleth implies a qualitative distinction between oppressive, pointless work and the kind of labor that permits some measure of enjoyment.

Sisyphus, proletarian of the gods, powerless and rebellious, knows the whole extent of his wretched condition: it is what he thinks of during his descent. The lucidity that was to constitute his torture at the same time crowns his victory. There is no fate that cannot be surmounted by scorn.[54]

Both Camus and Qoheleth, in different ways, ask the question of what Sisyphus must have felt at the moment he knows he must descend back into the dark lair once again to push his rock, for something extraordinary happens. Camus asks why at this very point in which Sisyphus realizes the utter futility of his labors a smile breaks out on his face, a "silent joy."[55] For Camus, it is a clever joy that is motivated by scorn and defiance of the gods who have condemned him to such labor.

For Qoheleth, however, the reason Sisyphus breaks out into a smile as his rock rolls back into the valley is not motivated by hatred or even protest. It is no doubt tainted with a tired resignation, even sorrow, in the realization that the activity itself is patently absurd. Unlike Camus's Sisyphus, however, futile labor for Qoheleth is infused with an overwhelming sense of acceptance of one's lot in life that allows a person to cherish the few brief moments of rest when the boulder is delicately balanced and the cool breeze is savored before the chase begins again. The duration and quality of the rest are determined by God and received serendipitously in gratitude. Rest and sustenance are integral parts of the daily rhythm of toil, which has its own internal rewards. Such rewards are to be found within the strain of labor, the exercise of life. Qoheleth never specifically identifies what these rewards are; they are simply understood to lie outside the domain of net gain. Perhaps they are to be located within the uniquely subjective needs and desires of the laborer. In any case, such joy is paradoxically serendipitous:

> Sorrow is better than laughter,
> for by sadness of countenance the heart is made glad. (7:3)

Finally, it is death that paradoxically constitutes the ultimate reason behind Qoheleth's commendation of simple enjoyment. Death ultimately undermines all distinctions between the righteous and the wicked, even between humans and animals. It topples all lofty aspira-

---

54. *The Myth of Sisyphus*, 90.
55. *Ibid.*, 91.

tions and thus inspires a profound acceptance of life on its own terms. Instead of espousing suicide as the final solution, Qoheleth commends the fleeting, yet redemptive, nature of enjoyment (9:7-10).[56]

The Limitations of Virtue and Vice

Although Qoheleth espouses certain virtues, he does it in recognition that there are limitations, even dangers, to living the virtuous life. Eccl. 7:15-18 is a good case in point, a passage that is notoriously difficult to understand and hence has generated a number of interpretations:

> In my vain life I have seen everything; there are righteous people who perish in their righteousness, and there are wicked people who prolong their lives in their evil-doing. Do not be too righteous, and do not act too wise; why should you destroy yourself? Do not be too wicked, and do not be a fool; why should you die before your time? It is good that you should take hold of the one, without letting go of the other; for the one who fears God shall succeed (lit., "go forth"; *yēṣēʾ*) with both.

Is Qoheleth advocating a golden mean, as some have suggested,[57] or is he counseling against excessive striving for righteousness?[58] Contrary to Aristotle, Qoheleth juxtaposes the very categories of virtue and vice.[59] Qoheleth's admonitions are no doubt tinged with bitter irony, since he notes that the social responses to righteous and wicked people are easily reversed (7:15). Elsewhere, Qoheleth concludes that the wicked and the righteous suffer the same fate (2:14; 3:17-19). These are the facts of life,

56. Cf. James L. Crenshaw, "The Shadow of Death in Qoheleth," 210-11.

57. Cf., e.g., Williams, "What Does it Profit a Man?" 186. Cf. Aristotle, *Nichomachean Ethics* 3.7-4.9.

58. So Hans Wilhelm Hertzberg, *Der Prediger*, 152-55; Albert Strobel, *Das Buch Prediger*, 112-15; Walther Zimmerli, *Das Buch des Predigers Salomo*, 209-10; E. Glasser, *Le procès du bonheur par Qohelet*, 116-17.

59. Identifying Aristotelian thought with Ecclesiastes is the result of confusing two different levels of abstraction regarding moral categories. Aristotle located virtue between two extremes of *concrete action*. Courage, for example, was the mean between cowardice and recklessness, while self-control was situated between self-indulgence and insensitivity. Qoheleth, on the other hand, attempts to establish normative character between the *abstract categories* of righteousness and wickedness (7:16-17). See Murphy, *Ecclesiastes*, 72.

and they are reflected in the rhetorical questions in 7:16b and 17b. Self-ruin and early death are the inevitable outcomes of the extremes of virtue and vice. Neither path by itself leads to gain; rather, they must be balanced against each other.[60]

The wider context fills out these ironic injunctions. Qoheleth observes that there is no righteous person who is without sin (7:20; cf. v. 22; 8:11). Indeed, striving to maintain a state of "super righteousness" is nothing more than an illusion, a matter of arrogant presumption.[61] Righteousness, like wisdom, remains essentially unreachable (7:23-24). To think otherwise is an exalted estimation of one's moral faculties, which will result only in ruin.[62] The extremes of virtue and vice are exposed for what they are, elusive quests to obtain desired gain, analogous to the situation of toil. Righteousness is unable to ensure long life and happiness; indeed, quite the opposite. The pretense of blamelessness accompanied by the lofty expectations of reward will only result in utter despair, if not self-destruction.[63] Indeed, it appears that Qoheleth has already cited two examples of self-ruin that illustrate quite well the obsessive love of riches and a life devoid of enjoyment.[64] Both stem from increasingly higher expectations of fulfillment *as the result* of further toil and hoarding of material gain.

Similarly, in his statement warning against being overly righteous, Qoheleth attacks the causal nexus between righteousness and fortune, countering the extreme, albeit logical, conclusion that super righteousness will afford ultimate joy and fulfillment. Implicit is the recognition that all efforts that strive to fulfill the pure ideals of righteousness ultimately stem from the self-serving desire to reap ideal rewards, a matter of arrogant presumption. Yet to caution against consideration of the other extreme, Qoheleth immediately points out that wickedness will also result in early death.

The key to understanding the relationship between these two extremes and the alternative Qoheleth suggests is found in the positive statement, "One who fears God shall go forth with both of them"

60. See James L. Crenshaw, *Ecclesiastes*, 140-41.

61. Elsewhere, Qoheleth highlights the presumption of the wise (8:17).

62. R. N. Whybray vigorously argues that 7:16 argues primarily against pretense, given the slight change in parallel wording between 16aα and 17aα ("Qoheleth the Immoralist?"). Though his linguistic arguments are overly subtle, particularly in the nuance of *ṣāddîq* in v. 16a, the overall context partially confirms his thesis.

63. The reflexive hithpoel of the verb *šmm* can include such a nuance.

64. See 4:7-8; 5:13-17; cf. 6:1-6.

(7:18b). The precise nuance of "go forth" (*yēṣē'*) is a matter of dispute.[65] Some have taken it to mean to "escape, avoid."[66] However, rendered this way the verse simply repeats what has already been stated. More commonly accepted is Robert Gordis's rendering of the verb with a legal nuance akin to the Mishnaic formula "will do his duty by both."[67]

This generic verb, however, need not have such a restricted legal focus in 7:18. In conjunction with v. 18a, the conveyed image is a physical one of carrying the two precepts in vv. 16-17, one literally in each hand. "Going forth" denotes general conduct in life, guided by the balance between the extremes of wickedness and super righteousness. Moreover, the Greek translation suggests well-being, the outcome of moral conduct.[68] In any case, the traditional association of moral conduct with the way of wisdom remains in the background.[69] Qoheleth is not against traveling along the path of life; rather, he suggests a new set of guidelines that dismantles all obsessiveness in practice, based on the presumption that such a path will secure wisdom once and for all. Conversely, the path that Qoheleth commends is one that allows for freedom to enjoy the simple pleasures of life within the day-to-day rhythm of work and rest. In a passage strikingly similar to 7:15-18, Qoheleth again notes the travesty of justice that afflicts the righteous and concludes by recommending enjoyment:

> There is a vanity that takes place on earth, that there are righteous people who are treated according to the conduct of the wicked, and there are wicked people who are treated according to the conduct of the righteous. I said that this is also vanity. *So I commend enjoyment,* for there is nothing better for people under the sun than to eat, and drink, and enjoy themselves, for this will go with them in their toil through the days of life that God gives them under the sun. (8:14-15, italics added)

In summary, Qoheleth pointedly unmasks the danger brought on by a form of works righteousness: the obsessive striving to outdo oneself and each other in righteousness. Such righteousness is rooted in the

---

65. See Whybray's discussion of the options ("Qoheleth the Immoralist?" 200-201).

66. E.g., W. Zimmerli, *Das Buch des Predigers Salomo,* 209-10.

67. *Koheleth — The Man and His World,* 267-68.

68. Cf. the LXX: *exeleúsetai tà pánta.*

69. See Chapter 2.

pretension of thinking that one can exhaustively know the work of God (8:16). The unknowable future and a God who transcends the laws of moral retribution are unavoidable realities that decisively shatter all yearnings for grand rewards, which can generate a meticulously obsessed righteousness. But for the sage who has stepped back and viewed the enterprise of wisdom in its absurd entirety, the rewards are sparingly few, disappointingly mundane, yet deceptively worthy to be received appreciatively when accepted on their own terms. In the end, Qoheleth does not forge a middle way or golden mean, but lifts the level of moral discourse to the realm of theological discourse. The one who will successfully go forth is the one who fears God, "the highest accolade of moral virtue that can be bestowed."[70]

Fear of God

As with Proverbs and Job, the fear of God for Qoheleth most comprehensively shapes the contours of right character, but in radically different ways. Reference to fear or reverence of God occurs in five passages (3:14; 5:6[7]; 7:18; 8:12; 12:13) in Ecclesiastes. Although once described as the "kernel and the star of the whole book,"[71] 12:13 reflects more the theology of Ben Sira than authentic Qoheleth.[72] As suggested in 7:15-18, the fear of God is Qoheleth's chief virtue, but what it means for Qoheleth is a different matter.

In 3:14, Qoheleth combines his commendation of enjoyment (v. 13) with the immutability of God's sovereign providence (v. 14a). God has made everything "suitable" (lit., "beautiful"; *yāpeh*) in its time (v. 11), but humans cannot fathom time on God's terms, much less alter what God has determined. Self-determined destiny is an illusion before God, whose work is cloaked perpetually in mystery. Yet Qoheleth does claim some knowledge of God's ways: "I have seen . . ." (v. 10); "I know

---

70. Whybray, "Qoheleth the Immoralist?" 201.

71. Franz Delitzsch, *Ecclesiastes*, 438.

72. Nowhere other than in 12:13b does the book mention "commandments" (*miṣwôt*) or make any allusion to *torah*. However, it was self-evident to the final editor of the book that fearing God, along with keeping the commandments, was the key to Qoheleth's treatise, and to some degree such a claim is correct. See Gerald T. Sheppard, *Wisdom as a Hermeneutical Construct*, 120-29; idem, "The Epilogue to Qoheleth as Theological Commentary."

that . . ." (vv. 12, 14). Qoheleth is aware of the "business" God has allotted human beings, putting "eternity" into their minds (v. 11bα).[73] In this verse, Qoheleth contrasts punctiliar time (v. 11a; 'ēt) with duration[74] or the *totality* of time.[75]

Qoheleth claims that God has placed an all-encompassing temporal perspective within every human mind. Similar to his notion of the absurd, Qoheleth's meditation on time illustrates well the human capacity to "step back" in order to gain the most comprehensive picture possible of one's relationship to the world and the self. In this transcending movement toward self-consciousness, Qoheleth views the whole course of time with objective detachment (cf. 3:1-8) and concludes that even though human beings have the capacity to transcend the transient moments of their absurd lives, there is still a ceiling of the incomprehensible that no one can breach. The capacity to transcend one's self, the ability to view the overarching sweep of cyclical time, leads to a profound realization of the mystery of God's involvement in time. Yet despite this wall of impenetrable mystery — perhaps even because of it — Qoheleth is cognizant of the enduring permanence of divine providential involvement.

How "fearing God" fits in the context of God's mysterious involvement in history is not clearly specified. What is clear, however, is that "fear" is not a reversion back to the primitive notion of divinely inspired terror, as some have claimed.[76] A God who extends the blessings of enjoyment, the highest good according to Qoheleth (3:12), is by no means a jealous or terrorizing despot. Far from it, Qoheleth depicts a generous deity who has set limits to human discernment as well as instilled in human beings the intellectual capacity to be fully aware of

---

73. The translation of 'ōlām ("eternity") in this verse has generated much discussion (see Charles F. Whitley, *Koheleth: His Language and Thought*, 31-33; Murphy, *Ecclesiastes*, 34-35). Parallel to v. 11a, the term maintains its temporal nuance, as also evinced in the Greek translation aiŏna. Attempts to render it with the meaning "hiddenness" or "unknown," though supportable linguistically through minor emendation, fail in light of Qoheleth's consistent temporal use of 'ōlām elsewhere (*contra* Crenshaw, *Ecclesiastes*, 97-98, who appears undecided in 98 n. 55). See 1:4, 10; 2:16; 9:6; 12:5.

74. So also Ernst Jenni, "Das Wort 'ōlām im Alten Testament," 24-27; Murphy, *Ecclesiastes*, 34-35.

75. Emmanuel Podechard, *L'Ecclésiaste*, 295. His translation of the disputed term is "la durée entière" (292).

76. Cf. Gordis, 233; Crenshaw, *Ecclesiastes*, 100.

them. Qoheleth's fear of God is reached at the conclusion of his remarks on God's unsearchable providence and the permanency of divine action. It is the latter that specifically leads Qoheleth to refer to "fear" as the appropriate response before God. Fear is rooted in the recognition that all human action and thoughts are only fleeting and will not be remembered (cf. 1:4, 11). Human life and action pale against the work of the eternal, immutable God. God's plans are irrevocable and no one can alter them. They must be accepted on their own terms; hence, Qoheleth's advice is to welcome *both* toil and joy within life's ever-changing rhythms. To fear God is to embrace one's creaturely status as well as acknowledge the impenetrably enduring work of God, who freely extends the blessings of joy to finite, ephemeral beings.

Qoheleth's injunction to fear God in 5:6(7) is embedded in a meditation on religious observance in which brevity in piety is advocated. A minimum of words is urged in addressing God (5:1, 2[2, 3]); listening is valued over sacrifice; and speedy fulfillment of vows is advised (5:3-5[4-6]). It is not clear what is precisely meant by reference to dreams (5:2, 6[3, 7]),[77] but in any case, Qoheleth identifies dreams as a form of verbosity, and thus of obsessive concern. In 4:17–5:6(5:1-7), the reference to fearing God effectively sums up the specific liturgical injunctions listed in this section. To fear God is to be quietly receptive in the domain of the Holy, where human initiative is to be minimized. Qoheleth has brought the ideal of the reserved, unassuming sage into the realm of the divine presence, the temple. To fear God is to acknowledge the unsurpassable chasm between the transcendent God and the frail human being. Deference is equated with sincere reservedness in matters pertaining to the divine.

In 8:12, Qoheleth appears to grant some measure of well-being (*tôb*) to those "who fear God." Unlike the rhetoric of traditional wisdom, Qoheleth's argument concedes the empirically confirmed thesis that "sinners" prolong their lives (v. 12b), even more so than the righteous. But the well-being to which Qoheleth refers includes the ability to find

---

77. The conceivable range of possibilities that fit the context (or, more accurately, lack of context) extends from dreams that result in lack of sleep due to burdensome cares and worries (see 8:16) to prophetic incubation. I would suggest that Qoheleth is referring to (allegedly) divinely inspired dreams, since such an injunction against cultic (apocalyptic? see Joel 3:1[2:28]) reception of dreams accords well with his insistence in Eccl. 5:2(3) upon the unsurpassable distance between God and humankind.

joy *(ṭôḇ)* in one's work (e.g., 2:24; 3:12). The wicked, on the other hand, are rendered joyless by their obsessive conduct. Qoheleth does not mitigate the tension between the fact of the wicked's continuing prosperity and his judgment on the wicked in 8:13.[78] Qoheleth appears to concede proverbial wisdom's claim of the demise of the wicked despite all empirical evidence to the contrary. Yet by bowing to this tenet of traditional wisdom, Qoheleth recontextualizes the notion of prosperity that is associated with normative character. Well-being is not measured quantitatively by life span or by the number of achievements, but by the grateful reception of joy and acceptance of life. The wicked, with all of their ambitious machinations notwithstanding, are likened to a shadow (8:13a). In contrast, standing in awe before the mystery of God is the only life-affirming stance possible.

In summary, sincere reverence of God in Qoheleth shifts the focus of moral discourse away from specific maxims of conduct, those paths in traditional wisdom that were meant to lead to success and reward. As in 7:15-18, proper reverence of God marks a step beyond the ways of righteousness with which a follower can easily become obsessed. The "fear of God" is not so much a specific injunction for righteous living by which one receives just reward as it is a simple, dynamic profile of right character. To stand in awe before the God of mystery is to position one's character in relation to God, as opposed to defining correct behavior that presumes the ways of God. According to the final shape of the book of Proverbs, the fear of God is foundational for the myriad of collected instructions and proverbial maxims.[79] Without denying its foundational position in the quest for wisdom, Qoheleth recasts such reverence in a way that breaks the endless cycle of obsessive striving for righteousness (and wickedness, for that matter) that can consume the individual. Not only does reverence for God correct the rigid logic and extremes of the sapiential enterprise, it constitutes the source from which all virtues and right conduct are to flow. Qoheleth has given godly reverence its orthodox due without reducing it to primitive terror, on the one hand, or human pretense, on the other.

The benchmarks of proper reverence involve a profound acceptance of life on its own terms, with both its absurd limitations and redemptive

---

78. Such a contradiction may be the result of the work of a glossator who has added 8:12b-13. See discussion in Murphy, *Ecclesiastes*, 85, 87.

79. See Chapter 2.

joys. Sincere reverence is the simple acknowledgement of divine supremacy and transcendence and thus the open reception of life's vicissitudes without premeditated calculation. Qoheleth recognizes that joy and toil, life and death, are essentially incalculable entities, unplanned except by the mysterious providence of God. Fear of God is the final conclusion in the process of stepping back and discerning no ultimate relevance to the striving for gain and, hence, for permanence within one's life. To fear God is to surrender the human desire and proclivity to carve out a praise-worthy, lasting existence. As Qoheleth states in his opening passage, even the successive generations pass away into oblivion (1:4, 11). Proper reverence is rooted in a faith that is devoid of expectations and thus of ulterior motives, a faith in the transcendent Power that stands forever behind the workings of the cosmos, inaccessible to human inquiry.[80]

Carpe Diem

The lasting result of divine reverence is a certain attitude toward life that is rooted in the full reception of its serendipitous joys. Faced with the absurd fact that life cannot provide the means for permanence, Qoheleth encourages one to exhaust each moment life has to offer as God's gift (3:12, 22; 5:17-19[18-20]; 8:15; 9:7-9; 11:9-10). Conversely, Qoheleth condemns wallowing in nostalgia:

> Do not say, "Why were the former days better than these?"
> For it is not from wisdom that you ask this. (7:10)

For Qoheleth, it is the present that is of utmost importance: The past is dead and forgotten, and except for the certitude of death, the future is forever cloaked in uncertainty. All human schemes to ensure the fulfillment of self-interests, to control the future, are necessarily preempted. Only the present warrants attention. It is no accident, then, that Qoheleth in the end identifies the figure of the young man as his primary audience (11:9). Youth serves as an effective metaphor to illustrate vividly the importance of living in the present. Indeed, the young man incarnates such an approach to life. Tempered with the realization of divine judg-

---

80. See Hans-Peter Müller, "Wie sprach Qohälät von Gott?" 516; Michel, "Vom Gott, der im Himmel ist," 286-87.

ment, Qoheleth urges the young man to revel in cheer and banish anxiety and pain, for "youth and the dawn of life are vanity" (11:10). Here, *hebel* denotes ephemerality;[81] however, such a conclusion is reached only by critically viewing human life in its *absurd entirety*, from birth to death, which Qoheleth introduces to the young man in an allegorical meditation on old age (12:1-7).[82] The profound recognition of the absurdity of human life requires nothing less and nothing more than exhausting every present moment as God's gift.

VI. CONCLUSION

According to the modern sage James L. Crenshaw, Qoheleth's skepticism stems from a "heightened sense of justice and possess[es] a vision of a better world."[83] Qoheleth's brand of skepticism, however, stems from something more basic, namely from a heightened degree of self-consciousness. By stepping out of the character that traditional wisdom forged, Qoheleth is able to cast into question the profile of traditional character and its formation, namely the unquestioned appropriation of the accumulated wisdom of the past. And yet it is from his step backward that Qoheleth can construct a new character, a character fashioned for the most part without the wisdom of the past.

Like Job, Qoheleth places enough weight on his own experience to tip the scales against many of the "truths" of inherited tradition. However, beyond Job, Qoheleth has turned his experience into an epistemological method that is singularly rooted in his autobiographical style. Qoheleth revels in "introspective reporting."[84] Intrinsic value is placed on personal perception and experience. Qoheleth's style places high value on the role of the individual and personal intellect to make moral coherence of one's life and world.

Yet by striking out on a new path toward wisdom, Qoheleth has "struck out," having found all paths leading ultimately to dead ends. As

---

81. See Fox's partial admission that *hebel* in 3:19 and 11:10 may "not denote absurdity" ("The Meaning of *Hebel* for Qohelet," 421).

82. See Fox's insightful, albeit one-sided, treatment of 12:1-7 in "Aging and Death in Qoheleth 12."

83. James L. Crenshaw, "Ecclesiastes: Odd Book In," 33.

84. Fox, *Qohelet and His Contradictions*, 93.

the preeminently royal sage, Qoheleth searches for and tests wisdom, exhausting all means at his disposal, but in the end comes up wanting. Wisdom forever remains irretrievable for Qoheleth, and yet the failed pursuit of wisdom affords Qoheleth a view of the world and the human condition in their absurd totalities. It is in the quest itself that the contours of character are reshaped.

Qoheleth does not condemn his lifelong search as a veil of tears. Instead, he commends unqualified acceptance of the absurd life in all of its vicissitudes and fleeting moments of joy. It is from his step backward that Qoheleth returns to life changed. The profile of this new character is admittedly only faintly sketched by Qoheleth, but it is one that is fashioned from a humble and grateful acceptance of the few fleeting moments of joy one receives from the hand of God. Indeed, it is this attitude of acceptance and seizing the moment that enables him to exhort one to embrace enjoyment. The capacity of enjoyment is rooted in an inner freedom that is unassailable,[85] a freedom that can only be reached in the deliberate, interior act of self-consciousness. By exploring the depths of failure and despair and arriving at a pervasive sense of the absurd, Qoheleth espouses a radical openness to life, a life lived without pretensions, an exploration without delusions of grandeur. Qoheleth's brand of *carpe diem*, of exhausting the fleeting moments of enjoyment, comes from a profound realization of one's finitude to the world and to God, the Inscrutable.

The book of Ecclesiastes is at root a confession of disillusionment about life in general and the frustration of work in particular. For an achievement-oriented society, Qoheleth's message speaks persuasively to those who with great and ambitious plans for success are ripe for disillusionment, whether in the business world, politics, raising children, ministry, or academia. In every vocation there is the personal struggle over the perceived lack of effectiveness and progress that can bring one to the brink of burnout and despair. For clearly misguided reasons, Qoheleth points out, it is all too easy to fall into the trap of pinning one's hopes on the *human* capacity to fulfill dreams and goals, no matter how lofty and worthy, only to have many of them sacrificed upon the altar. One experiences a disillusionment of the most intractable kind, a disenchantment that cuts like a knife, perhaps fatally wounding everything one had held dear in one's vocation. Qoheleth's message speaks to such universal experience, made even more urgent in an industrial

85. *Ibid.*, 75-76.

age. In almost Humian fashion,[86] Qoheleth demonstrates that the means and the end, effort and result, work and gain, bear no necessary connection in the real world. Attaining a goal, any goal, can be as elusive as striving after wind.

For Qoheleth, in working through the depths of despair that question the very meaning of life and work, there is an answer, and it lies in the fervent desire to live and work despite the absurdities and contradictions of life. The answer is admittedly anticlimactic: eat, drink, and find enjoyment in one's labors. All noble and honorable goals and ideas are whittled down to everyday simple pleasures received in gratitude. Yet there is something more. The elusive enjoyment Qoheleth describes is one that thrives not on the result, not on the goals achieved, but rather in the very doing, in the process of toil. It is a joy that accompanies one's work at every step in the process. Qoheleth is not saying that one should not have goals and objectives. Work could not exist without them. Rather, the danger lies in attaching personal fulfillment to the end result, for God alone knows what the result might hold. Qoheleth's message is in the end a liberating one.

To be sure, Ecclesiastes is not a very optimistic book. But it is a treatise on joyful perseverance. Qoheleth is at base a preacher of joy, of joy found through hard work and rest. Do not dwell or even count on what can be achieved, Qoheleth seems to say. Rather keep on working, keep toiling under the sun, keep crying out for justice and right relationships, keep ministering to others, and do it all for all you're worth. Feel the cool breeze when it comes, accepting the support and fellowship of others. Then let the chips fall where they may. For wherever they fall, God's mercy is to be found. And as that stone tumbles down the mountain one more time, as it always has and always will, and as each of us begins to descend again back into the valley to retrieve it, Qoheleth urges us to go forth in reverence and joy.[87]

86. Reference is made to the Scottish philosopher David Hume, who argued against the philosophical claim that material cause and effect bore a *necessary* connection.

87. Qoheleth has ably set the stage for a successor on the quest for wisdom to say, "The fear of the Lord delights the heart, and gives gladness and joy" (Sir. 1:12b).

6 Conclusion: The Journey of Character

According to a rabbinic tradition, Proverbs was written by Solomon in his prime while the book of Ecclesiastes was codified in his old age.[1] Historical naiveté notwithstanding, the rabbis appropriately recognized the developmental nature of wisdom as one rooted in the continuum of character. All three wisdom books, including Job, depict the formation of character as an interactive process through time, an "emplotment" of the self.[2] This temporal aspect of character formation is indicated in the frequently repeated motif the "way of wisdom." Moreover, the nature of this path highlights the fact that the journeying self is no island, as noted in Proverbs. The way of wisdom is the prescribed way of the community. The development of the self is consistently framed in relation to other selves: God, parent, friend, or foe, flat or full. Character in and of itself is necessarily character *in relation*.[3] It is only in encounter that interaction takes place, whether in receptive silence, caustic protest, or mutual edification. Things are bound to happen, and the development of character is inevitable.

---

1. According to Song of Songs Rabbah I:VI.17.H, the Song of Solomon was written in Solomon's youth (Jacob Neusner, *Song of Songs Rabbah*, 1:50).

2. See Paul Ricoeur's investigation of narrative "emplotment" in relation to character in *Time and Narrative*, 1:31-51.

3. See Chapter 1.

I. THE SELF MOVING OUTWARD

What holds the three books in common from a character standpoint is that all three chart the self starting from a central, familiar locale that provides expected security and identity. But the moral subject does not remain in this position for long; it moves into certain realms of liminality, to the frontiers of community, creation, and knowledge, which can pose particular dangers.

The character of the silent son, sitting deferentially at the feet of his elders, is pointed outward toward a community that is sharply divided between the righteous and the wicked, his peers and the sages, between the alien woman and woman wisdom. The father commends to him the way of wisdom and warns him against his rapacious friends (Prov. 1:8-19). The mother details the tragic story of a young man dragged down to his death by the predatory outsider (Prov. 7).[4] In both cases, the parents compel the son to step back and look at the motivations and consequences of potentially disastrous actions. Together, the parents present a rhetorically persuasive case for maintaining the familiar and the family. The familiar and the family operate in consort in maintaining the viability of communal life. Conversely, the strange is resisted as the archetypal threat to both family and, thus, community at large. With the stranger, all covenants are overturned, from marital to Mosaic (Prov. 2:17).[5] The stranger is the veritable black hole that subsumes all that is wrong, and can potentially go wrong, with the community.

Guided by the familial spirit of wisdom on his journey beyond the cloistered walls of hearth and home, the son is instructed to avoid all that is strange and wicked as he makes his way through the winding alleyways of public engagement in the larger community. Wisdom provides the inextricable link between family and community, no less youth and age. As the straight pathway to maturity, she gently and gradually replaces the parental hand of guidance that has brought the child to the threshold of adulthood. The book of Proverbs is about letting go as much as it is about holding firm.

Similar to Proverbs, the book of Job is about leaving the security of domicility and patriarchal norms, naturalized domains that become thoroughly undermined soon after Job's character is established in ch.

4. See Athalya Brenner, "Proverbs 1–9: An F Voice?" 113-130.

1. As a result, Job is estranged from his family and community and, thus, exceeds the traditional boundaries of normative character. Unlike the proverbial son's journey, the movement of Job's anomalous character requires a deconstruction of the traditional norms and marks of character. Through turgid and circuitous deliberations, Job replaces his posture of humble submission with one of grievance and protest. Job's *chutzpah* becomes a crowning mark of his integrity in transition.[6] Yet Job's journey does not simply end with impassioned protests against his friends and God. Like wisdom's leading the son outward into the community, Yahweh offers Job a new vision of cosmic community that explodes his restrictive moral worldview. Estranged from family, Job finds himself in a strange world order whose horizons embrace the very margins of the created order, exempt from human control and dominance. Job himself embodies strangeness. The wild creatures that Yahweh presents to Job become his new relatives and peers. Compelled to step back and look beyond his provincial world, Job discovers humility and awe before the grand sweep of creation as well as solidarity with it and thus finds a new responsibility toward all of existence. Reaching out to the extremes of moral and created order, Job's journey blurs the boundaries between the familiar and the strange.

Qoheleth's odyssey is much more individualized. There is no God or personified wisdom to lead Qoheleth to new visions of social engagement. Nevertheless, his journey outward is no less relevant, for it cuts to the core of conscious existence. Catapulted by despair, Qoheleth transcends the self that is consumed with relentless, tiring engagement with the world and finds his world profoundly lacking in progress and meaning. Qoheleth journeys from self to non-self, a search ostensibly for wisdom that unavoidably leads to the negation of meaningful existence. In Qoheleth's step back, all of existence becomes estranged. Finding the cosmos a stranger, Qoheleth legitimately asks whether there is any purpose to effort and existence. Unlike Job, Qoheleth cannot identify himself with the strangeness of creation and consequently find his liberation. Qoheleth's journey has taken him to the void of existence and he is repulsed.

---

5. Cf. Prov. 5:15-20; 7:14-18; Mal. 2:10-16. See Claudia V. Camp, "What's So Strange about the Strange Woman?" 20-23.

6. Not surprisingly, the "virtue" of *chutzpah* is absent in William J. Bennett's *The Book of Virtues*.

II. THE SELF RETURNING

Each of the wisdom books, however, does not conclude with the self in limbo, severed from its point of departure. With the step backward is the forward, return step, a re-entry into the naturalized environment from which the self first departed. It is in this return that the development of character reaches its conclusive formation. Proverbs concludes with a return to family life, the point of departure for the silent son. Making his way through the normalities and abnormalities of a divided community, through the competing voices that vie for his attention and allegiance, the blossoming patriarch establishes himself in the end as one who has reached his vocational goal: finding the ideal spouse, raising the ideal family, and securing the esteem of his fellow patriarchs. Proverbs begins and ends with the familial context. But the community is no mere detour to and from the family; it is the goal and result of life within the family.

Similarly, Job ends his story back within the family fold. Rather than a reconstitution of his earlier family, however, Job's new family is a profoundly innovative one. Unprecedented attention is devoted to the daughters, as it is to the "woman of excellence" who overshadows her spouse in the final chapter of Proverbs. In addition, Job's community and family, once the source of castigation, welcomes the sufferer with open arms and material offerings, redeeming where Job's wise "friends" have failed. Job returns a different man with a reconfigured family and a new moral vision. Job and his world are reconciled.

Qoheleth also makes his return to the vicissitudes of everyday existence. And indeed, like Job, his re-entry comes at some cost. Whereas Job returns with renewed commitment, ready to embrace the risks of communal obligations, Qoheleth returns with the deep sigh of resignation. Qoheleth reenters the self, having played spectator over himself and life. He has no other choice. Qoheleth cannot live with or as a disembodied self, forever juxtaposing a life consumed with the desire to achieve greater things with a life resigned to unresolved futility and meaninglessness. Qoheleth does not ultimately find death to be the remedy of a divided, unreconciled life, though it is life's natural outcome. Nonetheless, his entry back into life does not mark a happy resolution of life's intractable contradictions. Without satisfying answers, Qoheleth reinvests in self by focusing on life's fleeting, yet redemptive moments of joy and work. His character is reconstructed to relish them, receiving them as gift rather than as earned gain.

III. FORMATION OF CHARACTER: WHAT IS GAINED IN THE JOURNEY

All three main characters in the wisdom books end with a full profile of character formed or reformed. The silent son has become a responsible citizen of the community, having established his own family. The familiar and familial virtues that he and his spouse embody work toward maintaining the structures of the community, ensuring their stability amid threats from the outside. The "woman of excellence" profiled in the concluding chapter provides not only for the welfare of the family but also the well-being of the community, particularly the poor. In consort, the new parents lead a life of *service* and *security*, an interdependent balance of virtues. Their household is a mighty fortress, impregnable to the ravages of climate and chaos. And yet the door of this domicile remains open as the matriarch conducts commerce outside and extends her hand to the poor, while her spouse takes his seat among the elders, exercising his duties over community affairs. Security for the household translates into security for the community and vice versa. The inextricable bond is also reflected in acts of service to the community. No form of "amoral familism," by which the family becomes the exclusive aim of moral conduct, is espoused here.[7] In short, the establishment of a family, in the eyes of the proverbial sages, represents an indispensable form of engagement with the community.

Job's return to the family in the final chapter of his story comes, however, at the cost of upsetting the delicate balance between security and service established in Proverbs. His journey begins with the destruction of his family and ends with its renewal and reconfiguration. In the transition, Job is afforded a new moral vision that embraces the margins of the cosmic community, a no-man's-land. Job moves much beyond his days as the once dutiful and successful son. Having secured his

---

7. This phrase is borrowed from James Q. Wilson's reference to E. C. Banfield's study of a southern Italian village, whose extreme poverty is attributable to an intractable unwillingness to cooperate beyond the families' material interests (*The Moral Sense*, 228).

position in the community, he is forced to relinquish all social esteem and unwittingly must seek his solitude at the fringes of civilized life. There he finds true solidarity and an enlarged field of vision that embraces the greatest and least of God's creation. No longer based on mechanical laws of reaction and retribution, the cosmos is conceived as a veritable ark and play field of the Creator, with all creatures living in a vibrant network of freedom and interdependence.

It is with such a vision that Job makes the painful transition back into his provincial community, and it is with such a vision that Job is restored. Job has discovered God's gratuitous delight in a creation characterized by an orchestration of fiercely dynamic, sometimes competing forces. And so Job attends to his family in delight and giving, fully aware that the guarantees of security no longer have their place in a life of gratuitous service. Job assumes a life of risk, uncalculating and undaunted, overturning established norms of familial conduct. Job is the prototype of the father in Jesus' parable of the prodigal (Luke 15:11-32).

This new moral vision enables Job to make the final and necessary move in the formation of his character. God's revelation is a rite of passage that compels him to transcend the ethos of grievance and entitlement, which he had perfected to an art form in the dialogues, and embrace a life of giving. Job's righteous anger is the required step toward a profound empathy with all of creation. His life of protest was the necessary, albeit insufficient, step toward the reformation of character. Indeed, Job's impassioned dissension does not fall short of heroic proportions, but in the end, like his ancient Near Eastern counterpart Gilgamesh,[8] he must return home in humble gratitude and service to his community.

8. The epic of Gilgamesh relates the Mesopotamian story of a tragic hero, who in traveling to the margins of the created order and seeking answers concerning death and immortality, ends in failure. At one crucial juncture in his expedition, the female tavern owner Siduri gives him worthy advice:

> Gilgamesh, whither rovest thou?
> The life thou pursuest thou shalt not find.
> When the gods created mankind,
> Death for mankind they set aside,
> Life in their own hands retaining.
> Thou, Gilgamesh, let full be thy belly,
> Make thou merry by day and by night.
> Of each day make thou a feast of rejoicing,
> Day and night dance thou and play!
> Let thy garments be sparkling fresh,

Qoheleth, too, attempts to penetrate the secrets of the cosmos, but, unlike Job, finds them wanting. His journey is to the void rather than to the vital diversity of life. And yet, like Job, Qoheleth also embodies a life-affirming stance. It is precisely through the veil of cosmic indifference and vocational despair that Qoheleth arrives at an unconditional acceptance of life on its own terms. Qoheleth is forced to realize that some things simply cannot be changed, whether it be the bureaucratic diffusion of responsibility, the endless cycles of celestial movement, or death itself. Nature and society mirror each other in a static continuum. Within the confines of indifferent natural and social structures fashioned by an inscrutable God, Qoheleth is able to commend a life of enjoyment received in gratitude and exercised in simplicity. Indeed, to strive to do more is rooted in delusions of grandeur, if not self-pride, resulting only in unmitigated despair.

So Qoheleth urges the young man to rejoice in his potent but fleeting youth and banish all anxiety (Eccl. 11:9-10). Qoheleth himself serves as an example that the aged, though racked with pain and bereft of vitality, need not lose the capacity for enjoyment. Qoheleth's call is to relish each moment in gratitude, however sparse they may be. These redemptive moments cannot be had or made, Qoheleth comes to realize in his lifelong pursuit as the royal sage. They are rather extended serendipitously, as "providential chances." The marks or virtues that Qoheleth commends all operate in consort with the reception and stewardship of such moments.

IV. A SYNTHESIS OF CHARACTER?

The authors of these three books would undoubtedly have much to say to each other in rebuke as well as in approval if they were seated together at table. All would argue, no doubt, over who — the aged or youth, the

---

Thy head be washed; bathe thou in water.
Pay heed to the little one that holds on to thy hand,
Let thy spouse delight in thy bosom!
For this is the task of [mankind]! (*ANET,* 90)

Siduri's sound advice commends Gilgamesh to return home and enjoy the life of familial simplicity.

established or dispossessed — could lay claim to the lion's share of wisdom, particularly if Elihu were invited. In addition, Job would chide Qoheleth for being such a stoic about matters, while Qoheleth would point out that Job's revelational experience is privileged. To be sure, both Job and Qoheleth would rebuke the editors of Proverbs for their naiveté and simplistic worldview. But perhaps the proverbial sages would have the last word by arguing that reverence of God and engagement in the community remain formative and irreducible virtues for every profile of normative character.

All, however, would recognize that the kind of interaction that leads to character formation is a rocky road, one full of crises and gifts. As the youth must let go of the familial moorings to embark upon the uncharted waters raging beyond the protective walls of hearth and home, Job and Qoheleth must let go of preconceived notions of ethical intuition and appropriate practice. Dead ends are inevitably encountered on their respective journeys. To pose the question of a standard, exhaustive profile of right character for all seasons is to some extent analogous to asking a chess master for the best move. The answer must be framed relative to the context and situation as the game progresses. As the game itself proceeds in a characteristic way, so there is a common thread that unites the wisdom books with their common focus. Each book contains snapshot profiles of works in progress, formulated in response to the social challenges and perceived crises of their times. Whether painted with the broad strokes of proverbial wisdom or with the fine, detailing brush of the Joban poet, these portraits of character are part of a larger canvas: the inclusive, empathetic community of God's good creation, one filled with enjoyment and potency as well as suffering and consolation. Such wisdom calls for a greater humility regarding humanity's place in the cosmos and, concomitantly, a greater sense of responsibility toward all of life. For this, wisdom offers a deeper sense of mystery of all that is: the reverberating laughter of wisdom witnessing the marvelous acts of creation, the majestic potency and freedom of all life, and the unfathomable nature of the God behind it all.

Creation is an indispensable feature of biblical wisdom, but not in isolation. Necessarily rooted in the perception and worldview of the inquirer of wisdom, the cosmic perspective is embodied and lived out in conduct. As suggested in the foregoing analyses, both creation and community are bound up with worldview. The litany of creation presented by God to Job is in part a radical reconfiguration of Job's community that results in his reformation of character. In Proverbs, the voice of wisdom, present at the advent of creation, is correlated with the voice of the sagacious community, whose duty is to educate youth and lead them to communal responsibility. For Qoheleth, only traces of community can be discerned, thereby making his quest all the more difficult. Qoheleth depicts communal institutions, such as the family and government, on the verge of collapse or plagued with the withering effects of indifference. Any vestige of community is discerned atomistically: isolated individuals eking out their own existence in oppressive toil. Indeed, any genuine sense of community or fellowship is just as fleeting as the moments of joy. Qoheleth's painful quest for character is conducted in large part without the benefits of community, much less wisdom. Whereas the community in Job failed miserably to sustain the sufferer, it is by and large absent in the rhetoric of Qoheleth's confessions. Consequently, Qoheleth's view of character is deficiently individualized and self-referential.

By contrast, the ideals of the sagacious community are vividly portrayed in Proverbs and the end of Job. Consoling and instructing, demonstrating solidarity and providing authoritative guidance, inviting and rebuking, the community has a diverse and far-reaching role in the formation of character. More than pedagogical, the community is to provide the arena of social interaction and praxis by which the contours of individual character are continually shaped and reshaped. That is not to say that the individual is subsumed by the community. The character of Job is one that is set off against the community as it initially attempts to silence his subversive words. In light of the kind of cosmic community Yahweh reveals to Job, the human community is critiqued and corrected to embody freedom within established structures of interdependence and support. Moral fascism, on the one hand, and divisive culture wars, on the other, are ways to be avoided by the community, for both roads cut off the possibility of genuine, informed dialogue as well as new frontiers of empathy and fellowship.[9]

9. Walter Brueggemann spells out this dimension nicely in "Scripture and an Ecumenical Life-Style."

V. THE LETTER OF JAMES: WISDOM FOR THE CHURCH

How does the character of Old Testament wisdom inform the Christian community today? Of all the books of the New Testament, the Letter of James best reflects the ethos of the Hebrew wisdom traditions.[10] Though the epistle does not profile a journey of character in the way its Old Testament counterparts do, there are nonetheless important points of correlation and revision between James and the wisdom books.[11] Echoing the exhortative language of Proverbs, James brings the insights of wisdom into a distinctly Christian context and community.[12]

Like that of the sages who preceded him, James's pursuit of consistency in conduct and conviction, the requisites of character, is not a quest for personal purity. As in Proverbs, James's overriding concern is the character of the community. James offers a vision of a mutually supportive community whose members confess their sins to one another, pray for one another, and encourage each other in moral integrity (Jas. 5:16, 19-20).[13] Moreover, much attention is devoted to the plight of the poor, as in the abhorrent case of favoritism displayed to the rich during worship (2:1-7).

> Has not God chosen the poor in the world to be rich in faith and to be heirs of the kingdom that he has promised to those who love him? But you have dishonored the poor. (2:5b-6a)

Without idealizing poverty, James takes the proverbial call to sustain and defend the poor one step further: He claims preferential status and vindication for the disenfranchised (2:5-6),[14] a view toward which Job's experience, which invests dignity in the dispossessed, tends. Pure reli-

10. Wisdom can also be readily discerned throughout the New Testament, from the parables of Jesus to the Gospel of John and the Corinthians letters of Paul. For a complete survey, see Ben Witherington III, *Jesus the Sage*, 117-380.

11. To begin with, the author of James identifies himself as a teacher in Jas. 3:1. For James, teaching is a vocation that must be taken with utmost seriousness and care, requiring a moral integrity above that of most other professions.

12. It is often noted that James's perspective is more theocentric than Christocentric, since Jesus' name occurs only twice (1:1; 2:1) and references to Jesus' death and resurrection are absent. On the other hand, James utilizes Jesus' sayings (1:6; 2:8; 5:12). See Luke T. Johnson, "James," 1272; Sophie Laws, "James, Epistle of," 3:624.

13. *Ibid.*, 627.

14. See Elsa Tamez, *The Scandalous Message of James*, 43-50.

gion is caring for the "orphans and widows in their distress" (1:27b), which has strong proverbial warrant.[15] With such a statement, James comes close to identifying religion with the exercise of virtue. Corrupt religion, on the other hand, is evinced in the sin of partiality, which introduces "distinctions" within the community of faith (2:4) as well as fragments the law:

> If you show partiality, you commit sin and are convicted by the law as transgressors. For whoever keeps the whole law but fails in one point has become accountable for all of it. (2:9-10)

In short, partiality leads to the fragmentation of self and community.

The sin of the compartmentalized self, or "double-mindedness,"[16] is particularly evident in the failure to translate faith into works. Faith must issue in works to be a living faith (2:14-26). Again, the prime example is service to the poor:

> If a brother or sister is naked and lacks daily food, and one of you says to them, "Go in peace; keep warm and eat your fill," and yet you do not supply their bodily needs, what is the good of that? (2:15-16)

More broadly, what typifies such sin for James is the sin of hypocrisy: knowing the right thing to do but failing to do it (4:17), the sin of "double-mindedness." At base is a divided loyalty or "friendship": One can either be a friend of the world or a friend of God (4:4). Echoing the opposing calls of wisdom and the stranger in Proverbs, the moral life is divided between two irreconcilable allegiances, a wisdom "from above" and one "from below" (3:15). The latter is rooted in envy and results in social upheaval (3:16–4:2). The perspective such "earthly" wisdom offers is one that views human beings in irresolvable competition with each other, leading inexorably to murder, the elimination of rivals.[17] Wisdom from above, on the other hand, seeks peace (3:18). Like wisdom in the role of host and friend in Prov. 8–9, God overflows with generosity, giving generously to all who sincerely inquire (Jas. 1:5; 4:6). One cannot live committed to both kinds of wisdom, confessing allegiance to God but contradicting it in action consonant with the way

---

15. See Chapter 2.
16. See 1:8; 4:8.
17. Johnson, 1275.

of the world. By likening faith without works to the body without the spirit, James suggests that separating faith from action results in a bifurcated self and death (2:26). James, like the company of sages that preceded him, seeks to profile the unitary nature of character in an age of challenge and conflict.

This integrity of character is demonstrated in consistent action. Doing the word is the necessary compliment of hearing the word (1:22-25). Inconsistency, by contrast, is most blatantly illustrated in the misuse and abuse of speech for James. As repeatedly noted, prudent speech is a theme that runs consistently throughout the wisdom corpus. For James, restraint in speech bespeaks religious integrity (1:26). Speech should be straightforward and truthful (5:12; cf. Prov. 8:8-9; Eccl. 4:17–5:3[Eng. 5:1-4]). Conversely, James condemns speaking evil in judgment against one another (Jas. 4:11-12), the very sin of Job's friends. The one who slanders asserts superiority over others and the law. Not surprisingly, James lifts up the example of Job, commending his endurance amid great suffering (5:10-11).[18] Elsa Tamez appropriately speaks of such patience as "militant," the antithesis of passive submission,[19] as was also the case with Job.

The road to maturity is marked by trials and testing. As implicit in the book of Job,[20] James hesitates to cast God in the role of tester: It is not God who tests and tempts (2:13).[21] God cannot be blamed for one's own moral failure. Trials are the result of external hardship, as in the case of human persecution (1:2-4), and temptation is the con-

---

18. To be sure, lifting up the *patience* of Job fails to take into account Job's impassioned complaints against his friends and God. Job does endure, but it is hardly an example of patience. Perhaps James is relying more on the revisionist Testament of Job than on the biblical Job (čf. T. Job 27:7). However, it is clear that James is fully aware of the fact that the biblical Job never renounced his integrity or faith (Ralph P. Martin, *James*, 188-89).

19. Tamez, 52-56.

20. See Chapter 3 on the role of God in the prologue of Job.

21. The Greek words used for "test," "tempt," and "trial" are synonymous (*peirázō* in Jas. 1:2, 12a, 13, 14 and *dokímion/dókimos* in 1:2, 12b [see textual note in Martin, 12]). Though there appears to be a distinction in meaning between external testing and internal temptation (see Johnson, 1272-73), what is clear is that neither is directly attributable to God. Rather, God generously provides the means and rewards for endurance. God is untouched by evil, a claim that admittedly revises the prologue of Job, but one that is in keeping with the outcome of God's character, as discussed in Chapter 3. See Bo Reicke, *The Epistles of James, Peter, and Jude,* 17; Martin, 30-31.

sequence of "one's own desire," evident in the perennial struggle of everyday life (1:13).[22] The pedagogy of testing is internalized, rooted squarely in the painful process of maturation within a culture that is hostile to the Christian faith, within a divided Christian community of competing factions, and in the personal struggle to cultivate virtue. But whether external or internal, hardship and temptation can lead to wholeness of character, depending upon how one responds. Character is both a work in progress and an end in itself.[23]

One should rejoice in this painful process of trial, according to James (1:2-4; cf. Prov. 1; 8; Sir. 2:1; 4:17-18). As in Ecclesiastes, James repeatedly refers to the phenomenon of joy and blessing (Jas. 1:2, 12, 25; 5:11). Such joy is distinguished from the kind of joy that seeks either fulfillment in the end times or masochistic pleasure in suffering.[24] Like Qoheleth's enjoyment, joy for James is built into the process and result of active endurance and hardship.

> But those who look into the perfect law, the law of liberty, and *persevere*, being not hearers who forget but doers who act — they will be *blessed in their doing*. (2:25)[25]

Joy is the result of service, yet it is also a gift (1:5, 12b; 5:11b).

James even draws a healthy dose of Qoheleth's view of the absurd, particularly in his attack on the rich. Like Qoheleth, James sees humility as a cardinal virtue that counters self-exaltation and pride (4:10). More specifically, life is likened to a "mist that appears for a little while and then vanishes" (v. 14). As with Qoheleth, such a realization guards against all pretentious boasting (v. 15). The antithesis to boasting — an illegitimate form of speech — is humble prayer (cf. Eccl. 5:1 [5:2]). With wisdom as its object, the act of prayer is a wholehearted, bold enterprise that, if done with integrity, ensures fulfillment of what is requested

---

22. See 1 Pet. 1:6-7, which uses the same phrase for "trials of any kind," that is, external hostility and persecution (cf. 3 Macc. 2:6; 4 Macc. 17:7; Rom. 5:3-4). See Sophie Laws, *A Commentary on the Epistle of James*, 51, 69-70.

23. The latter is stressed by Laws, *ibid.*, 52.

24. Tamez, 36-37.

25. Italics are added for emphasis. Compare Qoheleth's statement: "So I commend enjoyment . . . for this will go with them *in their toil* through the days of life" (Eccl. 8:15, italics added). For James, "blessing" and "joy" are inseparable, if not coextensive in meaning. Similarly, Qoheleth finds enjoyment to be exclusively the gift of God.

(1:5-7; 4:3). According to James, the problem of unanswered prayer lies with the one who prays and the appropriateness of the request (1:5-8; 4:2-4).[26] Placed in its proper context, the act of prayer, like service, approximates Qoheleth's high esteem of work. Accompanied by action and coherence in character, prayer is fundamental to the Christian life. But Qoheleth would no doubt insist, lest James be misinterpreted, that prayer, like any form of work, does not ensure personal gain. Both the mystery of the sovereign God and the integrity of human character must be preserved. Both in work and in prayer, necessary components of the daily rhythm of life, one's character is molded and shaped to perceive more readily the gracious dimensions of living, regardless of fulfilled requests. Prayer is what restores the physical as well as communal body and makes "gratitude palpable" (5:13-16).[27] To pray unceasingly and boldly without contingency, whether in praise or petition, whether fulfilled or unfulfilled, may very well be the highest exercise of virtue: the merging of service and gratitude.[28]

Finally, James has much to say about wisdom itself. He echoes his predecessors by capturing the dynamic, character-based nature of wisdom:

> Who is wise and understanding among you? Show by your good life that your works are done with gentleness born of wisdom. But if you have bitter envy and selfish ambition in your hearts, do not be boastful and false to the truth. . . . The wisdom from above is first pure, then peaceable, gentle, willing to yield, full of mercy and good fruits, without a trace of partiality or hypocrisy. And a harvest of righteousness is sown in peace for those who make peace. (3:13-14, 17-18)

Wisdom is demonstrated in character that is consistently gentle, impartial, and "willing to yield." The final test of wisdom and character is the quality of community it engenders, a community of peace and righteousness whose arms can stretch wide enough to welcome the Kingdom of Peace.

---

26. The model of prayer as a reflection of character is conveyed by Elijah (5:17-18).

27. Tamez, 71.

28. Such precedent is most clearly evident in Ecclesiastes. See Chapter 5.

Works Cited

Abrams, M. H. *A Glossary of Literary Terms,* 4th ed. New York: Holt, Rinehart, Winston, 1981.

Allen, Diogenes. *The Traces of God in a Frequently Hostile World.* Cambridge, Mass.: Cowley, 1981.

Alonzo-Schöckel, Luis, and Sicre Diaz, J. L. *Job: Comentario teológico y literario.* Nueva Biblia Española. Madrid: Ediciones Cristiandad, 1983.

Alter, Robert. *The Art of Biblical Narrative.* New York: Basic Books, 1981.

————. *The Art of Biblical Poetry.* New York: Basic Books, 1985.

Althusser, Louis. *Lenin and Philosophy.* London: Monthly Review, 1972.

Aristotle. *Nicomachean Ethics,* trans. Martin Ostwald. LLA 75. Indianapolis: Bobbs-Merrill, 1962.

Auerbach, Erich. *Mimesis: The Representation of Reality in Western Literature,* trans. Willard R. Trask. Garden City: Doubleday, 1957.

Baechler, Jean. "Virtue: Its Nature, Exigency, and Acquisition," in *Virtue,* ed. John W. Chapman and William A. Galston. *Nomos* 34. New York: New York University Press, 1991, 25-48.

Bar-Efrat, Shim'on. *The Art of the Biblical Story.* Tel Aviv: Sifriat Hapoalim, 1979.

Baskin, Judith R. "Rabbinic Interpretations of Job," in *The Voice from the Whirlwind,* ed. Leo G. Perdue and W. Clark Gilpin. Nashville: Abingdon, 1992, 101-110.

Becker, Joachim. *Gottesfurcht im Alten Testament. Analecta biblica* 25. Rome: Pontifical Biblical Institute, 1965.

Bennett, William J., ed. *The Book of Virtues: A Treasury of Great Moral Stories.* New York: Simon & Schuster, 1993.

Berlin, Adele. *Poetics and Interpretation of Biblical Narrative.* BLS 9. Sheffield: Almond, 1983.

Birch, Bruce. *Let Justice Roll Down.* Louisville: Westminster John Knox, 1991.

―――, and Rasmussen, Larry. *Bible and Ethics in the Christian Life,* rev. ed. Minneapolis: Augsburg, 1989.

Blanchard, Kenneth H., and Peale, Norman Vincent. *The Power of Ethical Management.* New York: William Morrow, 1988.

Boecker, Hans-Jochen. *Law and the Administration of Justice in the Old Testament and Ancient East,* trans. Jeremy Moiser. Minneapolis: Augsburg, 1980.

Bondi, Richard. "Character," *Westminster Dictionary of Christian Ethics,* ed. James F. Childress and John Macquarrie. Philadelphia: Westminster, 1986, 82-84.

―――. "The Elements of Character," *JRE* 12 (1984): 201-218.

Brenner, Athalya. "God's Answer to Job," *VT* 31 (1981): 129-137.

―――. "Proverbs 1–9: An F Voice?" in *On Gendering Texts: Female and Male Voices in the Hebrew Bible,* ed. Athalya Brenner and Fokkelien Dijk-Hemmes. Leiden: E. J. Brill, 1993, 113-130.

Brown, William P. "Divine Act and the Art of Persuasion in Genesis 1," in *History and Interpretation: Essays in Honour of John H. Hayes,* ed. M. Patrick Graham, William P. Brown, and Jeffrey K. Kuan. JSOTSup 173. Sheffield: Sheffield Academic, 1993, 19-32.

Brueggemann, Walter A. *In Man We Trust.* Richmond: John Knox, 1972.

―――. "Scripture and an Ecumenical Life-Style: A Study in Wisdom Theology," *Interpretation* 34 (1970): 3-19.

―――. "The Social Significance of Solomon as a Patron of Wisdom," in *The Sage in Israel and the Ancient Near East,* ed. John G. Gammie and Leo G. Perdue. Winona Lake: Eisenbrauns, 1990, 117-132.

Budziszewski, J. "Religion and Civic Virtue," in *Virtue,* ed. John W. Chapman and William A. Galston. *Nomos* 34. New York: New York University Press, 1991, 49-68.

Camp, Claudia V. "What's So Strange About the Strange Woman?" in *The Bible and the Politics of Exegesis: Essays in Honor of Norman K. Gottwald,* ed. David Jobling, Peggy L. Day, and Gerald T. Sheppard. Cleveland: Pilgrim, 1991, 17-31.

―――. *Wisdom and the Feminine in the Book of Proverbs.* BLS 11. Sheffield: Almond, 1985.

Camus, Albert. *The Myth of Sisyphus and Other Essays*, trans. Justin O'Brien. New York: Alfred A. Knopf, 1955.

Cessario, Romanus. *The Moral Virtues and Theological Ethics*. Notre Dame: University of Notre Dame Press, 1991.

Chatman, Seymour B. *Story and Discourse: Narrative Structure in Fiction and Film*. Ithaca: Cornell University Press, 1978.

Clements, Ronald E. *Wisdom in Theology*. Grand Rapids: Wm. B. Eerdmans, 1992.

Clifford, Richard J., S.J. *The Book of Proverbs and Our Search for Wisdom*. Milwaukee: Marquette University Press, 1995.

Clines, David J. A. *Job 1–20*. WBC 17. Waco: Word, 1989.

Covey, Stephen R. *The Seven Habits of Highly Effective People: Restoring the Character Ethic*. New York: Simon & Schuster, 1990.

Crenshaw, James L. *Ecclesiastes*. OTL. Philadelphia: Westminster, 1987.

————. "Ecclesiastes: Odd Book In," *BibRev* 31 (1990): 28-33.

————. *Old Testament Wisdom: An Introduction*. Atlanta: John Knox, 1981.

————. "The Shadow of Death in Qoheleth," in *Israelite Wisdom: Theological and Literary Essays in Honor of Samuel Terrien*, ed. John G. Gammie, et al. Missoula: Scholars Press, 1978, 205-216.

————. "Wisdom and Authority: Sapiential Rhetoric and its Warrants," *Congress Volume, Vienna, 1980*, ed. J. A. Emerton. *VTS* 32 (1981): 10-29.

Crüsemann, Frank. "The Unchangeable World: The 'Crisis of Wisdom' in Koheleth," in *God of the Lowly: Socio-Historical Interpretations of the Bible*, ed. Willy Schottroff and Wolfgang Stegemann, trans. Matthew J. O'Connell. Maryknoll: Orbis, 1984, 57-77.

Curtis, John Briggs. "On Job's Response to Yahweh," *JBL* 98 (1979): 497-511.

Dahood, Mitchell. "*Mišmār* 'Muzzle' in Job7$_{12}$" *JBL* 90 (1961): 270-71.

Davis, Ellen F. "Job and Jacob: The Integrity of Faith," in *Reading Between Texts: Intertextuality and the Hebrew Bible*, ed. Danna Nolan Fewell. Louisville: Westminster John Knox, 1992, 203-224.

Day, Peggy L. *An Adversary in Heaven: śāṭān in the Hebrew Bible*. HSM 43. Atlanta: Scholars Press, 1988.

Delitzsch, Franz. *Proverbs, the Song of Songs and Ecclesiastes*. 1872. Repr. Grand Rapids: Wm. B. Eerdmans, 1984.

Douglas, Mary. *Purity and Danger: An Analysis of the Concepts of Pollution and Taboo*. London: Routledge and Kegan Paul, 1966.

Ellul, Jacques. *The Reason for Being: A Meditation on Ecclesiastes,* trans. Joyce M. Hanks. Grand Rapids: Wm. B. Eerdmans, 1990.

Engel, Helmut. *Die Susanna-Erzählung: Einleitung, Übersetzung und Kommentar zum Septuaginta-Text und zur Theodotion-Bearbeitung.* Freiburg: Universitätsverlag and Göttingen: Vandenhoeck & Ruprecht, 1985.

Fineman, Howard. "The Virtuecrats," *Newsweek,* 3 June 1994 ["The Politics of Virtue: The Crusade Against America's Moral Decline"], 30-36.

Fisch, Harold. *Poetry with a Purpose: Biblical Poetics and Interpretation.* Indiana Studies in Biblical Literature. Bloomington: Indiana University Press, 1988.

Fishbane, Michael. "The Book of Job and Inner-Biblical Discourse," in *The Voice from the Whirlwind,* ed. Leo G. Perdue and W. Clark Gilpin. Nashville: Abingdon, 1992, 86-98.

Fohrer, Georg. "The Righteous Man in Job 31," in *Essays in Old Testament Ethics,* ed. James L. Crenshaw and John T. Willis. New York: Ktav, 1974, 1-22.

Fontaine, Carole R. *Traditional Sayings in the Old Testament.* BLS 5. Sheffield: Almond, 1982.

———. "Wounded Hero on a Shaman's Quest," in *The Voice from the Whirlwind,* ed. Leo G. Perdue and W. Clark Gilpin. Nashville, Abingdon, 1992, 70-85.

Forster, E. M. *Aspects of the Novel.* Harmondsworth: Penguin, 1963.

Fowl, Stephen E., and Jones, L. Gregory. *Reading in Communion: Scripture and Ethics in Christian Life.* Grand Rapids: Wm. B. Eerdmans, 1991.

Fox, Michael V. "Aging and Death in Qoheleth 12," *JSOT* 42 (1988): 55-77.

———. "The Meaning of *Hebel* for Qohelet," *JBL* 105 (1986): 409-427.

———. "The Pedagogy of Proverbs 2," *JBL* 113 (1994): 233-243.

———. *Qohelet and His Contradictions.* BLS 18. JSOTSup 71. Sheffield: Almond, 1989.

———. "Wisdom in Qoheleth," in *In Search of Wisdom: Essays in Memory of John G. Gammie,* ed. Leo G. Perdue, Bernard Brandon Scott, and William Johnston Wiseman. Louisville: Westminster John Knox, 1993, 115-131.

Frankena, William K. *Ethics,* 2nd ed. Foundations of Philosophy. Englewood Cliffs, N.J.: Prentice-Hall, 1973.

Freedman, David Noel. "The Elihu Speeches in the Book of Job: A Hypothetical Episode in the Literary History of the Work," *HTR* 61 (1968): 51-59.

Fuchs, Gisela. *Mythos und Hiobdictung, Aufnahme und Undeutung altorientalischer Vorstellungen.* Stuttgart/Berlin/Cologne: Kohlhammer, 1993.

Galling, Kurt. "Kohelet-Studien," *ZAW* 50 (1932): 276-299.

———. *Der Prediger.* HAT 18. Tübingen: J. C. B. Mohr (Paul Siebeck), 1969.

Galston, William A. "Introduction: The Revival of the Virtues," in *Virtue,* ed. John W. Chapman and William A. Galston. *Nomos* 34. New York: New York University Press, 1991, 1-22.

Gammie, John G. "Behemoth and Leviathan: On the Didactic and Theological Significance of Job 40:15–41:26," in *Israelite Wisdom,* ed. John G. Gammie, et al. Missoula: Scholars Press, 1978, 217-231.

Garrett, Susan R. "The 'Weaker Sex' in the *Testament of Job*," *JBL* 112 (1993): 55-70.

Gese, Hartmut. "The Crisis of Wisdom in Koheleth," in *Theodicy in the Old Testament,* ed. James L. Crenshaw. IRT 4. Philadelphia: Fortress, 1983, 141-153 (trans. from "Die Krisis der Weisheit bei Koheleth," in *Les sagesses du Proche-Orient ancien.* Colloque de Strasbourg, 1962 [Paris: Presses Universitaires de France, 1963], 139-151).

———. *Lehre und Wirklichkeit in der alten Weisheit.* Tübingen: J. C. B. Mohr, 1958.

Gilkey, Langdon. "Power, Order, Justice, and Redemption: Theological Comments on Job," in *The Voice from the Whirlwind,* ed. Leo G. Perdue and W. Clark Gilpin. Nashville: Abingdon, 1992, 159-171.

Girard, René. *Job, The Victim of His People.* Stanford: Stanford University Press, 1987.

Glasser, E. *Le procès du bonheur par Qohelet.* LD 61. Paris: Editions du Cerf, 1970.

Good, Edwin M. *In Turns of Tempest: A Reading of Job.* Stanford: Stanford University Press, 1990.

———. "Job," in *Harper's Bible Commentary,* ed. James L. Mays. San Francisco: Harper & Row, 1988, 407-432.

———. "Job and the Literary Task: A Response," *Soundings* 56 (1973): 470-484.

———. "The Problem of Evil in the Book of Job," in *The Voice from the Whirlwind,* ed. Leo G. Perdue and W. Clark Gilpin. Nashville: Abingdon, 1992, 50-69.

Gordis, Robert. *Koheleth — The Man and His World.* 3rd ed. New York: Schocken, 1955.

Gunn, David M. *The Fate of King Saul: Interpretation of a Biblical Story.* JSOTSup 14. Sheffield: JSOT Press, 1980.

———. *The Story of King David: Genre and Interpretation.* JSOTSup 6. Sheffield: JSOT Press, 1978.

Habel, Norman C. *The Book of Job.* OTL. Philadelphia: Westminster, 1985.

———. "The Role of Elihu in the Design of the Book of Job," in *In the Shelter of Elyon: Essays on Ancient Palestinian Life and Literature in Honor of G. W. Ahlström,* ed. W. Boyd Barrick and John R. Spencer. JSOTSup 31. Sheffield: JSOT Press, 1984, 81-98.

———. "In Defense of God the Sage," in *The Voice from the Whirlwind,* ed. Leo G. Perdue and W. Clark Gilpin. Nashville: Abingdon, 1992, 21-38.

Hauerwas, Stanley. *Character and the Christian Life: A Study in Theological Ethics.* TUMSR 3. San Antonio: Trinity University Press, 1975.

———. *A Community of Character: Toward a Constructive Christian Social Ethic.* Notre Dame: University of Notre Dame Press, 1981.

———. *The Peaceable Kingdom: A Primer in Christian Ethics.* Notre Dame: University of Notre Dame Press, 1983.

———. "The Self as Story: A Reconsideration of the Relation of Religion and Morality from the Agent's Perspective," in *Vision and Virtue: Essays in Christian Ethical Reflection.* Notre Dame: Fides, 1974, 68-89.

Hengel, Martin. *Judaism and Hellenism: Studies in their Encounter in Palestine during the Early Hellenistic Period,* vol. 1, trans. John Bowden. Philadelphia: Fortress, 1981.

Hermisson, Hans-Jürgen. "Observations on the Creation Theology in Wisdom," in *Israelite Wisdom,* ed. John H. Gammie, et al. Missoula: Scholars Press, 1978, 43-57.

Hertzberg, Hans Wilhelm. *Der Prediger.* KAT 17/4. Gütersloh: Gerd Mohn, 1963.

Hunter, James D. *Before the Shooting Begins: Searching for Democracy in America's Culture War.* New York: Free Press, 1994.

———. *Culture Wars: The Struggle to Define America.* New York: Basic Books, 1991.

Jaeger, Werner W. *Paideia,* 1. Oxford: Basic Blackwell, 1939.

Janowski, Bernd. *Rettungsgeweissheit und Epiphanie des Heils.* WMANT 59. Neukirchen-Vluyn: Neukirchener, 1989.

Janzen, J. Gerald. "Creation and the Human Predicament in Job 1:9-11 and 38-41," *Ex Auditu* 3 (1987): 45-53.

————. *Job: Interpretation.* Atlanta: John Knox,1985.

Janzen, Waldemar. *Old Testament Ethics: A Paradigmatic Approach.* Louisville: Westminster John Knox, 1994.

Jenni, Ernst. "Das Wort ʿōlām im Alten Testament," *ZAW* 65 (1953): 1-35.

Johnson, Luke T. "James," *Harper's Bible Commentary,* ed. James L. Mays. San Francisco: Harper & Row, 1988, 1272-78.

Kaplan, L. J. "Maimonides, Dale Patrick, and Job XLI 6," *VT* 28 (1978): 356-57.

Kayatz, Christa. *Studien zu Proverbien 1–9.* WMANT 22. Neukirchen-Vluyn: Neukirchener, 1966.

Keel, Othmar. *Jahwes Entgegnung an Ijob.* FRLANT 121. Göttingen: Vandenhoeck & Ruprecht, 1978.

Kermode, Frank. *The Genesis of Secrecy: On the Interpretation of Narrative.* Cambridge, Mass.: Harvard University Press, 1979.

Kovacs, Brian W. "Is There a Class-Ethic in Proverbs?" in *Essays in Old Testament Ethics,* ed. James L. Crenshaw and John T. Willis. New York: Ktav Publishing House, 1974, 171-189.

Kuhn, Thomas S. *The Structure of Scientific Revolution.* Chicago: University of Chicago Press, 1970.

Lang, Bernhard. *Wisdom and the Book of Proverbs: An Israelite Goddess Redefined.* New York: Pilgrim, 1986.

Laws, Sophie. *A Commentary on the Epistle of James.* San Francisco: Harper & Row, 1980.

————. "James, Epistle of," *The Anchor Bible Dictionary,* ed. D. N. Freedman. New York: Doubleday, 1992, 3:621-28.

Levenson, Jon D. *Creation and the Persistence of Evil.* San Francisco: Harper & Row, 1988.

Lichtheim, Miriam. *Ancient Egyptian Literature,* vol. 1: *The Old and Middle Kingdoms.* Berkeley: University of California Press, 1975.

Loretz, Oswald. *Qohelet und der alte Orient.* Freiburg: Herder, 1964.

MacDonald, Duncan B. *The Hebrew Literary Genius: An Interpretation.* Princeton: Princeton University Press, 1933.

MacIntyre, Alasdair. *After Virtue: A Study in Moral Theory.* Notre Dame: University of Notre Dame Press, 1981.

McKane, William. *Proverbs: A New Approach.* OTL. Philadelphia: Westminster, 1970.

de Man, Paul. "The Rhetoric of Temporality," in *Interpretation: Theory and Practice,* ed. Charles S. Singleton. Baltimore: Johns Hopkins University Press, 1969, 173-209.

Martin, Ralph P. *James.* WBC 48. Waco: Word, 1988.

Mettinger, Tryggve N. D. "The God of Job: Avenger, Tyrant, or Victor?" in *The Voice from the Whirlwind,* ed. Leo G. Perdue and W. Clark Gilpin. Nashville: Abingdon, 1992, 39-49.

Michel, Diethelm. *Untersuchungen zur Eigenart des Buches Qoheleth.* BZAW 183. Berlin: Walter de Gruyter, 1989.

————. "Vom Gott, der im Himmel ist (Reden von Gott bei Qohelet)," *Untersuchungen zur Eigenart des Buches Qohelet,* 274-289 [repr. from *ThViat* 12 (1975): 87-100].

Moore, Rick D. "The Integrity of Job," *CBQ* 45 (1983): 17-31.

Morrow, Lance. "The Search for Virtues." *Time,* 7 March 1994, 78.

Morrow, William. "Consolation, Rejection, and Repentance in Job 42:6," *JBL* 105 (1986): 211-225.

Müller, Hans-Peter. "Der unheimlische Gast: Zum Denken Kohelets," *ZTK* 84 (1987): 440-464.

————. "Wie sprach Qohälät von Gott?" *VT* 18 (1968): 507-521.

Murphy, Roland E. *Ecclesiastes.* WBC 23A. Waco: Word, 1992.

————. "Qoheleth's 'Quarrel' with the Fathers," in *From Faith to Faith: Essays in Honor of Donald J. Miller,* ed. D. Y. Hadidian. Pittsburgh: Pickwick, 1979, 235-245.

————. "Wisdom and Creation," *JBL* 104 (1985): 3-11.

Nagel, Thomas. "The Absurd," *Journal of Philosophy* 68 (1971): 716-727.

Nelson, Daniel M. *The Priority of Prudence: Virtue and Natural Law in Thomas Aquinas and the Implications for Modern Ethics.* University Park, Pa.: Pennsylvania State University Press, 1992.

Neusner, Jacob. *Song of Songs Rabbah: An Analytical Translation,* vol. 1. BJS 197. Atlanta: Scholars Press, 1989.

Newsom, Carol A. "Job," in *The Women's Bible Commentary,* ed. Carol A. Newsom and Sharon H. Ringe. Louisville: Westminster John Knox, 1992, 130-36.

————. "The Moral Sense of Nature: Ethics in the Light of God's Speech to Job," *PSB* n.s. 15 (1994): 9-27.

————. "Woman and the Discourse of Patriarchal Wisdom: A Study of

Proverbs 1–9," in *Gender and Difference in Ancient Israel*, ed. Peggy L. Day. Minneapolis: Augsburg Fortress, 1989, 142-160.

O'Connor, Kathleen M. *The Wisdom Literature*. MBS 5. Wilmington, Del.: Michael Glazier, 1988.

Pardee, Dennis. *Ugaritic and Hebrew Poetic Parallelism: A Trial Cut (°nt I and Proverbs 2)*. VTS 39 (1988).

Patrick, Dale. "Job's Address of God," *ZAW* 91 (1979): 268-282.

———. "The Translation of Job XLII 6," *VT* 26 (1971): 369-371.

Paul, Shalom M. "An Unrecognized Medical Idiom in Canticles 6,12 and Job 9,21," *Biblica* 59 (1978): 545-47.

Perdue, Leo G. "Cosmology and the Social Order in the Wisdom Tradition," in *The Sage in Israel and the Ancient Near East*, ed. John G. Gammie and Leo G. Perdue. Winona Lake: Eisenbrauns, 1990, 457-478.

———. "Job's Assault on Creation," *HAR* 10 (1986): 295-315.

———. *Wisdom and Creation: The Theology of Wisdom Literature*. Nashville: Abingdon, 1994.

———. *Wisdom in Revolt: Metaphorical Theology in the Book of Job*. BLS 29. JSOTSup 112. Sheffield: Almond, 1991.

Peters, Thomas J., and Waterman, Robert H., Jr. *In Search of Excellence*. New York: Harper & Row, 1982.

Pinckaers, Servais. "Virtue is Not a Habit," *Cross Currents* 12 (1962): 65-81.

Pincoffs, Edmund L. *Quandaries and Virtues: Against Reductivism in Ethics*. Lawrence: University Press of Kansas, 1986.

Pleins, John David. "Poverty in the Social World of the Wise," *JSOT* 37 (1987): 61-78.

Podechard, Emmanuel. *L'Ecclésiaste*. Ebib. Paris: Gabalda, 1912.

Pope, Marvin H. *Job*. AB 15. Garden City: Doubleday, 1965.

Priest, John F. "Humanism, Skepticism, and Pessimism in Israel," *JAAR* 36 (1968): 311-326.

———. "Where is Wisdom to be Placed?" in *Studies in Ancient Israelite Wisdom*, ed. J. L. Crenshaw. Library of Biblical Studies. New York: Ktav, 1976, 281-88 [repr. from *JBR* 31 (1963): 275-282].

Pritchard, James B., ed. *Ancient Near Eastern Texts Relating to the Old Testament*. 3rd ed. Princeton: Princeton University Press, 1969.

von Rad, Gerhard. *Old Testament Theology*, vol. 1. New York: Harper & Row, 1962.

————. *Wisdom in Israel.* Nashville: Abingdon, 1972.

Reicke, Bo. *The Epistles of James, Peter, and Jude.* AB 37. Garden City: Doubleday, 1964.

Ricoeur, Paul. *Time and Narrative,* vol. 1, trans. Kathleen McLaughlin and David Pellauer. Chicago: University of Chicago Press, 1984.

Rimmon-Kennan, Shlomith. *Narrative Fiction: Contemporary Poetics.* New Accents. London: Methuen. 1983.

Ringgren, Helmer. *Sprüche/Prediger.* ATD 16/1. Göttingen: Vandenhoeck & Ruprecht, 1962.

Safire, William. *The First Dissident: The Book of Job in Today's Politics.* New York: Random House, 1992.

Sawyer, John F. A. "The Authorship and Structure of the Book of Job," in *Studia Biblica 1978,* vol. 1: *Papers on Old Testament and Related Themes,* ed. Elizabeth A. Livingston. JSOTSup 11. Sheffield: JSOT Press, 1979, 253-57.

Schmid, Hans Heinrich. "Creation, Righteousness, and Salvation," in *Creation in the Old Testament,* ed. Bernhard W. Anderson. IRT 6. Philadelphia: Fortress, 1984, 102-117.

————. *Gerechtigkeit als Weltordnung.* BHT 40. Tübingen: J. C. B. Mohr (Paul Siebeck), 1968.

Scott, R. B. Y. "Wisdom in Creation: The *'ĀMÔN* of Proverbs VIII 30," *VT* 10 (1960): 213-223.

Seow, Choon-Leong. "The Farce of the Wise King: Rhetoric and Subversion in Qohelet 1:12–2:11," paper read at SBL meeting, San Francisco, 1992.

Sheppard, Gerald T. "The Epilogue to Qoheleth as Theological Commentary," *CBQ* 39 (1977): 182-89.

————. *Wisdom as a Hermeneutical Construct.* BZAW 151. Berlin: Walter de Gruyter, 1980.

Simon, Yves R. *The Definition of Moral Virtue,* ed. Vukan Juic. New York: Fordham University Press, 1986.

Spiegel, Shalom. *The Last Trial: On the Legends and Lore of the Command to Abraham to Offer Isaac as a Sacrifice: The Akedah,* trans. Judah Goldin. New York: Schocken, 1969.

Spittler, Russell P. "Testament of Job," in *The Old Testament Pseudepigrapha,* vol. 1, ed. James H. Charlesworth. Garden City: Doubleday, 1983, 829-858.

Sternberg, Meir. *The Poetics of Biblical Narrative.* Bloomington: Indiana University Press, 1987.

Strobel, Albert. *Das Buch Prediger (Kohelet)*. Die Welt der Bibel. Düsseldorf: Patmos, 1967.

Tamez, Elsa. *The Scandalous Message of James*, trans. John Engleson. New York: Crossroads, 1990.

Terrien, Samuel. "The Play of Wisdom: Turning Point in Biblical Theology," *HBT* 3 (1981): 125-153.

Thomas Aquinas. *Summa Theologiæ*, vol. 23, trans. W. D. Hughes. New York: McGraw-Hill, 1969.

Towner, W. Sibley. "The Renewed Authority of Old Testament Wisdom for Contemporary Faith," in *Canon and Authority*, ed. George W. Coats and Burke O. Long. Philadelphia: Fortress, 1977, 132-147.

Tsevat, Matitiahu. "The Meaning of the Book of Job," *HUCA* 37 (1966): 73-106. Repr. in *The Meaning of the Book of Job and Other Biblical Studies*. New York: Ktav, 1980, 1-38.

Washington, Harold C. *Wealth and Poverty in the Instruction of Amenemope and the Hebrew Proverbs*. SBLDS 142; Atlanta: Scholars Press, 1994.

Westermann, Claus. "The Two Faces of Job," in *Job and the Silence of God*, ed. Christian Duquoc and Casiano Floristan. Concilium. New York: Seabury, 1983, 15-22.

Whitley, Charles F. *Koheleth: His Language and Thought*. BZAW 148. Berlin: Walter de Gruyter, 1979.

Whybray, R. N. *The Composition of the Book of Proverbs*. JSOTSup 168. Sheffield: Sheffield Academic, 1994.

———. *Ecclesiastes*. NCBC. Grand Rapids: Wm. B. Eerdmans, 1989.

———. "Qoheleth, Preacher of Joy," *JSOT* 23 (1982): 87-98.

———. "Qoheleth the Immoralist? (Qoh 7:16-17)," in *Israelite Wisdom*, ed. John G. Gammie, et al. Missoula: Scholars Press, 1978, 191-204.

———. *Wisdom in Proverbs: The Concept of Wisdom in Proverbs 1–9*. SBT 45. Naperville: Allenson, 1965.

Williams, James G. "Job and the God of Victims," in *The Voice from the Whirlwind*, ed. Leo G. Perdue and W. Clark Gilpin. Nashville: Abingdon, 1992, 208-231.

———. "Job's Vision: The Dialectic of Person and Presence," *HAR* 8 (1984): 259-272.

———. "What Does it Profit a Man?: The Wisdom of Koheleth," in *The Sage in Israel and the Ancient Near East*, ed. John G. Gammie and Leo G. Perdue. Winona Lake: Eisenbrauns, 1990, 375-389 [repr. from *Judaism* 20 (1971): 179-193].

Wilson, James Q. *The Moral Sense.* New York: Free Press, 1993.

————. *On Character: Essays.* Lanham: AEI Press, 1991.

Wintermute, Orval S. "Jubilees," in *The Old Testament Pseudepigrapha*, vol. 2, ed. J. H. Charlesworth. Garden City: Doubleday, 1985, 35-142.

Witherington III, Ben. *Jesus the Sage: The Pilgrimage of Wisdom.* Minneapolis: Fortress, 1994.

Ziegler, J. "Die Hilfe Gottes am Morgan," *Alttestamentliche Studien.* BBB 1. Bonn: Peter Hanstein, 1950, 281-88.

Zimmerli, Walther. *Das Buch des Predigers Salomo.* ATD 16/1. Göttingen: Vandenhoeck & Ruprecht, 1962.

————. "Concerning the Structure of Old Testament Wisdom" in *Studies in Ancient Israelite Wisdom,* ed. James L. Crenshaw, 175-207 [trans. from "Zur Struktur der alttestamentlischen Weisheit," *ZAW* 10 (1933): 177-204].

————. "The Place and Limit of the Wisdom in the Framework of the Old Testament Theology," in *Studies in Ancient Israelite Wisdom,* ed. J. L. Crenshaw. Library of Biblical Studies. New York: Ktav, 1976, 314-326 [repr. from *SJT* 17 (1964): 146-158].

————. *Die Weisheit des Predigers Salomo.* Biblische Reihe 11. Berlin: Alfred Töpelmann, 1936.

Zuckerman, Bruce. *Job, the Silent: A Study in Historical Counterpoint.* New York: Oxford University Press, 1991.

Index of Authors